EDISON
IN THE
BOARDROOM

EDISON
IN THE
BOARDROOM

How Leading Companies Realize Value from Their Intellectual Assets

JULIE L. DAVIS
SUZANNE S. HARRISON

JOHN WILEY & SONS, INC.

New York • Chichester • Weinheim • Brisbane • Singapore • Toronto

Library of Congress Cataloging-in-Publication Data:

ISBN 0-471-39736-9

Printed in the United States of America.

10 9 8 7 6 5 4 3 2 1

To Roger, without whom there would never have been an IP Value Hierarchy—in fact, without whom there would never have been anything of value.

Julie L. Davis

For my father and brother, who have helped make every one of my dreams come true. Thank you for having the tenacity to continue to push the boundaries of knowledge, even in the face of adversity.

Suzanne S. Harrison

FOREWORD

"YES" WAS MY unhesitating answer when Julie Davis and Suzanne Harrison asked me to write the foreword for their new book, *Edison in the Boardroom*. I respect the authors for their knowledge of intellectual assets, and I share their reverence for the famed innovator.

With a quarter century of IP consulting accomplishments between them, Julie Davis and Suzanne Harrison bring real corporate street smarts to an all-too-theoretical field. Through their work as consultants with Andersen and ICMG, these two are at the forefront of change in the intellectual property field.

Moreover, their choice of an icon is fitting. If Thomas Alva Edison stands tall in the history of science, he looms as a giant in the history of business. The inventor's contributions did not end in his laboratories. Instead, through his guidance, they evolved into vast business empires that exist to this day—notably personified in the legendary General Electric. The Edison emulated in these pages is not the Edison whose brilliant tinkering helped build our modern industrial world. Rather, it is the Edison whose methodical management of the entire IP process ensured that these inventions would build value for his companies' shareholders.

In my view, this is the Edison we need to emulate today. My book *Rembrandts in the Attic*, coauthored with David Kline, drove home one central point: IP may be neglected, like a painting in an attic, but once discovered, it can become extremely valuable. We showed readers how companies have made millions by planning their patents, mining them for value, and mapping a strategy. The instant success of our book in the marketplace showed that businesses around the world were hungry for such examples.

Edison in the Boardroom makes this same message even more immediate, showing executives and others exactly how to climb the "Intellectual Asset Value Hierarchy," a methodical approach worthy of the Edisonian name. Using examples from nearly two dozen companies, the authors guide readers through a logical sequence of steps, progressing from defense of intellectual property to the heights of strategic vision for all intellectual assets.

The Continuing Need for Practical IP Guidance

This manual comes none too soon in a field that craves practical guidance. I speak from experience. A decade ago, my business partner Irving S. Rappaport and I cofounded a small company (then called SmartPatents) that became Aurigin Systems, Inc. Irving and I wanted to create and market a software and research tool that could help IP attorneys and managers perform their jobs. Even back then, in 1992, we saw IP as far more than a fixed legal asset; we saw it as a dynamic business process. But sometimes it seemed that we were voices crying in the wilderness.

Our company's mission was simple. IP professionals could use our software and related management concepts to perform their functions at a higher level. In helping companies use our software, we urged them to avoid a reactionary approach to patents. Companies, we said, should not automatically file and renew patents in assembly-line fashion. Instead, they should actively *choose* what patents to pursue based on precise and telling competitive information. In a phrase, the Aurigin product enables companies to identify the IP rights they own, see how those rights fit into the competitive landscape, and decide where to focus their future R&D efforts.

But as any vendor of software applications knows, a company can have the best software and applications in the world, but unless company managements are prepared to use them effectively, these tools will fail to succeed in the marketplace. And while we took great satisfaction in the truth and beauty of our product, we wanted above all else to survive and thrive in the marketplace. That was one reason I decided to join David Kline in writing *Rembrandts in the Attic,* which exhorted companies to consider IP as a valuable structural asset that transcended mere ownership control.

To a large degree, we succeeded in this goal. *Rembrandts* sparked IP revolutions in many major companies, and still enjoys brisk sales after two years. Yet despite the publication of *Rembrandts*—and the many periodical articles we and others have written to pound home its major premise—much of the IP world remains anchored in the legal world. This is unfortunate. Corporate IP functions are often headed by astute professionals who have not only legal but also technical backgrounds. These pros are eminently qualified to make a difference. In fact, many of them are yearning to do so. Sadly, however, their internal campaign's efforts to bring IP into the twenty-first century often end in failure. They must cede power to a dying mentality—one still widespread in many major corporations—that sees IP as an asset separate from innovation, rather than as a process intimately linked to it.

A Useful Model for IP Progress

Edison does far more than drive yet another nail in the would-be coffin of this old mindset. Instead, Edison embraces the defensive ownership of IP as a necessary and first level in a dynamic "value hierarchy" for intellectual assets.

The upward journey described here is long but rewarding. It includes not only the defense of IP, but also the control of costs, the pursuit of profits, the integration of IP into the corporate fabric, and the creation of a lasting vision for IP and all of a company's intellectual assets.

I strongly recommend *Edison in the Boardroom* to all corporate leaders, managers, and advisors charged with maximizing the value of their companies' intellectual property. Whatever your challenges are, you will find solutions here.

Kevin G. Rivette
May 2001

ACKNOWLEDGMENTS

A S ANY AUTHOR can attest, a book is the result of a complex and interacting set of activities. Good ideas have many parents, and that was certainly the case with *Edison in the Boardroom*. The authors openly acknowledge that this book is the result of collaboration with a number of people who provided the inspiration, guidance, support, and ideas that have made this book possible. For these people we are deeply grateful. While we brought the original framework of ideas to the endeavor, the executives who donated their time, stories, and words of wisdom have enlivened and animated the bare bones with which we started.

We are particularly indebted to the corporate executives and thought leaders who made these contributions: Margaret Blair, Fred Boehm, Bob Bramson, Tom Colson, John Cronin, Joe Daniele, Steve Fox, Henry Fradkin, Bill Frank, Paul Germeraad, Rick Gross, Bob Gruetzmacher, David Kline, Bob McCall, Rob McLean, David Near, Sharon Oriel, Jim O'Shaughnessy, Jan-Erik Osterholm, Mark Radcliffe, John Raley, Jane Robbins, Jerry Rosenthal, Paul Rothweiler, Randy Stauffer, Bruce Story, Bill Swirsky, Graham Taylor, Elizabeth Thom, Tony Torres, Joe Villella, Lanny Vincent, Jeff Weedman, and Barry Young.

We are also very appreciative of our many clients who have challenged our thinking and forced us to articulate the concepts that have become the subject of this book. Other friends, including Rob Pressman and Michael Smythe, have also contributed to our thinking.

Edison was created by marrying the best practices of companies in the ICM Gathering with the depth of experience the authors have garnered through their consulting experiences. We are especially grateful to the companies of the ICM Gathering for sharing their knowledge, experiences, successes, and failures with us. Our firms, Andersen and ICMG, have worked together in a strategic alliance to share the results of the Gathering's collective learning with other companies.

In the course of our joint endeavor there have been a number of colleagues who have been instrumental in shaping and supporting our view of the art of intellectual property management. They include our colleagues at ICMG: Dr. Patrick Sullivan and Patrick Sullivan Jr.; as well as many current and former partners at Andersen: Mark Bezand, Richard Boulton, Dan Broadhurst, Paul Charnetzki, Barbara Duganier, Susan Gallagher, Ed Giniat, Mark Hargis, Bob Hiebeler, Todd Huskinson, Kathi Kedrowski, Gerry Keeler, Mark Kindy, Peter King, Carol Kone, Barry Libert, Mike Maloney, Cindy Munger, Jim Nawrocki, Heidi Rudolph, and Barry Sussman, along with several other current and former Andersen colleagues: Jason Ackerman, Doug Aguilera, Gary Bender, Cheryl Benes, Melissa Bennis, Darlene Butscher, John Coult, Meghan Doyle, Ron Epperson, Jim Ewing, Brandy Fernow, John Galiski, Clare Harding, Scott Hultgren, Rodger Jackson, Nancy Jessen, Deb Kiley, Jennifer Knabb, Doug Knoch, Jerry Kral, Catherine Madrid, Laura McLaughlin, Missy Metzl, Lori Morrison, Della Quimby, Tim Renjilian, Dawn Rice, Jill Rusk, and Kris Swanson. In addition, we couldn't have done without our administrative support staff—Joy Barrows, Kim Bhear, Tricia Lange, and Maria Munoz.

Intellectual capital management and its growing importance in both individual companies as well as in our national economy can be traced back to the efforts of several key individuals who had vision, patience, fortitude, and a gift for words. Their books and thoughts have opened our eyes and enabled a generation of managers to begin to harvest the value of their firms' knowledge. Kevin Rivette, Tom Stewart, and Karl-Erik Sveiby, thanks for pushing the boundaries.

We would also like to thank Martha Cooley for her patience and encouragement to share what we have learned. Thanks also go to Alexandra Lajoux for her research into Edisoniana and for her gift of words.

And finally, thanks to both of our husbands, Roger and Juan, for their support, suggestions, words of encouragement, and lost weekends and holidays.

CONTENTS

INTRODUCTION

THE EDISON PROPHECY

If the world wages on for many thousand years more, there would seem to be no reason why men should not go on discovering and inventing. No reason to doubt that new tricks and arrangements will be made so that Nature may work to man's advantage. The scientific journals will go on publishing . . . It is [for] the unreasonable men today to be afraid that they cannot find out any more; that all has been found. Men are just beginning to propose questions and find answers, and we may be sure that no matter what question we ask, so long as it is not against the laws of nature, a solution can be found.[1]

CORPORATIONS ARE ALWAYS on the lookout for exciting, new, novel, and discontinuous innovations. The light bulb, telephone, automobile, and personal computer are all examples of legally protected technology innovations that have created corporate empires and changed the course of history. In fact, the light bulb and its inventor, Thomas Alva Edison, have become synonymous with innovation. When we think of a bright idea, it is symbolized by a drawing of a light bulb. When we think of prolific inventors, Edison is usually at the top of the list. In today's world, innovation drives corporate profits and competitive advantage. Yet innovation, though key to the real "business" of most companies, has generally been treated as a separate activity.

In many companies, the research and development or "R&D" function, has been literally a "black box." Inventors—whether engineers, scientists, or web developers—have received special treatment—often keeping odd hours and receiving incentives for their ideas. Innovation has seemed like a magical event—the elusive "Eureka!" resounding at the birth of a new idea. It has been up to the business folks on the other side of the wall—or even in a different building altogether—to shape and refine that idea into a saleable product or service that can generate revenue. Functions such as legal, or marketing, or finance, or strategy have been tasked with creating linkages between ideas and cash flow.

For centuries, companies have linked ideas and money by embedding their new ideas (legally protected or not) into products to be sold or bartered. Today, however, an exciting new concept is revolutionizing the way companies extract value from their ideas: an idea no longer needs to be embedded into a product

1

or service to create value. Today ideas are licensed, sold, or bartered in their raw state for great value. IBM currently receives $1.5 billion in revenue a year from licensing its intellectual property, unrelated to its manufacturing of a single product! More and more companies are intrigued with this notion of turning their legal departments (where intellectual property is housed) from cost centers to profit centers. And an increasing number of pioneers are doing just that.

So how are companies getting value out of their ideas? In a phrase, they are getting value through *intellectual property management* (IPM). This book describes the unfolding of IPM through a series of true stories—beginning with the story of how the IPM movement began in the first place.

A Brief History

In October 1994, Tom Stewart of *Fortune* magazine published an influential article on *intellectual capital* ("IC"), which he defined as the intangible assets of skill, knowledge, and information. In late 1994, ICMG began contacting all the companies who were actively trying to manage their intangible assets. In January 1995, representatives from seven of these companies assembled for a meeting to share what their IC efforts entailed. At that first meeting, the group defined intellectual capital as "knowledge that can be converted to value." They also determined that IC has two main components: *human capital* (HC—ideas we have in our heads) and *intellectual assets* (IA—ideas that have been codified in some manner). Within intellectual assets, there is a subset of ideas that can be legally protected, called *intellectual property* (IP). (See Exhibit 1.)

The original group of seven companies that met in January 1995 has now grown to over 30 companies from around the world. Members meet three times a year to create, define, and benchmark best practices in the emerging area of ICM. This group is collectively known as the ICM Gathering. The Gathering has spent the past six years working on creating and defining systems and processes for companies to routinely create, identify, and realize value from intellectual assets.

When the principals of ICMG first met with Julie Davis of Andersen, they learned a great deal from each other. ICMG through the Gathering had discovered and tested best practices. For her part, Julie and her Andersen colleagues had developed a framework for organizing and using the best practices. Together, ICMG and Julie had been looking at patterns of behavior that helped to describe some of the activities leading-edge companies used in their quest for better ways to realize value—patterns that came to be known as the Value Hierarchy. *Edison in the Boardroom* melds these two sets of know-how. Now for the first time, by reading this book, companies can do three things. First, they can

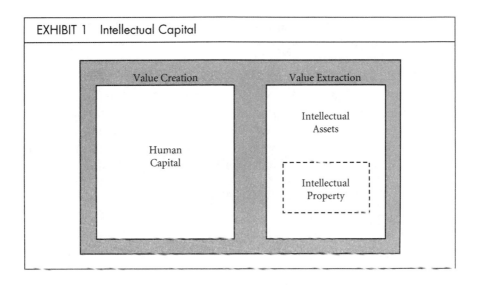

EXHIBIT 1   Intellectual Capital

Value Creation

Value Extraction

Human
Capital

Intellectual
Assets

Intellectual
Property

identify their current level of activity. Second, they can target the level they want to achieve. Finally, and perhaps most importantly, they can learn directly from other companies what systems and processes they need to put in place to get to their desired level.

WHY INTELLECTUAL PROPERTY IS IMPORTANT

IPM guidance is particularly valuable in the current era. Coming up with the "million-dollar idea" seems to be a global pastime these days. We have watched as companies from the new and old economies alike—Dow Chemical and IBM, to name just a couple—have made hundreds of millions of dollars on the basis of their ideas. Now is the time to join them—and our book is here to help.

We feel privileged to have worked in the field of patents over the past 10 years, during the greatest patent boom in U.S. history. We call it a "boom" because in the past full decade (1990–1999), the U.S. Patent and Trademark Office (USPTO) has issued more than 1 million patents—or about 100,000 per year. This rate of patent issuance is nearly triple the overall historical rate of patent issuance (36,000 per year on average since 1836). This does not count reissues, which have also grown in number (now numbering some 40,000 in total). In late 1999, the USPTO issued its 6 *millionth* patent.[2]

The current patent boom extends beyond the United States—a trend revealed in *A Technology Assessment and Forecast Report,* a March 1999 USPTO report available at uspto.gov. In 1998, the most recent year for which international data are available, organizations around the world filed a total of 147,520 patents in countries disclosing patent filings.

Of these patents, organizations in the U.S. filed 80,294—a majority, but not an overwhelming one. And of the 67,226 patents with non-U.S. origin, 30,841 were filed by Japanese organizations, and 16,233 by organizations in Germany, France, and the U.K. combined. Organizations in South Korea and Taiwan filed an additional 6,359 (over 3,000 each), and Canadian organizations filed another 1,582. All of these countries have active cultures of innovation in their leading companies.

The global nature of the patent boom also shows itself in a recent study by the Council on Competitiveness, a Washington, D.C. think tank. The Council has created a National Innovation Index, measuring real and projected innovations per million residents. In 1995, the U.S. ranked number one in this index. The Council now foresees the U.S. as number five on the index by 2005, and predicts that Japan will take the primary spot, with the U.S. falling behind to the sixth spot after several smaller nations, including Finland. And year after year, when the USPTO ranks companies most active in seeking U.S. patents, Japanese companies join U.S. firms at the top of the list.

The present rate of growth in patents is likely to continue in the new economy which is based in large part on new technology employed in a global marketplace. Moreover, this intense pace is overtaking the entire realm of intellectual property, including not only patents but also copyrights and trademarks—as well as trade secrets—as described in Exhibit 2.

This jump in the value of patents is being reflected in the bottom line. Corporations define value according to the standards put in place by the accounting profession. In accounting, value is not "accounted for" until it is realized or a transaction has occurred. Yet we all know that in-process R&D—as well as the entire patent portfolio—has immense value to the firm, even though it does not show up on balance sheets. Our view of the world has been shaped by double-entry accounting, which was first created in 1494 by Luca Pacioli, an Italian monk. This is fundamentally the same accounting system that is used by global corporations around the world today to calculate and report revenues, profits, and expenses, and make decisions about resource allocations, risk management, and investment returns. While accounting is very good at recording transactions that have occurred in the past, it is not good at predicting future revenue streams. In addition, accounting only records events and transactions, so financial statements routinely exclude ideas that have not yet manifested themselves in a transaction.

In recent years the percentage of company value attributable to intellectual capital has increased dramatically, according to one prominent source. In a

---

EXHIBIT 2   Intellectual Property: The Big Three-Plus

Patents. A patent is typically defined as a government grant extended to the owner of an invention (the individual inventor, or an entity that owns the invention) that excludes others from making, using, or selling the invention, and includes the right to license others to make, use, or sell the invention. Patents are protectable under the U.S. Constitution, and under the Patent Cooperation Treaty of 1970, in Title 35 of the U.S. Code. Patent protection can be extended to inventions that are novel (new and original), useful, and not obvious. Some corporations have patentable inventions but choose to protect some of them as trade secrets, rather than filing for a patent.*

Patents may be issued for four general types of inventions/discoveries: compositions of matter, machines, man-made products (including bioengineering), and processing methods (including business processes). To obtain a patent, the inventor must send a detailed description of the invention (among other formalities) to the U.S. Patent and Trademark Office, which employs examiners who review applications. The average time between patent application and issuance is about two years, although the process may be much shorter or longer, depending on the invention.

Under U.S. patent law, patents are issued for a nonrenewable period of 20 years measured from the date of application. Inventors being granted patents in the United States must pay maintenance fees. Federal courts have exclusive jurisdiction over disputes involving patents.

Trademarks. A trademark is a name associated with a company, product, or concept, as well as a symbol, picture, sound, or even smell associated with these factors. The mark can already be in use or be one that will be used in the future. A trademark may be part of a trade name, which is the name a company uses to operate its business. Trademarks may be protected by both Federal statute under the Lanham Act, which is part of Section 15 of the U.S. Code, and under a state's statutory and/or common law. Trademark status may be granted to unique names, symbols, and pictures, and also unique building designs, color combinations, packaging, presentation and product styles (called trade dress), and even Internet domain names. Trademark status may also be granted for identification that does not appear to be distinct or unique, but that over time has developed a secondary meaning identifying it with the product or seller.

The owner of a trademark has the exclusive right to use it on the product it was intended to identify and often on related products. Service marks receive the same legal protection as trademarks but are meant to distinguish services rather than products. A trademark is indefinite in duration, so long as the mark continues to be used on or in connection with the goods or services for which it is registered, subject to certain defenses. Federally registered trademarks must be renewed every 10 years. Trademarks are protected under state law, even without

(continues)

EXHIBIT 2   Continued

---

federal registration, but registration is recommended. Most states have adopted a version of the Model Trademark Bill and/or the Uniform Deceptive Trade Practices Act.

Copyrights. A copyright is the right of ownership extended to an individual who has written or otherwise created a tangible or intangible work, or to an organization that has paid that individual to do the work while retaining possession of the work. Copyright protection grew out of protection afforded by the U.S. Constitution to "writings." Subsequent law (U.S. Copyright Act, U.S. Code in Title 17, Section 106) has extended this right to include works in a variety of fields, including architectural design, computer software, graphic arts, motion pictures, sound recordings (for example, on CDs and tapes), and videos. Any type of work may be copyrighted, as long as it is "original," and in a "tangible medium of expression." (Computer software, although intangible, is considered a tangible medium.)

A copyright gives the owner exclusive rights to the work, including right of display, distribution, licensing, performance, and reproduction. A copyright may also grant to the owner the exclusive right to produce (or license the production of) derivatives of the work. A copyright lasts for the life of the owner, plus 70 years. "Fair use" of the work is exempt from copyright law. The fairness of use is judged in relation to a number of factors, including the nature of the copyrighted work, purpose of the use, size and substantiality of portion of copyrighted work used in relation to that work as a whole, and potential market for or value of the copyrighted work. Copyrights are protected under both state and federal law, with federal law superseding. A number of organizations promote the protection of intellectual property, including the World Intellectual Property Organization, which covers copyrights, patents, and trademarks.

---

*A *trade secret* is "information, including a formula, pattern, compilation, program, device, method, technique, or process" that is kept a secret and that derives value from being kept secret.[3] Many states have adopted the Uniform Trade Secrets law to govern this area.

---

study of thousands of nonfinancial companies over a 20-year period, Dr. Margaret Blair, of the Brookings Institution,[4] reported a significant shift in the makeup of company assets, which she measured by comparing market value to book value. She studied all of the nonfinancial publicly traded firms in the Compustat database. In 1978, her study showed that 83 percent of the firms' value was associated with their tangible assets, with 17 percent associated with their intangible assets. By 1998, only 31 percent of the value of the firms studied was attributable to their tangible assets, while a stunning 69 percent was associated with the value of their intangibles.

Why do intangibles now account for such a high percentage of company value? Reasons abound, but here are a few of the most pressing causes.

The changing legal environment. In countries around the world, there is a growing awareness of intellectual property rights. In the United States, the creation of the new Court of Appeals for the Federal Circuit in 1982 has had an immeasurably positive effect on the value of patents, one of the major forms of intangible assets in U.S. firms. The relatively high number of decisions in favor of the holder of intellectual property rights since the court's creation has made patent-holder rights more enforceable and therefore of greater value.[6] And around the world, companies are battling the menace of counterfeits with new strategies of prevention, recovery, and lobbying.

Effects of the Internet and information technology. The rapid rise of the Internet in parallel with the exponentially growing capabilities of information technology (computers, communications, and so forth) has effectively moved the industrialized world into a new economic paradigm: the economics of abundance. In the industrial era, tangible assets were the major source of value, and their value depreciated with use. In the "information age," by contrast, most value comes from information, which increases in value the more people use it.

The leverage of intellectual capital. Intellectual capital is often the "hidden value" within a firm. It involves the firm's knowledge, know-how, relationships, innovations, and structure. It comprises both the firm's tacit and codified knowledge. It is the engine behind a firm's ability to create new products, business processes, and business forms. In addition, intellectual capital can increase exponentially. We notice that companies today are upgrading their products by adding information and capability to them. For example, we often see companies providing more intelligence in the same amount of product volume, or providing the same amount of intelligence in a smaller amount of product volume. Examples of products containing more and more information per unit of volume are: telephones, computers, appliances, children's toys, credit cards with embedded chips, bar codes on retail products, and office copiers that self-diagnose their own operating problems—to name just a few.

THE EDISON MINDSET

The growing emphasis on ideas is not new to the times. Looking back over the last century we see a similar pattern emerging at the end of the nineteenth century. In Thomas Edison's time, the key inventions were related to the airplane, light bulb, telegraph, telephone, and automobile. Today inventions are emerging around the Internet, software, and business processes.

Thomas Edison may have marked a turning point in the history of innovation when he said (as quoted on page 1):

> Men are just beginning to propose questions and find answers, and we may be sure that no matter what question we ask, so long as it is not against the laws of nature, a solution can be found.[5]

The "we" here was no mere rhetorical device, but a new way of thinking. Thomas Edison is often romanticized as a lone inventor—the creator of the light bulb, the motion picture, the microphone, and a myriad of other technologies. Less well known is his invention of the modern research laboratory using teams of inventors.

To be sure, Edison will forever be the very symbol of brainpower. In his lifetime, he would obtain 1,093 patents, including one for the incandescent electric lamp—a prototype of the "light bulb" that would come to symbolize the "bright" idea. Other patents included those for the phonograph, the microphone, and the motion picture projector—technologies that would shape a century.

But despite the brilliance of these inventions, one might well say that Thomas Edison's greatest contribution to society was not any particular invention, but rather the creation of the world's first research laboratories—in fact, two of them, in Menlo Park and West Orange, New Jersey. As one source notes, his workshops were "forerunners of the modern industrial research laboratory, in which teams of workers, rather than a lone inventor, *systematically investigate a problem.*"[6] Edison, more than any other scientist of his day, knew that to generate ideas and successfully commercialize them required *sustained and methodical effort.* The history of the light bulb proves this point. (See Exhibit 3.)

Edison made his optimistic prediction about inventions in 1878, exactly four years *before* the beginning of a steady rise in patents that would continue for the next 120 years, boosted by innovations in telegraphy, electricity, automobiles, airplanes, synthetics, aerospace, and most recently, high technology including computers, computer software, and the new Internet economy they have spawned (as seen in Exibit 4).

At both our firms, we work with clients who hunger to find new sources of value—but where? Companies have already been reengineered, reorganized, and restructured. Their workforce has been downsized, right-sized, and empowered. Their inventory is just-in-time. Their core competencies have

---

EXHIBIT 3   The Light Bulb: A Brief History

The light bulb may symbolize the quick flash of invention, but it also represents the long, slow process of bringing an idea to the marketplace. Known technically as the incandescent lamp, a light bulb is simply a glass bulb enclosing an electrically heated filament that emits light. As simple as it may sound, this object was very difficult to produce, and had a significant impact on society. Today, light bulbs are one of only two major sources of electric light. The other source, fluorescent light, is generally considered to be inferior for ordinary use.

Before Thomas Edison began working on the light bulb, 20 inventors had similar insights, but nothing significant came of their efforts. For example, in 1802, Humphry Davy passed an electric current through a platinum wire and lit it up, but he did not protect or pursue this invention. In 1845, American J.W. Star received an English patent for a "continuous metallic or carbon conductor intensely heated by the passage of electricity for the purpose of illumination." Building on Star's invention, Joseph Swann experimented with lamps between 1848 and 1860, but never produced anything practical until 1877, when he renewed his efforts at exactly the same time that Thomas Edison was turning his attention to electricity.

Edison was by far the most persistent of this line of inventors. He experimented with a variety of materials—including mandrake bamboo from Japan—before he finally hit on a solution: the use of a filament made of carbonized cotton sewing thread. Edison patented this procedure, but lost a patent infringement case initiated by Swan. In order to make peace, the two men formed the Edison and Swan United Electric Light Company Limited in 1883. The company acquired several other companies and renamed itself Edison Electric. It eventually merged with another company, renaming itself General Electric, or GE in 1892.

Interestingly, it was a GE scientist who finally made the commercial breakthrough. Irving Langmuir tackled a persistent problem with the light bulb—the tendency of the filament to crumble, and the bulb to blacken, after short use. After three solid years of experimentation, Langmuir solved the problem in GE labs, and won the Nobel Prize for his discovery.[7]

---

been benchmarked and noncore functions outsourced. And companies have streamlined their factory operations, introduced many quality initiatives, and partnered with suppliers, customers, and communities. There are no more stones to turn—or so they think.

In our work together, we share the mindset of Thomas Edison. We agree with him that inventiveness will never end, but more important, we agree that

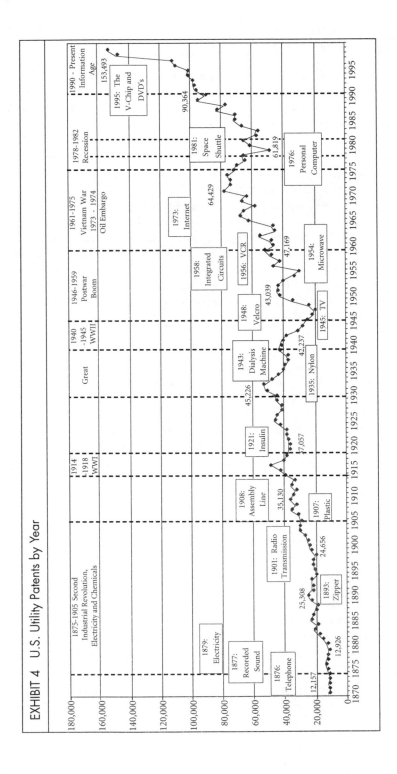

EXHIBIT 4   U.S. Utility Patents by Year

10

it is hard work and perseverance that have fueled this continuing flow of invention. This is a message that companies today can take to heart as they develop, protect, and enhance their intellectual assets day in and day out—for months, for years, and for generations.

The answer for our clients then and now has been a rediscovery of intellectual assets—current and future, legally protected or not. Intellectual assets are codified knowledge, which may or may not be protected by such laws. Know-how, brands, contracts, and architectural drawings are all examples of intellectual assets. Legal protection comes from patent, trademark, and copyright laws, as well as laws protecting trade secrets.

In our joint work with companies around the world, we have developed an appreciation for the best practices in the management of intellectual assets—and how those practices yield results that affect both profits and shareholder value. From working behind the scenes, we know from experience that the real value in intellectual assets lies not only in the inspiration that gives it life, but also in the perspiration that fully develops it and extracts its value. That is why Edison's oft-quoted maxims appeal to us.

Marching in step with Edison, we believe that inventions will continue to stream forth, and that each and every one of them will require *hard work* to bring into full value. Our own systematic work in investigating the extraction of value from patents (as a prototypical type of intellectual property) has led us to study their "sweat" component—the hard, methodical work of *defending ownership, controlling costs, extracting profits, integrating with other aspects of a business, and, finally, mapping out a future strategy.* We have identified the best practices of leading companies that relate to the realization of value from their intellectual assets.

We have found, though, that benchmarking best practices without any regard for the underlying culture of the firm can be problematic. For example, many firms want to make money from licensing fees. We have met many IP executives who have been told by their CEOs, "If IBM can make $1.5 billion dollars in royalties, by golly, so can we," and then in the next breath have also said, "but don't come back here and tell me I need to hire any more lawyers!" The point, of course, is that IBM makes a substantial investment in both R&D and legal resources to generate that royalty stream. Most CEOs are not prepared to make a similar investment. So we realized that it was important for companies to understand where they were in their awareness of IP as a business asset, and to create a way for them to articulate where they want to be, and then identify best practices to allow them to get there.

We call this the "hierarchy of value" for intellectual property (see Exhibit 5)—a model created at Andersen and developed further with ICMG.

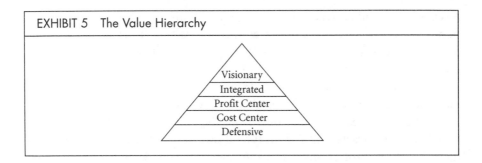

EXHIBIT 5   The Value Hierarchy

Visionary
Integrated
Profit Center
Cost Center
Defensive

THE VALUE HIERARCHY

The Value Hierarchy comes from our study of and work with many companies around the world. From that work we have developed an appreciation for the best practices in the management of intellectual assets, especially intellectual property, and how those practices yield results that affect both profits and shareholder value. The collective learnings of these companies are the foundation for the best practices of this book. But just a raw list of best practices is relatively difficult for companies to integrate into their existing processes and decision systems. And so the Value Hierarchy was born.

Think of the Value Hierarchy as a pyramid with five levels. Each level represents a different expectation that the company has about the contribution that its IP/IA function should be making to the corporate goals. Each higher level on the pyramid represents the increasing demands placed upon the IP function by the executive team and the board of directors. Like building blocks, each higher level relies on the foundation of the lower levels. Mastery of the practices, characteristics, and activities of the prior levels builds the foundation for greater increases in shareholder value. The more one builds on intellectual property on Level One, the better one is able to enhance the value of all intellectual assets—and more broadly, intellectual capital—at the higher levels.

- Level One of the Value Hierarchy is the Defensive Level. If a corporation owns an intellectual asset (such as a great business concept), it can prevent competitors from using the asset. By "staking a claim" on its valuable intellectual assets, a company builds a base from which to obtain more value from them. This is the most fundamental of the IP functions, which is why it is at the base of our pyramid. At this level, the IP function provides a patent shield to protect the company from litigation. By stockpiling patents, companies can not only gain valuable IP, but also shield themselves from litigation because they will be able to negotiate cross-licenses rather than go to court. The IP function of companies involved heavily in this level tends to be run by the company's intellectual property counsel, who often has experience in litigation. (IBM is a rare exception to this rule; its IP function has always been headed by a business person.) Companies at this level generally view IP as a legal asset.

- Level Two is the Cost Control Level, in which companies focus on how to reduce the costs of filing and maintaining their IP portfolios. Well-executed strategies in this area can save the company millions of dollars annually. Companies focusing on this activity may still put the function under the control of a defense-minded attorney, but he or she is more likely to have a background in business. Intellectual property is still viewed primarily as a legal asset.

- Level Three of the Value Hierarchy is the Profit Center Level. Having learned how to control many of their patent-related costs, companies at this level turn their attention to more proactive strategies that can generate millions of dollars of additional revenues while further continuing to trim costs. Passing from the previous levels of activity to this one requires a *major change* in a company's attitude—and even its organization In such a company, IP may have its own function, and the individual in charge may even become an IP "czar" as Vice President–IP. It is at this level that companies begin to view IP as a business asset, rather than just a legal asset.

- Level Four is the Integrated Level. In this level the IP function ceases to focus exclusively on self-centered activities and reaches outwardly beyond its own department to serve a greater purpose within the organization as a whole. In essence, its activities are integrated with those of other functions and *embedded* in the company's day-to-day operations, procedures, and strategies—much as quality programs have been embedded in companies that previously treated them as a separate function. Here the focus is on the process, not just IP. Hence the "process czar" in such a company will often hold a senior vice president title in a broad area such as strategy, information, or R&D.

- Level Five, the final level, is the Visionary Level. Few companies have reached this level of looking outside the company and into the future. In this level, the IP function, having already become deeply ingrained in the company, takes on the challenge of identifying future trends in the industry and consumer preferences. It anticipates technological revolutions and actively seeks to position the corporation as a leader in its field by acquiring or developing the IP that will be necessary to protect the company's margins and market share in the future. The IP function here is often headed by the director of business development or strategic planning—or a similarly future-oriented role.

Few, if any, corporations *in the world* have mastered all five levels and extracted maximum value from their intellectual assets. *Not every corporation needs to do so.* But *every* corporation has room for improvement. *Every* corporation has an opportunity to increase shareholder value by strengthening and building on its intangible assets.

Keep in mind that each of the levels on this pyramid serves as the foundation or building block for levels above it. Many, if not most, companies may actually be engaging in activities from several different levels. These same companies, though, can benefit by candidly assessing where they stack up compared to others. It is not a "bad" thing to recognize that your company may only be functioning in the bottom levels. It simply means that you have a greater opportunity to really make a difference and influence shareholder value in a noticeable way.

Moving from one level to the next in the Value Hierarchy requires discipline, organization, and leadership. And it requires a road map to avoid the mistakes made by similar organizations in the past. It is important for a company to know the best practices used by other IP leaders, both inside the company's industry as well as in other industries. By mastering all five levels, a company can get the most out of all its intellectual capital—including, perhaps most importantly, its patents.

In this book, we will focus on patents—but we will put them in a broader context. We know full well that intellectual property represents only a small fraction of all of the ideas and innovations of a firm. As mentioned earlier, intellectual capital includes human capital, intellectual assets, and, within that group, intellectual property.

The value hierarchy discussed in this chapter applies to the *entire* spectrum of intellectual capital, not just the intellectual property. In this book, however, we will focus on intellectual property, especially patents.

Of all types of intellectual property, the quintessential one is the patent. Indeed, it bears the very name of public protection. The term *patent* derives from *litterae patentes,* meaning something that is disclosed, rather than secret. By publishing—or rendering "patent"—an invention, the inventor protects his or her rights to it. The patent is also the most common form of intellectual property in most businesses, and as we say, "is the most tangible of the intangibles." Also, the protection it grants is arguably the strongest.

THE INTELLECTUAL PROPERTY MANAGEMENT SYSTEM

To fully understand the Value Hierarchy, one should have a way of viewing the systems used by companies to manage and extract value from their intellectual assets. Such a system can be referred to as the Intellectual Property Management System (IPMS). The following exhibit (Exhibit 6) depicts a generic IPMS as visualized by the Gathering companies.

Although no one company uses a system identical to the one shown below, the Gathering companies have agreed that if they were to start all over again, they would each likely design a system with the components described in the box below. In the chapters to follow, we focus on these components as they relate to the best practices detailed for each level of the Hierarchy. (See Exhibit 7 for further detail.)

Each firm involved in extracting value from its intangible assets inevitably uses a set of activities and decisions similar to that described below. Each such firm tailors the activities and decisions to suit its individual context. In addition to tailoring the activities and decisions involved in the management of the firm's intangible assets, there are also significant issues surrounding how a firm will organize itself to operate and manage this set of decisions and activities.

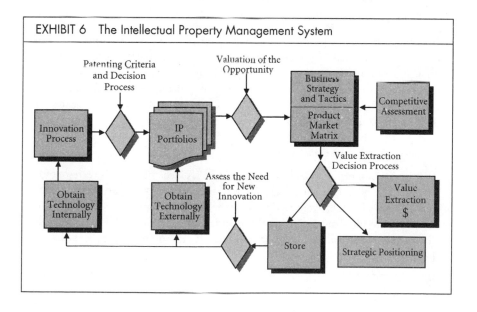

EXHIBIT 6   The Intellectual Property Management System

EXHIBIT 7   The Innovation Process

All firms have their own approach and method for developing new or innovative ideas that create value. For many technology companies the innovation process is an R&D activity; service companies, on the other hand, often have a creativity department; still others rely on their employees in the field to produce innovative ideas. Whatever the firm's source of new innovations, the generic system calls this the *innovation process*. This process has both decisions (represented by diamonds) and activities (represented by squares).

◇ *Patent Criteria and Decision Process*

Most firms have a method for evaluating the innovative ideas that emerge from the innovation process. Innovations that pass the screening—those that are deemed likely to be useful to the company in pursuit of its strategy—are selected for inclusion in the company's portfolio of intellectual assets. Some companies use the screening process to determine which innovations will be patented; the decision to patent requires an investment of at least $200,000 to obtain and maintain worldwide legal protection for an innovation over its 20-year life. This decision is important for all companies because it separates ideas that are of particular interest to the firm from ideas that, though they may be good and interesting, are not aligned with the firm's strategy. (When a firm decides not to patent, it often maintains an innovation as the know-how of its employees, sometimes formally protecting this knowledge as a trade secret.)

☐ *The Intellectual Asset Portfolio*

The intellectual asset portfolio is in fact a series of portfolios containing the firm's different kinds of intellectual assets. Some of the portfolios may contain intellectual properties; others may contain documents of potential business interest (e.g., customer lists, price lists, business practices, and internal processes); and others may contain ideas or innovations that are in the portfolio because of their potential to create profits.

◇ *Coarse Valuation of Opportunity*

Each innovation of potential interest should be "valued" before it is reviewed for use. "Valuation" in this sense is a bifurcated process. The first part of the valuation process is to narratively describe how the intellectual property is expected to bring value to the firm. Following this qualitative valuation, and where it is possible to do so, the firm should attempt to quantify the amount of value it expects the innovation to provide.

(continues)

EXHIBIT 7   Continued

☐ *A Simple Competitive Assessment*

While competitive assessments in business are commonplace, the competitive assessment contemplated here is one that is focused on the intellectual property of the competitition.

☐ *Business Strategy/Tactics/Product-Market Matrix*

This portion of the intellectual property management system involves a review of intellectual properties of interest matched with the firm's business strategy, tactics, and product/market mix. The outcome of this review is an assessment of the fit between this asset and the organization's strategy, and a decision about how to use or dispose of the intellectual property under review.

◇ *The Value Extraction Decision Process*

The decision concerning the disposition of reviewed intellectual properties may have several possible outcomes. The intellectual property may be commercialized, used to gain strategic position, or stored until another innovation is developed that makes the first one more marketable.

◇ *Assess the Need for New Innovation*

This decision process is invoked where it has been decided that a new innovation should be sought to add to an existing innovation to make the first more marketable. In this case, the question is whether to seek the new innovation from inside or outside the company (through, e.g., in-licensing, acquisition of a company, etc.).

CONCLUSION

We agree with Pat Sullivan of ICMG when he says, "Intellectual capital is the creator of cash flow!" Certainly a firm's market value includes the present value of the future cash flows the firm is expected to generate from its intellectual assets.

So the question really is, how exactly can a company convert its intellectual assets—particularly intellectual property—into the greatest amount of cash over time? As recently as five years ago, we would be hard-pressed to answer that question without resorting to generalities. Today, however, we have a wealth of best-practice knowledge about value extraction.

In our consulting careers we have been privileged to meet individuals who are clearly "ahead of their time" when it comes to realizing value from their companies' innovations and ideas. As mentioned earlier, we have learned much by working with the members of the Gathering. This book is a collection of their learnings, along with success stories of other leading companies we have encountered in our work with clients who were striving to do a better job in leveraging and monetizing their intellectual assets.

Like Edison, these practitioners are at the forefront of this value realization revolution. Many of the individuals we interviewed were tapped by their CEOs to find value—usually cash—in activities previously seen as little more than necessary cost. Many were expected to fail, but most succeeded. Like Thomas Edison the man, and like the companies he founded, the companies in this book uphold the value of sustained, collective effort. It was this kind of effort that would eventually enable Edison to create and realize value from his innovations, showing that the place for value creation and realization is not only the laboratory but also the boardroom.

In the following pages, we will help you use a forward-looking, yet methodical approach worthy of the Man from Menlo Park. For the remainder of this book, we authors, joined by the spirit of Thomas Edison, will travel with you as we build a Value Hierarchy for your company's intellectual property—and, beyond this, all its intellectual assets. So turn the page to take the next step of the journey.

1

LEVEL ONE—DEFENSIVE

IN THE GOLD rush days of more than a century and a half ago, "Forty-Niners" learned there were different levels of value to be obtained from gold mining. The first of these involved staking and defending a claim. Today too, the first step is protection. This is the spirit of the Value Hierarchy's *Level One, Defensive* shown in Exhibit 1.1.

Defense of intellectual property—including patents, trademarks, and copyrights, as well as ownership offered through various types of agreements— is a necessary and desirable activity. Indeed, protection is the foundation of value. For example, patents give inventors adequate time to apply and market an idea before others do.

Much as a miner must stake a claim in the land containing gold, or a shareholder must hold a stock certificate, a patent holder must own a patent. Only after staking claims can the owner of the intellectual property actually achieve the other levels of intellectual property value. To continue the "gold rush" metaphor, these might be seen as panning (Level Two, the initial savings of cost control), mining (Level Three, deeper profit-seeking), processing (Level Four, integration with other operations), and, finally, sculpting into new forms (Level Five, Visionary). These five levels constitute an overall process for the management of intellectual property—a process that depends on the foundation of *defense of ownership*.

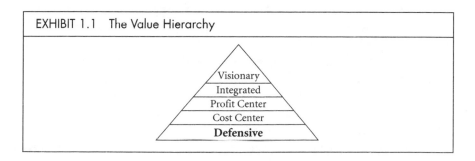

EXHIBIT 1.1 The Value Hierarchy

Visionary
Integrated
Profit Center
Cost Center
Defensive

We begin our discussion of best practices by focusing attention on the companies at the first level of IP management—the Defensive Level. Level One firms are concerned with the creation and management of sufficient numbers of patents protecting the firm's technologies to ensure defense against potential infringers. Companies at this level typically see the role of intellectual property as purely defensive. The primary concerns for companies at this level are the classical defensive objectives: protection, litigation minimization, and design freedom. Companies at this level are often focused on accruing a sufficient number and breadth of patents to provide the desired protection. These companies are involved with creating and implementing processes for identifying technologies offering patenting opportunities, screening these opportunities against the company's vision and strategy, prosecuting the patents through issuance, and enforcing the patents against infringers.

What Level One Companies Are Trying to Accomplish

At Level One, companies are trying to accomplish five things:

1. Generate a significant number of patents for their IP portfolio
2. Ensure that their core business is adequately protected
3. Initiate basic processes to facilitate patent generation and maintenance
4. Initiate basic processes for enforcing patents
5. Ensure that their technical people have freedom to innovate

Management activities for Level One companies often are pointed toward getting the largest number of applicable patents as quickly as resources will allow. Companies at this level are concerned with the quantity and quality of patent output (effectiveness). While costs are a natural concern, they are usually of lesser importance than the need to obtain the desired protection. According to Joe Villella, a partner with the Palo Alto law firm of Gray Cary Ware & Freidenrich, "Very often, companies at this stage are playing catch-up as they realize that their competitors have patent portfolios and they don't. Sometimes this point is driven home when they're on the wrong side of a license agreement and have to pay royalties to someone against whom they're competing in the marketplace."

At Level One, companies are concerned with only the portions of the IP Management System that are the province of the IP attorneys (see Exhibit 1.2).

IP attorneys at smaller Level One companies typically spend time with the innovative R&D people to learn what kind of new ideas or projects they are considering. Through informal conversations, IP attorneys seek out ideas that are patentable, and then gather them into a prioritized list. They give the highest

EXHIBIT 1.2   Decision System with Legal Focus

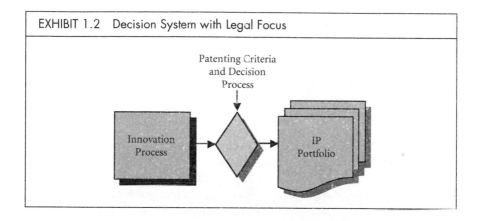

ranking to ideas related to the company's key innovations, and to those covering tactical or business opportunities. At larger companies, attorneys tend to branch out more, according to Henry Fradkin, Director, Technology Commercialization, Ford Global Technologies, Inc. (a wholly owned subsidiary of Ford Motor Company), "Attorneys may spend time with key client groups. They may also serve on patent committees to decide whether an invention should be patented. Attorneys may give presentations to draw out new invention disclosures."

This direct, dynamic approach to prioritizing and patenting the company's innovations has both advantages and disadvantages. On the advantage side, the method is simple, direct, inexpensive, and efficient—there is very little wasted effort. Nevertheless, there are some disadvantages that need to be mentioned. The process relies heavily on the IP attorneys' ability to know what is valuable to the firm—including what is strategic, tactical, and/or marketable. Further, it assumes that the IP attorneys are fully aware of competitors' business and patenting strategies, and can effectively use the company's patent creation process to neutralize competitor IP actions. Finally, the Level One approach assumes that the attorneys are constantly apprised of any changes in company strategy and tactics so that they may revise the criteria used to screen innovations for patentability.

All these expectations are worthy, but hardly realistic—especially in companies operating exclusively at Level One. Such companies are interested in IP primarily as a means to protect the ideas embedded in the products and services that they sell. Here intellectual property is used as a legal means to keep others out of their markets. Indeed, intellectual property in Level One companies is viewed as a *legal* asset. Fortunately, thanks to the progress made in the past few decades of patent law, IP can indeed be such an asset. (See Exhibit 1.3.)

EXHIBIT 1.3   A U.S. Example: The Federal Circuit

Defense is integral to IP management in any company. Fortunately, in many countries, staking a claim in intellectual property is easier today than ever before, especially where patents are concerned. In the United States, for example, patent appeals are now centralized in one court: the U.S. Court of Appeals for the Federal Circuit, known as the "Federal Circuit,"[1] which has exclusive jurisdiction over all patent appeals from other federal courts.

When viewed in light of nearly 200 years of patent law evolution, the Federal Circuit is relatively new—just two decades old. It was created with the merger of the U.S. Court of Claims and the U.S. Court of Customs and Patent Appeals—a consolidation ordered as part of the Federal Courts Improvements Act of 1982.[2] The courts certainly did need improving from a patent law perspective. Indeed, before 1982, it was not only ineffective to defend a patent by suing over infringement; it was plain risky. In the so-called Black-Douglas era (named for the Supreme Court Justices Hugo Black and William O. Douglas), the courts feared the monopoly potential of patents and discouraged them accordingly. In this era, "the chances of a patent being held valid, infringed, and enforceable, were one in three," ICMG cofounder Patrick Sullivan has noted.[3]

The courts, rather than focusing on the wrongdoing of the infringer, tended to focus on the protectability of the allegedly infringed patent, and often declared patents invalid. Consider the classic case of Westinghouse. Long before its restructuring and merger into CBS and later Viacom, the electronics giant sought to protect its circuit-breaker patents. In 1979, it petitioned the International Trade Commission to block imports on the grounds that Hitachi was infringing one of its patents. The federal courts ruled that the Westinghouse patent was not valid.[4] Westinghouse's attempt to defend its own rights caused those rights to be taken away.

This sad era in patent law is now long gone. The Federal circuit of today is handing down decisions more favorable to patent holders—making defense more worthwhile than ever. The protectability of intellectual ideas is a new and valuable notion, says Mark Radcliffe, a senior partner with the Palo Alto-based Gray Cary Ware & Freidenrich: "It has only been in the last 20 years that intellectual property and especially patents were regarded in U.S. courts, not as the tools of monopolists, but as critical to national economic well-being. Furthermore, it is now generally accepted that such innovation cannot occur unless companies that succeed in the marketplace can recoup their research, development, and marketing costs. The upshot is that intellectual property is now viewed as playing a key role in developing technologies for the next century."

Best Practices for the Defensive Level

What, then, is the best way to defend IP assets? The current practice of defense is adequate, but not ideal. Having an exclusive, permanent defensive mentality can cause companies to incur unnecessary costs and forsake opportunities for revenue. To be an "Edison in the Boardroom" requires a pragmatic approach—one that adopts certain best practices.

So let us look at the practical application of defensive IP management, and examine some of the best practices used by other defenders.

In our work, we have seen five best practice areas at this level. They are listed in Exhibit 1.4.

Best Practice 1: Take Stock of What You Own

The value of research and development (R&D) is often invisible—not only to outsiders, but to IP managers as well. That great new technology just perfected by your R&D department and patented by your legal group will never appear as an asset on your company's balance sheet because it was internally generated, rather than purchased from someone else. Will you remember that it is there?

It is not unusual for us to interview corporate officers and find that they have no idea how many patents their company owns. Even with the few who do, it is often the case that they have no real understanding of what resides in their portfolios. This is not surprising. Prior to introduction of recent computer software programs designed to help manage intellectual property, the only way for a company to really understand what comprised its patent portfolio was to read each individual patent.

Some time ago, the authors met with the new licensing manager at an electronic components company that held 700 patents. We asked him how he was planning to "get his arms around" the portfolio and learn its contents. He replied that he planned to read each of the patents in full. "How long do you

---

EXHIBIT 1.4   Defensive IP: Best Practices

Best Practice 1: Take stock of what you own.
Best Practice 2: Obtain intellectual property while ensuring design freedom.
Best Practice 3: Maintain your patents (don't let the good ones lapse).
Best Practice 4: Respect the IP rights of others.
Best Practice 5: Be willing to enforce, or don't bother to patent at all.

expect that to take?" we asked. "Well," he replied, "I think I'll be able to make it through about two patents a week." He was in for several long years of work! In another instance, when we met with the chief patent officer of a Fortune 500 firm, and asked what was contained in his portfolio, he sighed and pointed to some 20 file cabinets containing all of his company's patents.

Companies are now able to download the contents of their patent portfolios from a variety of online sources. If nothing else, companies should create a list of all of their intellectual property that has been granted, filed, and is currently pending.

According to John Cronin, CEO of *ip*Capital Group, Inc., a professional services firm specializing in creating and executing intellectual property

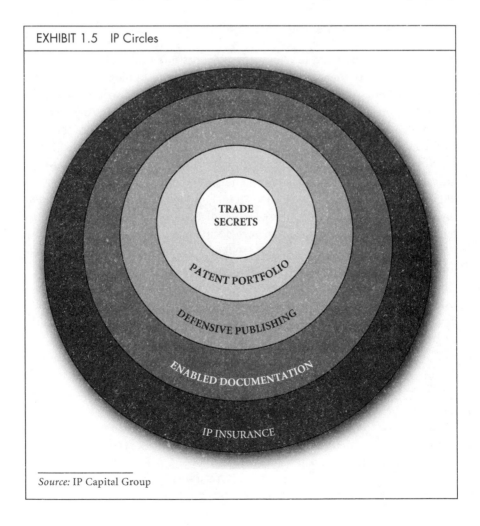

EXHIBIT 1.5   IP Circles

TRADE SECRETS

PATENT PORTFOLIO

DEFENSIVE PUBLISHING

ENABLED DOCUMENTATION

IP INSURANCE

Source: IP Capital Group

strategies and portfolios, "We need to remember that intellectual property is not just patents. The way we help our clients think about intellectual property is to visualize it in terms of protected innovation, as illustrated in Exhibit 1.5 by a set of concentric circles.

The inner circle illustrates trade secrets. We always recommend that inventors maintain some portion of their invention as a trade secret. A trade secret is a company's know-how, in other words a combination of things that individually are well-known but in combination are not known and provide leverage, but would not be patented because the patent would expire before the product leaves the market (like Coca Cola®) or by the time a patent would issue, the technology would change again. In terms of defensively protecting your intellectual property, this is core to a good strategy. If you have patents, and you don't have a formalized trade secret program, then chances are the company doesn't understand the elements that make up a comprehensive and well-protected IP system. This is key, because in our experience, too many people patent an invention without reserving the appropriate piece as a trade secret. To maximize the value of the patent, you always want to patent what no one else can do, and you never want to give away the complete recipe.

The next circle illustrates another layer of strategic protection: defensive publishing. We believe the concept of prior art management and defensive publishing will continue to grow as a focused strategy primarily because companies are constantly in the position of having to incrementally justify the cost of the volume of patents it believes it needs. By integrating defensive publications into the picture, a company can employ a tactic that strengthens the position of its basic patents by publishing—in volumes if necessary—around the patents.

Next is the circle containing all the enabled documentation, which is really where it all begins. Nothing can progress to a patent, a publication, a trade secret, or any other intellectual property instrument unless you have the enablement documented. In any IP portfolio there will be some initiatives that are documented, but not converted to trade secrets or patents or publications. They are documented, nonetheless, as confidential subject matter.

The outer circle illustrates an emerging best practice called IP insurance. Surveys of CEO's around the globe demonstrate that they all agree on one major issue: Creative ideas rapidly converted into enabled innovation are mandatory to success. And no matter how well you cover the bases, mistakes will be made. We believe that IP insurance will continue to grow as a standard risk management best practice."

As a part of this inventory, companies should also look beyond the narrow definition of intellectual property to include IP-related documents such as license agreements. A *license agreement,* often referred to simply as a license, is an agreement between two parties (companies and/or individuals) regarding the use of intellectual property. License agreements can be for an in-license or an out-license. An in-license agreement means that one company can use, adapt, sell, or otherwise benefit from another company's invention. An out-license does the opposite. The inventory of licensing agreements should include both "in" licenses, requiring the company to pay for another party's intellectual property, and "out" licenses. Some companies engage in numerous cross-licenses—discussed further below.

Licenses are essential to the ability of a corporation to continue to conduct its business. Therefore, the IP function should ensure that all such necessary licenses are current and in good order. In order to use licenses effectively, a company should review the proper documents pertaining to licenses, including:

- All intellectual property licenses where the company is a *licensee,* including names of parties, dates of expiration, rights granted, and any pertinent restrictions such as territory or transferability.
- All intellectual property licenses where the company is *licensor,* including names of parties, dates of expiration, rights granted, and any pertinent restrictions.

In addition, the inventory needs to take into account nondisclosure and noncompete agreements, joint venture agreements, and any partnerships related to the exchange of intellectual property.

EXHIBIT 1.6   An Intangibles Audit List

- All inventions that are not the subject of issued patents, but may be the subject of patent applications, or where the company may be able to establish dates for invention, discovery, or reduction to practice dates.
- All software developed by or for the company
- All known trade secrets from which the company derives economic benefit by keeping it secret
- Documents reflecting the company's policies and procedures relating to the creation, maintenance and protection of trade secrets, such as the company's written confidentiality policies and nondisclosure agreements
- Documents relating to hiring and exit interviews of technology and other sensitive personnel
- Nondisclosure agreements (often called NDAs) with R&D staff
- All license agreements whether the company is the licensor or licensee
- Any documentation relating to proprietary know-how such as a description and the place or person in whom it resides

According to Gray Cary's Villella; "The first step in getting a handle on your intellectual property, is to know what you own. We advise companies to inventory their intellectual property that has been granted, filed and is currently in process and update it routinely." For a more detailed description, see Exhibit 1.6.

Best Practice 2: Obtain Intellectual Property while Ensuring Design Freedom

Whether your inventory turns up only a few patents or many, it is wise to encourage the creation of more patents. This means, in part, encouraging innovation—an important aspect of patent acquisition. (In addition, patents can be acquired from other companies, but this is not always possible or optimal.)

Jim O'Shaughnessy, Vice President and Chief Intellectual Property Counsel, Rockwell International, believes strongly in the importance of not only generating but also protecting new technology. His company has not always emphasized protection, however. "Think about what Rockwell has always been—at least within our lifetime. It's been a pioneer in air and space. We are the company that made B-1 bombers and space shuttles." With such grand programs, sometimes patents got overlooked, he notes wryly, "It was more important to know four star generals than to know the top patent attorneys."

In 1996, Rockwell sold its aerospace and defense operations to Boeing Company. The remaining company had to build on its nondefense technology—which required an expansion of its IP profile. At first, many managers thought that they could simply go out and buy the technology. But recently, the company has come to realize the importance of generating technology at home. "We will continue to buy, but we will buy with one hand, and build and protect with the other," says O'Shaughnessy.

As IBM's top inventor and, now, as a CEO of an intellectual property professional services firm, John Cronin has been able to live every step of the creative process that goes into building new technology. "I firmly believe that at the core of all well protected innovation is understanding what an invention is, and then understanding the supporting elements that must be included in the documentation. More opportunity is lost and liabilities incurred because people don't pay enough attention to the art of documenting invention. If it's a publication, it must be documented as 'enabled prior art.' A trade secret, same thing. It is the ability to enable and document invention, including never losing sight of the constantly evolving requirements of IP, that creates the envelope of protection. No matter what strategy you employ, no matter how vision you are, no matter what your licensing-out program is, it never gets anywhere, really, unless the core engine of intellectual property is the inventor documenting his invention. We tell our clients, if you do this one thing well, you will be miles ahead of every company. In fact, we advise our clients, as an exercise in due diligence, to include in the process of a product release one last look at the thinking that went into the product, at the inventions surrounding the product, the publications, the trade secrets and most importantly, the credibility of the documentation. I have yet to meet a company that has the required discipline built into its product release cycles, not one. Unfortunately, I've met many companies who wish they had, so we have a long way to go."

Tom Colson, CEO of IP.com, a popular repository for prior art management, adds, "We created IP.com as the world headquarters for prior art management because we knew that the number one challenge that goes hand-in-hand with patenting is that it is extremely expensive to protect all corporate innovation with patents alone. But we also know that it is potentially far more expensive to go without patenting. As the patent race becomes more and more aggressive, patenting becomes more and more expensive. After you add up the legal fees, government fees, maintenance fees, translation fees, inventors' time, and more legal fees, it's hard to believe that anyone can afford to file patents for even a small fraction of their inventive ideas. And when you consider that the number of inventive ideas in most companies is approximately 10 times the number of developers, engineers, and researchers per year, it becomes clear that patenting all corporate innovation is an impossibility."

"But, what if you don't patent? And worse, what if your competitors patent the innovation that you leave in a drawer? Now the costs get out of control: litigation fees (Average legal fees for a patent infringement case in the US are over $1.5M, regardless of the outcome.), adverse verdicts (It is now common to see eight and nine figure verdicts, and recently there have been a few 10 figures verdicts.), royalty payments *to your competitors,* downstream redesign (sometimes post product launch), and lost time to market (preliminary injunctions, wasted time of developers in depositions and trial, and permanent injunctions)."

"So how do you protect your freedom to practice without patenting? You can publish defensively, an activity that is becoming increasingly important to the overall strategy of protected innovation."

So how exactly can an organization obtain intellectual property by encouraging innovation? One source of good ideas is the Human Capital division of Andersen, which has worked with many companies seeking to encourage innovation through their systems for employee management, recognition, and reward.[6] Here are some techniques companies are using.

- *Institute a formal "innovation initiative."* Senior management can adopt a slogan or phrase that expresses a commitment to the continuous generation of ideas that can be brought to market. One famous example of this is the new Hewlett-Packard logo, which shows an imperative slogan, "INVENT," under the HP signage.

- *Dedicate resources to innovation*—including the resource of time and a climate of cooperation. Some of the biggest killers of innovation are inhuman workloads and an excessive degree of interdepartmental competition.
- *Ensure employees' intellectual development by instituting a program for training and job transfers.* Nothing dulls creativity like routine; and nothing enhances it more than new challenges. Do not let your employees get in a professional rut.
- *Encourage work groups.* Structuring work groups not only improves performance but also contributes to self esteem and sense of empowerment.
- *Communicate, communicate.* Organizations can encourage innovation by showcasing successful innovations through vehicles such as company newsletters, press releases, and rallies. If senior management sees barriers to innovation in the organization, the communications can explore these as well.
- *Include innovation in the company's appraisal program.* Leadership skills, technical competence, relationships with others, judgment, and creativity, can all be measured, coached, communicated, and encouraged. Such attributes should be a part of the assessment of all employees, especially those who are managing R&D staff.
- *Support "intrapreneurs."* If an employee goes against the grain, others may chafe. Senior managers must look beyond criticism based on personality clashes and see if the individual's ideas have merit worthy of financial support.
- *Design an innovation reward and recognition program.* Compensation literature is full of ideas for how to incentivize behavior—and creative behavior is no different. Employees respond to nonmonetary as well as monetary awards.[7]

On this last point, most companies offer incentives to encourage their scientists, engineers, and other inventors to notify the IP function of potentially patentable discoveries. Indeed, all but one of the companies we interviewed used some sort of patent incentive system. ICMG's benchmarking studies on incentives have found this typical pattern for incentive programs:

$25 to $100 for each disclosure submittal

$500 to $1,500 for each inventor upon submittal of patent filing

$500 and/or a plaque upon patent issuance

And some companies also increase the reward to their inventors by adding an extra incentive for company usage of the new technology.

Not all companies reward their inventors in dollars. Most companies combine dollars and peer recognition as integral parts of their incentive structure. The ultimate determination of the incentive structure should be based on the culture of the firm and also recognition of whether patenting is in the job descriptions of the technical personnel. (See Exhibit 1.7.)

As the scope of what is patentable continues to increase (now including business methods, for example) incentive systems may need to be broadened as well to include nontechnical (i.e., business and administrative) personnel under the heading of "innovators." In doing so, a company may need to mount

---

EXHIBIT 1.7   Recognizing and Rewarding Innovation

An innovation reward and recognition program might contain the following elements:

Nonmonetary awards

> Extravagant luncheons or dinners celebrating innovation
> Gift certificates or catalogue gift awards
> Plaques, ribbons, and other recognition awards
> Honorable mention in the company newsletter
> Free time off
> Free educational courses
> Election to an Innovation Circle or Innovation Committee
> Innovation trips (offsite meetings focusing on innovation)

Monetary awards

> Raises in base salary (better annual pay for successful inventors)
> Cash bonuses (awarded to individuals or teams for successful inventions)
> Promotions (granting a better title to inventors)
> Phantom stock (paying "dividends" on increasing value of innovation)
> Gain sharing (group shares in income from their invention)
> Funded pools (setting aside revenues from invention for key individuals only)
> Performance incentives (same as gain-sharing, but tied to efforts at commercialization)

Adapted from *HR Director: The Arthur Andersen Guide to Human Capital* (New York: Profile Pursuit, 1999), pp. 142–144.

a strong IP education and process to indoctrinate nontechnical personnel into the ways of intellectual property.

The criteria used to screen patents should be a part of any incentive program the company may have to generate patents. Most companies will typically offer incentives to encourage their scientists, engineers, and other inventors to notify the IP function of potentially patentable discoveries.

According to John Cronin of *ip*Capital Group, "When I was an inventor at IBM, we surveyed 30,000 employees/inventors. And we tried to determine the number one reason why inventors invented. Out of 30,000 people, do you know what the number one response was? Most inventors invent because they like to solve problems—intrinsic motivation! They like the challenge, OK? But you know the number one reason why people actually wrote the patent up? For the money. The remuneration we gave them was considered compensation for the administrative efforts they had to go through to submit the patent. The real self-satisfaction came from solving problems, but we still needed the inventors to write up the invention, and to care about doing it right."

At IBM, the screening process determines the award given for each disclosed invention. A small award is given even for invention disclosures that ultimately result only in defensive publications. Larger awards are given for disclosures deemed patent-worthy by the screening process. Plateau awards sit atop the individual filing awards, and factor in both invention disclosures rated for publication and those rated for patenting, encouraging disclosure generally, quality in particular, and "repeat" business. The program has helped IBM generate thousands of invention disclosures and thousands of patent applications a year.

Rockwell, for example, has abandoned its old incentive approach that rewarded engineers and managers for filing a large number of patents. Instead, the company is focusing on the *quality* of the innovations. It is currently working on a plan to offer nonvoting restricted stock keyed to the value of the innovation, according to Rockwell's Jim O'Shaughnessy. A unique approach used at Avery Dennison was to issue gold and silver coins. Paul Germeraad, former VP and Director, Corporate Research explains "issuing collectable coins was a clear statement that the true value of an asset extends well beyond its face value. The coins had face values of one dollar, but a market value of between $10 and $150 depending on the date and precious metal content. These coins were valued more highly than any of the cash awards we offered."

Some companies worry that incentive programs for innovators can become entitlements. Steve Fox of HP has found a way around that. "We try to avoid having the incentive become an entitlement, so we say the incentive program is for a one-year period and renewable for a subsequent one-year period upon the decision of the general manager of the business based on what he or she sees as the results of the program. This permits the manager to stand up in a coffee talk and say 'Our program did great last year, we're going to renew it; and this coming year we'd really like to see more invention disclosures in such and such an area.' You'll pick a technology—let's say Internet interface printers—and the incentive program permits you to steer inventions into that area."

Even aside from the commercial value of patents, obtaining patents can be valuable as a potential counterdefense. Having a great number of patents helps shield a company from lawsuits by giving it the wherewithal to countersue. Competitors think twice before filing a patent infringement lawsuit against a company that could turn around and sue them on a different patent. When filing for patents, one need not stop at one. The great defenders develop a literal "thicket" of patents surrounding single inventions. Gillette is famous for utilizing this practice to sustain a market choke hold. According to John Bush, Gillette's former vice president of R&D,

> We patented the key design features in the cartridge, the springs, the angle of the blades, that sort of thing. There were also patents covering the handle and some of its characteristics. We even patented the container that had the proper masculine sound and feel as it was ripped. We covered all the features that we thought would be of value to the consumer. We created a patent wall with those 22 patents. And they were all interlocking so that no one could duplicate the product.[8]

Lee Benkgay, general counsel for the biotechnology firm Incyte, likens patents to a "protective" shield and, furthermore, to money: "Patents are like currency," he says. "The more, the better."[9]

For attorney Joe Villella; "One approach to building a portfolio is known as the "coal pile" approach. If the coal pile is big enough, there's bound to be a diamond or two somewhere in the coal pile." Villella continues:

> A problem with this approach occurs when you're dealing with a sophisticated potential licensee who actually searches through your coal pile and doesn't find any diamonds. Companies are not willing to pay diamond prices for chunks of coal. It can also be more than a little embarrassing when you have to tell your CEO that despite all the patents that you've been able to obtain, not a single one of them covers the products of your biggest competitor.

To ensure broad coverage, Hewlett-Packard initiated a program to increase its pace of patenting in 1996. In two years' time, the program achieved a 60 percent increase in the number of patents issued. The program, now five years old, pays various awards to inventors. There is a small cash award on submitting an invention disclosure, and then a larger cash award when the patent application is filed. A personalized plaque is presented when the patent is granted. The company also recognizes its inventors in public gatherings such as coffee talks or annual banquets. Financial aspects of the program are handled by the R&D functions, while the legal department identifies the inventors and handles the creation of the plaques.[10] Ford Motor Company has a similar program that also has been very successful in soliciting new ideas and inventions for quality patents.

HP is not the only company that has made valiant efforts to increase the level of its patented inventions. This is one of Microsoft's keys to marketplace success. At the beginning of 1990, the company had only five patents. The leadership team, headed by CEO Bill Gates, made a strategic decision to increase the number of patents. By the end of 2000 Microsoft owned nearly 1,500 patents.[11]

Yet another example of a proactive patenter is Celera. Robert Millman, Celera's general counsel, regularly attends research meetings to discuss genetic inventions, helping engineers to decide which are worth patenting, and which would receive better protection as trade secrets.[12]

Setting goals for a high number of patents can have negative (but preventable) side effects. A single patent attorney working in a corporation cannot do it all. In the words of Bill Frank, chief patent counsel for S.C. Johnson:

> The patent lawyers will put a lot of time into intellectual asset management. When they do, they will recognize that they also cannot file "x" number of patent applications that year. If they are trying to accomplish both tasks, the "x" will usually win, and the asset management will fall by the wayside. You have to give them relief on that and allow them to use outside counsel.

IBM has struck this balance using an entity it refers to as the "virtual law firm." The company recruits its retiring patent attorneys, along with nonretirement eligible attorneys seeking a stay-at-home work/life balance. It associates these proven performers with one of its outside counsel, and guarantees them levels of patent filing and prosecution work at fixed fees. The win-win generates a large stable of company-savvy, technology-experienced patent practitioners at rates untouchable in a traditional law firm relationship. It is one of the cornerstones of IBM's push for a high-quality, cost-effective filing strategy.

Companies working to build up a large number of patent applications would be wise to heed Bill Frank's advice—and look for quality as well as quantity. One company that has mastered the high-quality or "strategic" patent is Hitachi. In 1980, the company suffered a "bitter lesson" when it lost a countersuit against Westinghouse. A recent article about Hitachi tells the tale:

Patents are valuable, of course, when the company uses them, but their true value shows up when other companies have no choice but to use them. Hitachi realized there was no point in obtaining a mountain of patents if they were not going to give the company any competitive leverage in crunch situations.[13]

In short, not every invention should be patented. Indeed, to paraphrase William Shakespeare's Hamlet, *To patent or not to patent? That is the question.* Unfortunately, it is a question that is not asked often enough in the halls of the great defenders. The mentality in such companies was born in a time when the best defense was a good offense—ownership of as many inventions and patents, in as many areas as possible.

Rather than patenting everything, it may be best to consider a spectrum of patenting options—including patenting nothing at all (which may be a valid strategy for some businesses at certain times).

Here are the main choices, based on our experience with a variety of companies:

- Do not patent anything.
- Patent the occasional discovery of quite exceptional importance.
- Patent discoveries that have a clear application to your own company's products or processes.
- Patent discoveries that have a strong chance of technical success regardless of potential business application or use.
- Patent discoveries that might block or delay products implementing similar later discoveries by other companies within or outside one's industry—"strategic patents."
- Patent in order to have a portfolio with which to negotiate business agreements (licenses, joint ventures, alliances, and so forth) with other companies.
- Patent everything that is patentable.

This leads us to another important aspect of encouraging invention. As much as technologists would like to design every aspect of the company's products and technologies, no one company can design everything relating to their products. According to Jerry Rosenthal, Vice President of Intellectual Property and Licensing at IBM,

Cross-licenses are very valuable to IBM. We can't invent everything. It is important to keep your business growing. To grow in the IT industry you need to have access to inventions of others. We have patents that our competitors need, and they in turn have patents we need. We view cross-licensing as a strategic opportunity rather than a compromise. For example, we make inventions in businesses we are not in or won't go into. We use these inventions not only for revenue generation, but also to gain access to others' portfolios outside the core of the IT industry.

According to Steve Fox, Associate General Counsel of Hewlett-Packard:

Getting patents does two things for you: not only does it establish your prowess in the business, but it also gives you trading material so that if somebody else happens to be better at a disruptive technology than we are—for example some smaller start-up companies who can move very quickly—they may wind up with patents in key areas in disruptive technologies and beat us to the punch. But on the other hand, it is only a matter of time before this start-up company moves into our competitive space, infringing our patents, and then we often end up agreeing to cross-license.

So what does it mean to ensure design freedom and have access to the technology of others? Well, it means that a company's technical team can invent in a given area without the threat of infringement from a third party. It also means that a company can be immune from litigation, as we learned from Fred Boehm, chief patent counsel for IBM:

Back in the early 1970s we did a cross-license agreement with RCA. We did a cross-license and had a valuable patent portfolio and it turned out that RCA had some very basic patents that went to what is known today as the TFT/LCD architecture and displays on your laptop. This was before there were displays. Even before PCs.

We formed a joint venture called DTI with Toshiba in 1989 to make these displays. They make them according to IBM's design specifications and so all they are is a manufacturing facility. RCA still had some old but very valuable patents and went out to DTI and they said we are licensing everybody in the world to these patents and you will have to pay significant amounts of money.

Of course, they called us up and called Toshiba up and told us about this. I reminded RCA that under the license agreement we had these products were being built for IBM and also Toshiba. They were covered under the license agreement we signed in 1981. Although RCA was able to collect significant royalties from the entire industry, the IBM products DTI builds for us that go into our displays today are covered by that old agreement. This has given us a significant advantage in the marketplace.

Best Practice 3: Maintain Your Patents (Don't Let the Good Ones Lapse)

Check to make sure all maintenance fees have been paid, so that all the patents you own are truly active. If a patent lapses, you can lose it. Consider the loss this represents for a company that has made substantial investments in research and development.

Achieving strong defense does not require any complicated systems. As mentioned earlier, one can use a simple docketing system—a tickler file to remind the company of when to pay the maintenance fees. Without these basic docketing systems, there is always the risk that patents can be accidentally abandoned, because the company fails to pay the fee on time. However, larger and worldwide portfolios require more sophistication. IBM has created an end-to-end patent management system it calls WPTS—worldwide patent tracking system. Among its many functions, WPTS automatically tracks patent aging in all countries in which a patent family has issued, ensuring timely payment of maintenance fees with sensitivity to currency factors and deposit accounts available in some major patent offices.

One major company discovered during one patent maintenance review that it had allowed 10 percent of its patents to lapse. We know of another company executive who learned, while drafting a license for one of its foreign patents, that his company no longer owned those patent rights because it had failed to pay the maintenance fees on time. In a third more fortunate circumstance, one of our clients discovered that a competitor's patent on an important diesel engine technology had been allowed to lapse. Our client is now using that technology to compete in a new and profitable market.

Fradkin notes that the flip side to this is that a "good" company should have a process to evaluate the strategic and the tactical values of their patents. A default of "renew unless you hear otherwise" can lead to an expensive carrying of patents that have no value to the company and should be sold, donated or abandoned (see Level Three).

Best Practice 4: Respect the IP Rights of Others

The topic of ensuring ownership leads naturally to the subject of compliance with the law. This is another obvious best practice to pursue at the defensive level. A company must be careful not to infringe patents, trademarks, and copyrights held by others—otherwise, its ability to protect its own intellectual property will be weakened.

It is not always possible to avoid patent infringement, since inventions may occur simultaneously. However, by keeping a lab book and other records, a company can show that the infringement was unwitting—that is, that it stemmed from a simultaneous invention, not from an attempt to copy someone else's proprietary technology.

Note that patent, trademark, and copyright law are not all-inclusive when it comes to compliance. Companies must also be sensitive to trade secrets. That is, if one company uses a trade secret from another company without authorization, it may be guilty of theft under common law of "misappropriation."

The information taken in both cases is considered proprietary, even if it is not protected under patent, trademark, and copyright law. Some companies opt not to obtain patents and instead rely on the laws enforcing trade secrets.[14]

As a part of compliance, companies should avoid obtaining trade secrets by hiring employees or subcontractors from other organizations considered to be competitors. If the departing employee or the subcontractor brings valuable technical knowledge, it is important to make sure the employee owns that knowledge, and that it is not a trade secret proprietary to the previous employer. As such, employers should be aware of *assignments and transfers* of intellectual property to or from employees and subcontractors. These documents include:

- Documents showing assignments of intellectual property to or from the company, including grants of security interests
- Documents showing the recording of assignments of applications for intellectual property rights, including grants of security interests
- Documents showing releases of security interests in intellectual property, as well as the recording of such releases
- Agreements with persons or entities that may create, work with, or have access to the company's intellectual property (including employees and independent contractors), showing assignment to the company of rights in intellectual property and confidentiality of trade secrets
- Agreements relating to data base, processing services, and/or software
- Agreements pertaining to know-how, research and development, and technology
- Joint venture, partnership, and strategic alliance agreements
- Government grants and related agreements
- Agreements pertaining to domain names, source codes, and the like
- Noncompete and nonsolicitation agreements [15]

One good way to avoid lawsuits is to use product clearance techniques. The defense-savvy company is constantly exercising a product clearance process to avoid spending hundreds of millions of dollars of R&D to develop a new product only to find that it cannot lawfully sell the product because it is covered by someone else's patent. Early detection of these issues prior to the marketing of the final product ordinarily provides an opportunity to license-in any necessary patents at more favorable terms than might be available when the product's success is more evident.

New technology offers improved ways to avoid infringement. General Electric—heir to the Edison legacy—stays cautious by using Patent Adviser, its own proprietary version of the new "Jnana" software developed by New York-based litigator Frederic Parnon. The basis for Jnana software is a decision tree (if/then) that simulates legal questions. GE's version is used to avoid patent infringement. The computer queries the user about a proposed invention, and then searches a series of databases to find conflicting patents. It then assesses the level of infringement danger for the proposed patent or patents.[16]

IBM uses Delphion, an Internet-based company housing the entire repository of modern U.S. patents, along with patents issued in other major countries. Through traditional keyword/Boolean searching, as well as more sophisticated data-mining and mapping techniques available through Delphion, adverse patents are identified prior to product introduction.

Using Delphion, IBM has taken the clearance process a step further by integrating it into the patenting process. When an invention disclosure is searched for existence of close prior art, the prior art works both as a check against patentability and as a caution flag signaling adverse patent problems. This level of integration is in turn made possible by close correspondence between invention disclosures and products. IBM's WPTS system ensures and documents correspondence by prompting for relevant product data during disclosure submission. WPTS also includes an expert software component called the Patent Value Tool (PVT). The PVT poses a series of structured questions for use by investors and evaluators to determine the likely licensing value of an invention. Included in the PVT are questions directed to use in current or future IBM products. Actual or likely use results in a higher PVT score, increasing the likelihood of the invention being selected for patent protection. Thus, from a disclosure submission forward, IBM's IP system interlocks to integrate the clearance process (defensive) with the patenting process.

Such a product clearance process is not easy to implement but it only takes one big "find" for it to pay for itself. General Electric is now able to avoid a repeat of the patent litigation brought by Fonar years ago on one of GE's important new MRI products. The lawsuit itself resulted in an adverse judgment of nearly $129 million. And that figure does not include attorney fees or the costs of the time and energy invested in the R&D effort to develop the product and launch it commercially.

Infringement, unwitting or otherwise, costs money. For many companies, the corporate focus is on speed to market. Therefore many R&D and marketing folks are loath to engage the patent attorneys in the product development process until the very end because they perceive the legal process as "slowing everything down." As Kevin Rivette and David Kline note in *Rembrandts in the Attic,*

> Perhaps a better question to ask is, Who has the time (or the million-plus dollars) it takes to defend against a patent suit? And who can afford to devote a year or more of R&D effort on a product only to have to abandon it later because of an infringement problem that could easily have been spotted and designed around early in the process?[17]

A clear benefit of all this compliance activity is avoidance of payment to litigants in intellectual property lawsuits. It is also now possible to buy insurance to cover the company in the event of patent litigation. (See discussion of Finance and Tax in Best Practice 2 of Chapter 4.)

Best Practice 5: Be Willing to Enforce, or Don't Bother to Patent at All

A final defensive Best Practice. Once you obtain the patents, you must be willing to enforce them. Otherwise, don't patent at all. (What is the point of patenting if you are not willing to make the patent stick?) Remember, a patent is only worth what you are willing to spend to enforce it. This does not of course mean that every patent must be enforced. According to Steve Fox, Associate General Counsel and Director of Intellectual Property for Hewlett-Packard:

> We have had to struggle with our "Boy Scout" reputation. Other companies thought they could infringe our patents with impunity—and over the years it made litigation more expensive. Now we have a rather aggressive defensive posture—and also a rather aggressive offensive posture in certain areas—to protect our patents through litigation.

In addition Fox notes:

> There are some neophytes out there who hear about intellectual property management and suddenly say "Wow, I've got a patent—I'm going to go out and assert it!" And the next thing they know is that they get sued on counter claims by the party they asserted against and they get embroiled in a huge legal battle that may be difficult to get out of. For example, Xerox sued HP a couple of years ago on a single inkjet patent and they asked for a lot of money. So we went through our portfolio and found a patent they infringed and we sued

them back. Then Xerox went back into their portfolio and found another patent they thought we infringed and sued us. All in all there were six lawsuits pending before we got finished with it. And there would have been more had we not settled it, because we could have gone on endlessly based on all the patents we could choose from. A large, broad, and deep portfolio is really useful in those kinds of situations.

The goal of enforcement is for the company to create a reputation of willingness to litigate, balanced with an awareness of the rising costs of litigation. Often managers' pay is tied to division profitability, so they are reluctant to litigate in case there is a negative impact to the bottom line. Alternatively, the corporation does not want to be perceived as being unwilling to litigate.

Today, patent infringement is an increasingly significant issue, both in number and dollar amount of judgments awarded.[18] (See Exhibit 1.8.)

EXHIBIT 1.8 Top 10 Damage Awards* for the Period 1982–2000		
Case	Decision Year	Damages Awarded
Polaroid Corporation v. Eastman Kodak Company	1991	$873,158,971
Johnson & Johnson (Cordis Corp.) v. Boston Scientific Corp.	2000	324,400,000
Johnson & Johnson (Cordis Corp.) v. Medtronic/AVE Inc.	2000	271,000,000
Haworth Inc. v. Steelcase Inc.	1996	211,499,731
Smith International, Inc. v. Hughes Tool Co.	1986	204,809,349
Johnson & Johnson v. Amgen, Inc.	1998	200,000,000
The Procter & Gamble Company v. Paragon Trade Brands, Inc.	1997	178,400,000
Viskase Corporation v. American National Can Company	1999	164,900,000
Fonar Corporation, et al. v. General Electric Co., et al.	1997	128,700,000
3M v. Johnson & Johnson Orthopaedics	1992	116,797,696

*Reported in USPQ or Lexis/*Reported elsewhere.*

Conclusion: Building beyond the Defensive Level

Defense is necessary and desirable. Indeed, as a basis for future activities, defense can be a valuable way to gain IP territory for future development. And there are times for any company when the majority of attention and energy must be devoted to defense. But companies should not get "stuck" at Level One, refusing to operate outside it. Instead, they should use defense pragmatically, as one of many activities.

The five best practices in defense described in this chapter—taking stock of what you own, obtaining patents while ensuring design freedom, maintaining patents, respecting the rights of others, and being willing to enforce your patents—all can help a company stake a claim in its own future.

Claim-staking is a wise move for all kinds of companies—not just the companies with a high percentage of intangibles on their balance sheets. True, intangibles-rich companies are more successful in the current environment, as noted in our introduction. But this is partly because the managers of these companies spend the necessary time and energy creating or acquiring those intangibles, and then *claiming and protecting* them in order to develop them.

Any company can do this! Returning to our opening metaphor of a gold rush, it is useful to note that James Marshall, the man first credited with spotting gold in California, spotted it while on the job in a sawmill. He recognized its value, and immediately reported it to his employer. The rest is history.

In a similar vein, the "sawmills" of today need to be on the lookout for intellectual assets. We will see this more clearly in the next five chapters as we move beyond Level One defensive activities to review activities in the other levels: Level Two (cost control), Level Three (profit center), Level Four (integration with other operations), and Level Five (visionary).

Yes, even sawmill businesses and similar "old economy" businesses have assets that require protection. In fact, ICMG cofounder Patrick Sullivan often tells the story about a client of his:

> The CEO of a forest products company once lamented to me about the lack of intellectual capital in his industry. He defined intellectual capital as some form of sophisticated technology. In an effort to impress me with his company's attempts to fill this IC void, he told me that his firm had recently purchased and installed some sophisticated computer-controlled machinery for milling logs, but that it had been unable to produce the same amount of usable lumber per log as the company's human sawmill operators. When I pointed out to him that the mill hands and their knowledge and know-how were the very essence of intellectual

capital for his firm, he looked surprised, and then acknowledged that he had never considered intellectual capital in that way.

As in the "gold rush" that started more than a century and a half ago, the most important step is protection—the staking of a claim. So before going off into your next "gold rush," make sure that your company has staked its proper claims. Like James Marshall of Sutter's Mill, and like Thomas Edison—who followed in Marshall's claim-staking footsteps—keep your eyes open for hidden value, and then secure ownership of that value for a more prosperous future. To build that future, continue on the journey toward the boardroom, moving to the next step, cost-cutting.

2

LEVEL TWO—COST CONTROL

LEVEL TWO IS the second level of IP management evolution for firms involved with intellectual property. (See Exhibit 2.1.) Companies at Level Two are in defensive mode, just as they were at Level One. The difference is that Level Two companies have realized that IP is an expensive form of defense and they are looking for ways to manage the cost-benefit relationship so that they get greater results for their IP investment dollars. Indeed, companies at this level have come to realize that IP is an investment and it is one that requires management. Getting a real (or even a perceived) return on that investment requires that the costs be controlled as well as the outputs. For this reason, companies at Level Two find themselves interested in activities that reduce cost, increase efficiency, increase effectiveness, and raise productivity.

According to Joe Daniele, Senior Vice President of IP and Technology Commercialization at SAIC,

> What you find is, if the work is well organized, there's actually less work to do and more output. It's a matter of efficiency—less in and more out. If you're going to be competitive, and you're spending millions of dollars a year to support your portfolio, you want to make sure that portfolio is doing something for you. It's not just sitting there gathering dust. It's there to allow for licensing, cross-licensing and trade, to protect your products, to allow proprietary positions, and to allow you to

EXHIBIT 2.1   The Value Hierarchy

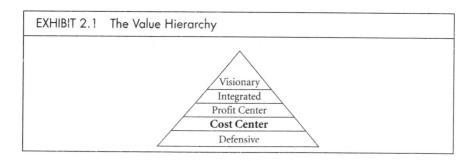

do partnerships and various equity-based arrangements as well. An IP portfolio can be a really valuable asset, and you want to make sure you're actively and efficiently managing that asset.

What Level Two Companies Are Trying to Accomplish

Companies at Level Two look beyond the defensive focus of Level One firms, although both use similar elements in their IP management decision systems. At Level Two, companies are trying to accomplish two things:

- Reduce costs associated with their IP portfolios
- Refine and focus the IP that is allowed into their portfolios

At the same time, companies continue to be engaged in two *creative* processes, as they continue to generate patents, and to refine the processes used to manage patents and the patenting process.

At Level Two, patents in the portfolio and the patenting processes are by now in place. Management efforts in Level Two are directed at improving the patenting and patent management processes in order to minimize the costs and to maximize the defensive benefits from patents.

In the previous chapter, we did not mention cost control, and for a good reason. Companies operating primarily at the Defensive Level (Level One in our pyramid) often lack any formal cost-control measures. They merely review each patent individually when it comes up. As a result, they may be blind to costs in the aggregate.

By contrast, companies operating at the Cost Control Level, or Level Two, take a higher view. They see the pattern and can aggregate costs. They separate small-dollar from large-dollar decisions—dealing with the former routinely, while giving the latter an extra level of review.

The benefits of such scrutiny are obvious. By reducing costs, companies increase their profits. This is particularly true in the later years of the life cycle of patents, when costs become higher. For example, renewing a patent in Sweden can cost up to $1,000 per patent. This may not seem like a lot to a company with millions of dollars in patent revenue, but multiplying it by 500 yields half a million dollars—not an unusual amount for a very large company. In fact, Fortune 100 companies that have studied their patenting costs have learned that their patents cost them approximately $250,000 to $500,000 per patent worldwide to obtain and maintain it over its average two-decade lifespan.

In our consulting practices, it is not unusual to find that anywhere from 5 percent to 50 percent of a company's portfolio is no longer useful and could be eliminated. Thus, just by reviewing their portfolios, many firms could realize immediate savings of hundreds of thousands of dollars! This chapter will describe how and where companies should begin to cut costs.

Companies operating at the Cost Control Level are much more proactive about patents than are companies operating at the Defensive Level. For Level Two companies, it is important to understand what patents the company holds and what patents the company is currently in the process of obtaining. Technology applications have greatly enhanced this previously tedious process. For example, many companies offer special software that can automate docketing:

- Patent Management System (Computer Packages Inc.)
- Global IP Estimator (Computer Software Associates)
- Patent Management System (Dennemeyer)
- PC Master (Master Data Center)

The electronic IP inventory systems used by Level Two are more functional than simple reminder systems. They help companies better understand how to link their innovations to cash flow, by allowing easy access to information which allows the routine evaluation about whether the patent is worth maintaining or whether it should be permitted to lapse. Some companies have even gone so far as to create their own internal applications, as IBM has done, which we will discuss later in this chapter.

It is also easier to get information about what competitors are doing. Until November 2000, patents remained confidential during the filing phase, but were published at the time they were issued. The law changed at that time such that, except under certain circumstances, all patent applications are now published 18 months after filing. To find out what patents have been issued by the U.S. Patent and Trademark Office, one merely needs to look up the agency's web site: uspto.gov.

Furthermore, the following sites—some free, some fee-based—offer not only basic information about patents, but also various kinds of analysis as well (all beginning with www. in the address):

- delphion.com
- cas.org/stn.html
- derwent.com
- dialog.com
- micropatent.com
- questel.orbit.com
- Aurigin.com

All of these analytical tools can help move a company from being a merely "defensive" firm operating at Level One, to a proactive firm operating at Level Two and beyond.

BEST PRACTICES FOR THE COST CONTROL LEVEL

These tools are valuable as far as they go, but Level Two companies go further. They adopt a series of best practices—often including these five. (See Exhibit 2.2.)

Best Practice 1: Relate Patent Portfolio to Business Use

Fundamental to the intent of companies at Level Two is the need to increase the efficiency and effectiveness of their patenting activities. In accomplishing this goal, companies must be able to match patents with the firm's business strategies and objectives. Any system or framework that increases the degree of alignment of the patent portfolio with business strategies will enhance the effectiveness and efficiency of the patent activity. Several best practices companies, all early participants in intellectual property management, have devised frameworks or schemes for categorizing current or prospective patents (and innovations) in ways that facilitate both tactical and strategic decisions about the patents in their portfolio.

To more effectively manage their intellectual property portfolios, companies must first know what their portfolios contain. This involves knowing not only simple portfolio demographics (e.g., numbers of patents and technologies, technology groupings, remaining patent life), but also information about the content or usability of the patents. Such information is useful for three reasons:

1. To obtain a clear picture of corporate technology assets and their value to support further strategic decisions and transactions
2. To be able to capitalize on technologies and their value as they become less valuable for internal use (usually due to changes in corporate strategy, etc.)

EXHIBIT 2.2   IP Cost Control: Best Practices

Best Practice 1: Relate patent portfolio to business use.
Best Practice 2: Establish an IP committee with cross-functional members.
Best Practice 3: Establish a process and criteria for screening patents.
Best Practice 4: Set detailed guidelines for patent filing and renewal.
Best Practice 5: Regularly and systematically review the portfolio to prune patents not worth maintaining.

3. To have a capability for providing information to stakeholders (investors, customers, employees, etc.) on the state of development and use of company technology assets

There is no single right way to categorize. Some companies may make a conscious decision to keep only patents related to their core technology. Others may obtain patents that do not relate to their core technology, but that can protect against competition. Japanese firms are more likely to use this approach than are U.S. firms. One-third of Japanese firms reported holding 1,000 patents they do not use in their business, compared with 7 percent of U.S. firms.[1] In firms like this, as few as 3 percent of patents may be used to support current business. Is this practice good or bad? The answer depends on the nature of the company's industry and the nature of the invention being patented. The important thing is to establish a classification scheme for the portfolio.

Companies categorize their intellectual property portfolios differently. Some companies classify the portfolio based on technology areas (IPC codes for example). Other companies classify their portfolio by business division. And yet others categorize their portfolio as "must have," "nice to have," and "junk"—not currently used by the company. When one company reviewed its patents vis-à-vis the above criteria, it found that only 20 percent were in the "must have" category," 30 percent were "nice to have," and 50 percent were "junk." Today, by following the "best practices" described for Levels One and Two in this book, the company has a different profile. It has more than doubled its percentage of "must have patents" to 45 percent, and it maintains few if any "junk" patents.

IBM uses all of these approaches. It has developed a detailed framework of technology categories optimized to the IT business, which it calls patent portfolio management codes. Every patent is placed in one or more PPM codes, enabling IBM's portfolio managing attorneys to quickly access patents related to a given competitor's technology, to group patents for maintenance evaluation, and to understand overall portfolio strength across particular technologies. IBM's codes are continuously updated based on its research activities, ensuring a forward-looking applicability IPC codes are unable to match.

At the same time, IBM assigns and maintains one or more division codes for each patent, supporting correlation of the portfolio on a business unit basis. Finally, every patent is given a relative value score from 1 to 3, indicating overall value to the portfolio. This score is based on factors such as claim scope, applicability to a standard, past usefulness in licensing, association with Nobel Prize or other major award, coverage over an industry-wide practice, etc.

Patent scores are regularly updated as patents issue and age. The scores are then used in making maintenance decisions.

All three categorization approaches are recorded in IBM's WPTS which supports full relational queries across categories. The categories thus integrate to generate value-revealing intelligence not obtainable from a single category in isolation.

One consideration should be the use of the patent. How does the company plan to use each patent? Will it be used to support an existing technology, to prevent a competitor from using a technology, or to reserve a technology for future use? All are valid goals, and should be spelled out as part of the company's criteria for assessing intellectual property.

Fortum (formerly Neste Oy) a Finnish company, is one of the largest energy companies in the Nordic region operating in oil and gas exploration and production, oil refining and marketing as well as in power and heat generation and electricity distribution. In 1994, Neste Oy was faced with the prospect of spinning off its petrochemical and polyolefin business and combining it with the Norwegian state-owned Statoil into a new company called Borealis. Neste, in anticipation of the merger, undertook a technology audit to help it better understand the contents of its existing portfolio, separate the petrochemical and polyolefin related technology assets to better understand the effect the Borealis merger would have on Neste's profitability and ability to extract more value from the company's existing intellectual assets. In Exhibit 2.3 Jan-Erik Osterholm, Technology Asset Manager for Fortum, tells the story.

A simple variant of the methodology developed at Fortum was utilized at Avery Dennison. "Our financial community had rank-ordered the 60 or so operating divisions into those that were in a growth mode, those whose operations we needed to sustain, and those that were cash cows that we either needed to milk or sell. We had also assigned our patents to each division the patent protected. Working with senior corporate and divisional staff, patents for each division were sub-categorized by use into those that were protecting products in current production, those in the division's strategic plan, and those outside the plan. It was quick and easy to make these determinations. Plotting the patents on a decision grid formed by the rank ordered divisions on one side and patent use on the other allowed our patent committee, division and corporate staff to quickly see which patents should be abandoned, maintained, licensed, or enhanced via continuing patent applications," reports Paul Germeraad, former VP and Director, Corporate Research.

EXHIBIT 2.3　Relating the Portfolio to Business Use—Fortum

The purpose of the project was to optimize the value of Neste's technology assets by ensuring the ability to use technology assets (including intellectual property, IP) where it has the highest long-term return for Fortum, whether internally or through licensing, partnering, or spin-offs, and by minimizing the costs associated with acquiring, maintaining, and defending IP rights. To achieve such monumental change, the project was divided into several sub-projects, which included auditing technologies, establishing IP strategies and policies, creating a corporate IP organization and ownership structure, developing a trade secret identification and protection program, and establishing programs to educate employees and management about the IP and its expanded role within Neste and now within Fortum.

The original intent of the program was to audit the technology portfolio and determine its value based upon three different criteria: technology transfer potential, management purposes, and increasing shareholder value.

In the first phase of the audit, detailed information on all the technologies selected for the audit had to be collected. To simplify the process, we created a standardized questionnaire. We also created a Technology Classification Scheme for each technology.

As each technology (along with its associated patents) was examined, there were four main questions that needed to be answered:

1. What stage of development was the technology in?
2. What was its legal ownership status?
3. What type of technology was it?
4. What were its commercialization options?

In principle, we divided the technologies into either existing or preexisting. *Existing,* meaning the technologies are currently being utilized by the company; and *preexisting,* meaning they are currently under development. Regarding the ownership structure, they can be totally owned by the company, jointly owned by us and a third party or we could have licensed rights to use the technology. Next we looked at R&D, or development structure; had the technology been based wholly or in part on Fortum research, engineering, or development efforts, or entirely acquired through a license or other arrangement with someone outside Fortum.

Commercial exploitation status is the strategic importance of the technology to the Fortum portfolio. A key technology is a technology that provides competitive advantage to Fortum; it is not widely used in the industry or available to competitors. A "base technology" is used and readily available in the industry; it is necessary for Fortum, but not sufficient alone to provide competitive advantage. A "spare technology" is not currently in commercial use by Fortum.

(continues)

EXHIBIT 2.3   Continued

A "pacing technology" is a technology under development that has not yet been exploited on an industrial scale, although it might have monetary value and could be exploited through technology transfer. An "emerging technology" is in an early stage of research or development that has not been and cannot be exploited internally or through technology transfer. Emerging technologies generally have not generated any patents or research results of monetary value so far.

After creating the classification scheme, we spent the next year interviewing the R&D staff to inventory and classify approximately 200 technologies within Fortum. The interviews were conducted jointly by members of the technology asset management function and by the R&D business unit management. The information was entered into an Access database and made available to corporate management.

Prior to the audit, many Fortum managers assumed that its businesses actively used the majority of their technologies for product research and development. They also believed many of the technologies were probably being underutilized and could be capitalized in cash flow by granting licenses to other companies and by selling or exchanging rights of use. The results showed something altogether different.

More than 50 percent of the patent portfolio was classified as excess! The excess patent portfolio has, during the years, been and is continuously actively exploited for profit. A substantial number of the excess technologies have been spun off into new companies as well as licensed. In addition we also had several other key learnings; some divisions and business units are already using the information generated by the new database as a planning tool for future activities. Some are rethinking their patenting and licensing policies. One of the first reactions to the audit was that the information was "dangerous" because it revealed that many patents could be categorized as excess and that a big portion of the rest were not the focus of future business. As a result, some businesses began to wonder whether filing patents was necessary at all, or whether they could build their business only on know-how and trade secrets.

We found out that many of our technologies were not transferable. Their primary value was in the know-how, expertise, and processes that are not necessarily patentable but that could be used when selling our engineering consultant services.

The Microsoft Access database created for the audit is an excellent tool that can be used effectively as a database for annual planning and budgeting for different businesses. Using the database, business units can create technology leverage in their portfolios by benchmarking what others are doing and determining what competitors are active in their business. To maintain its reliability, we update the database once a year.

Jan-Erik Osterholm, Fortum

Best Practice 2: Establish an IP Committee with Cross-Functional Members

The IP Committee is typically the body charged with the responsibility of deciding in which of the employees' innovations the company will invest. A decision to pursue a patent is also a decision to invest a substantial amount of money into an innovation. The committee should receive guidelines from the corporation as to what kinds of patents are desired for the portfolio, as well as what the corporation intends to use the patent portfolio to accomplish. With these inputs in mind, the IP Committee may be formed.

"Formation of an IP Committee involves several things," said Patrick Sullivan, of ICMG. "First of all, it requires that the corporation decide what kinds of decisions or actions it wants the committee to make. With this in mind, one can determine the kind of membership (i.e., functions and organizations to be included as well as individuals) the committee must have. It can also determine how often the committee must meet in order to fulfill its mission for the corporation. Knowing the kinds of decisions that are desired (and the frequency with which these decisions must be made), the company can determine what kind of information the committee will require as input to their decision process. Information is either currently available through existing databanks, company information systems, or external information sources, or, it must be created. Information that must be created typically involves the creation of new work processes within the corporation to develop and provide information to the IP Committee."

Barry Young, a partner in the Palo Alto-based law firm of Gray Cary Ware & Freidenrich, L.L.P., recommends that the patent committee be charged with two main duties:

1. Develop clear screening criteria for determining what patents should be included in the portfolio.
2. Review invention disclosures submitted by technology staff involved in R&D to determine those that meet the predefined screening criteria, and ensure breadth and depth of claims coverage.

One of the goals of the patent committee is to show the technical community that the company is proactively managing its IP. Many technical folks become discouraged if they do not see many patents filed or granted each year. Why should they waste their time if nothing ever comes of it? Active patent committees encourage engineers to submit their disclosure forms, and to provide full information in those forms. Such encouragement is important.

In our experience, some engineers see disclosure forms as "paperwork." They would rather be doing their primary work (i.e., scientific discovery and application).

Looking first at the committee's membership, it should typically include representatives from the business units, research and development, marketing, legal, and possibly finance. The committee should operate as a permanent "standing" management committee, reporting directly to the individual in charge of intellectual property management at the company. It should meet regularly. Members often hold senior management positions, and have the power to delegate tasks as they see fit.

The business representative should be able to evaluate how this patent relates to the current and future business strategy of the company or business division filing the patent. The technical representative should be able to evaluate the technical capability covered by the patent and relate it to the current or future research being conducted. The marketing representative should be able to evaluate how this patent differentiates any current or proposed product or feature from the competitors, or if it is going to help differentiate any product/market offering. The legal function representative needs to be able to evaluate the quality, scope, depth, and breadth of the legal coverage of the patent. Finally, the finance representative can provide a useful perspective on the financial implications of strategies.

Rockwell International Corporation has used committees for many years. Recently, it has changed the committees' focus from "invention committees" to "innovation committees." Jim O'Shaughnessy explains.

> What we've found in the past is that our old invention review committees would sit around and get people working real hard to make the right decisions. Each committee focused closely on its business sector in relation to its competitors. But if someone came up with an idea that was a little out of the box, it was rejected because it doesn't fit that business. The committee members would say, "Oh, well we don't do this." It was a classic case of local optimization. It was a sound decision for that committee but a poor decision for the company at large.

Furthermore, the committee is adding more members, since it can use the Internet to communicate.

> Our typical innovation review committee right now has four engineers, plus one patent attorney. In the future, we could have 30 or 40 engineers, a few people from sales and marketing, the company nurse if she has relevant expertise and 10 patent attorneys. After all, they don't have to be in the same place at the same time nor do they need to weigh in on every aspect of every decision. Now we can target

the considerable expertise of the company on making the best holistic decisions that will impact our future.

There are many variations on this theme. John Raley, the former Global IP Manager for a Fortune 500 company describes a process he has seen implemented at several companies:

> The decision of whether or not to file a patent is made by a committee—a group—in each business or technology unit. The committee is typically composed of a cross-section of experts: technical managers, inventors, marketing people, and lawyers. Overall, there is a common decision-making template that has been developed at the corporate level so that there is a basic consistency in the decision-making processes used in each group. However, each group can add to the template as appropriate for their unique business or technology considerations.
>
> Typically present in the common decision-making template are a few basic questions that focus on and drive home the business relevancy of the invention being considered for patent application. In general, these few questions take the form of:

> First: Do we really care if others use our invention? If they did, would it really have that much of an impact on our business?
>
> Second: How likely would others be to use this invention? The likelihood may be low if the invention is incompatible with the processes or product designs of competitors.
>
> Third: Would having a patent deter others from practicing the invention? How likely is this deterrent benefit? It is fair to assume that companies will respect the patent rights of others, however, as Ronald Reagan said, "Trust but verify." A subset of this is the "policeability" aspect—that is, how would you detect infringement? If it's not policeable, then is it really worth the time and money to file a patent application?
>
> Fourth: What is the plan for utilizing the invention? The point being that if the invention is going to be commercialized, patent applications need to incorporate considerations that would dissuade competitive reengineering or "invent around" so as to obtain the same benefits as the invention yet not infringe the patent.

Of these four questions, says Raley, "the first three are 'extrospective'— only the fourth is introspective. For years, many companies have asked only the fourth question. A big change is the transformation in corporate mindset from patents being an introspective decision logic to an extrospective decision logic. Or put another way, having a patent really does not enable you to practice the invention, but having a patent can disable your competition from practicing the invention."

Ford Global Technologies, Inc. (FGTI), according to Fradkin, uses a similar patent committee process at Ford Motor Company. A key determinant in whether a disclosure should proceed to a patent is its support of the business. Bill Coughlin, FGTI's new President & CEO (January 2001), wants to take this process one step further by requiring an economic impact statement as part of the disclosure and decision making by the patent committees.

Determining how often an IP committee should meet is often an issue to be addressed. For companies involved in industries with short product life cycles and rapid changes in the competitive marketplace, IP committees should probably meet frequently. For companies in industries that are slower moving, with product life cycles measured in years (or even decades), IP committees may comfortably meet only quarterly.

In addition to the frequency of meetings, another concern is the amount of calendar time the committee may require to reach a decision. The companies whose external environment are highly competitive and rapidly changing may need to develop decision systems that provide very rapid turnaround on inventions presented for their review. For example, in Xerox, all transfers of IP into or out of the company are handled by a largely "virtual" committee, the Corporate Office for Management of Intellectual Property (COMIP). (See Exhibit 2.4.)

For patent filing decisions, many companies have technology assessment panels (TAPs), which are subcommittees of the company's patent committee. These TAPs are composed of technical, business, and legal people. They are set up by technical/product specialty areas and meet as frequently as needed. Meetings are called quarterly, or more often when there are a minimum number of inventions proposed in a technical area, or when there is a particularly "hot" invention. The invention proposals can be made available electronically ahead of time to all committee members for review and electronic comment prior to the meeting.

IBM's selection process uses a committee approach augmented by its expert software system, the PVT (Patent Value Tool). Committees known as Invention Development Teams (IDTs) meet regularly enough to process inventions within days of first disclosure on IBM's WPTS system. Meetings are called automatically by WPTS, based on inventor demographics and technology. Each IDT includes an IP attorney, a business person, at least one technical expert, and at least one inventor from the subject invention disclosure. Including the inventors on the team fosters positive invention *development* rather than a beauty contest atmosphere. The mission of the team is not reject/accept, but to broaden, sharpen focus, develop the disclosed idea into a valuable patentable

---

EXHIBIT 2.4   A "Virtual" Intellectual Asset Management Committee at Xerox

In firms with large IA portfolios, the transfer of IA into or out of the firm often involves the transfer of very valuable corporate assets and is usually reserved for senior management decision rights either at the divisional or corporate levels. For firms with autonomous divisions, and with the IA portfolio broken up and in part associated and controlled by specific divisions, this decision-making is done at the owning division. However, in firms where IA is considered a corporate asset shared across divisions, decisions on transfer are made at senior management often at office-of-the-president levels. At Xerox, this decision-making has been done centrally by the corporate office management of intellectual property (COMIP) committee consisting of the three senior vice presidents of corporate research and technology (chairman), corporate strategy, and the chief general counsel. The committee is managed by the corporate manager of intellectual property (the IAM).

At Xerox, the decision process is based on two principles:

1. All IA (and IP) are corporate assets and all decisions concerning their transfer are office-of-the-president-level decisions.
2. Time is of the essence in this decision making.

The COMIP committee meets monthly and reviews all transfers of IA (at Xerox, this includes know-how) into or out of Xerox and to subsidiaries. A proposal for IP transfer must be sponsored at the division president level and submitted on a form. The form includes a description of the IP to be transferred, to whom, the business reason, the value of the IP, any issues or liabilities, and a summary of the terms and conditions of the arrangement.

After preliminary review and revision for clarification, the proposals are electronically distributed to a group of MIP champions reporting to all division presidents or their equivalent worldwide. These MIP champions are given ten days to review and comment on any of the cases up for review. If they have not commented within ten days, then by the rules of the process they have answered in the affirmative. A Lotus Notes database is used to provide these cases and background documents to the intellectual property managers and champions, and to collect their comments. After the ten-day review period is over, the comments are reviewed, and case briefs, including the background of the case, the proposal, issues, and the recommendation of the IAM, are drawn up. The committee meets monthly to review these briefs and make their decisions. The results are distributed electronically worldwide within hours of the close of the monthly meeting.

Joe Daniele, formerly of Xerox[2]

form. The IDT is aided in its work by the PVT, IBM's expert system that asks a series of structured questions about the invention: market size, market maturity, claim scope, avoidance, detectability, nature of problem, fit of solution to problem, standards applicability, prestige factor, etc. Using the answers input by the IDT, the PVT generates a numerical score for the invention. The score does not dictate the IDT decision, but assists the IDT in analytically isolating the advantages and disadvantages of the invention. It improves decision-making efficiency, ultimately linking back into WPTS to provide an early value measure for use in rating patent filings, and later tracking high-value patents.

Best Practice 3: Establish a Process and Screening Criteria for Screening Patents

One of the most critical activities for Level Two companies is patent screening. As Joe Villella reminds us, "It's extremely important to review your portfolio regularly so that not only do you keep the good patents from becoming abandoned, but you identify ones that should be abandoned. No one has unlimited funds for patents so it's really critical to review the portfolio to separate the wheat from the chaff."

Patent screening is a common activity for cost-conscious companies. Whereas companies at Level One are often devoid of processes and formal criteria, companies at Level Two have come to realize that there is value in some degree of formality and process. While no one likes excessive process or mindless bureaucratic procedures, it is also true that people don't like to waste effort or be forced to rebuild a go/no-go patent decision procedure every time a new patenting opportunity arises.

Successful "IP Best Practice" companies have learned that there are a number of key bits of information and process that can significantly improve both the efficiency and the effectiveness of their patenting decisions. Some companies are "innovation-poor"—that is, they do not spontaneously receive a sufficient number of innovations from their employees. Companies in this situation should be interested in creating processes and methods that encourage the creation of new innovations. Other companies are innovation-rich—that is, they receive more innovations from their employees than they can commercialize. These companies should be interested in creating screens and filters to identify the innovations of greatest interest to the firm. The point here is that not all best practices suit all companies at this level. Companies must diagnose their situation to determine which of the best practices cited in this chapter really relate to their circumstance.

The screening should begin as early as possible—not long after a company has accumulated a large stock of patents. We have discussed in Level One how a company can encourage innovation. At Level Two, this process continues, but with more prudence. ICMG's Patrick Sullivan cautions, "There are a number of pitfalls that are not obvious when companies first move toward creating incentives."

A story from Xerox illustrates this point. When Xerox hired George Pake in 1969 to head up what was to become its world famous Palo Alto Research Center (PARC), Jack Goldman, head of research at Xerox, told Pake that he should get the best people he could find and allow them the freedom to be creative. "Bottoms-up research is the only sensible philosophy if one wants to get the very good people,"[3] Goldman reportedly opined to Pake. Indeed, Pake was given a multimillion dollar research budget and a charge to create the information systems and technologies necessary to drive Xerox into the 1980s. Further, he was charged with putting together a research facility that would rival the legendary Bell Labs. Pake set about his task with gusto and hired the best and the brightest from universities. In the end, the researchers at PARC invented the first personal computer, as well as pop-down software menus and the ubiquitous computer mouse. Through a torturous process of evaluation and reevaluation, the executive management at Xerox, when presented with the opportunity of pursuing its commanding lead position in personal computing, decided not to invest. Why did Xerox opt out of pursuing its dominant entry position in personal computing? The after-the-fact consensus is that while the company understood and had experience with paper and toner products, it failed to understand the technology of personal computing or its market possibilities.

The lesson to be learned here from the Xerox story is two-fold. First, don't create an innovative process that produces new ideas you are incapable of leveraging; instead create a process that produces innovations that match your business strategy. Second, when your innovative process does produce ideas outside of your business capability, identify ways the corporation can benefit from them before moving on.

Many companies would like to be in the enviable position of having too many inventions to file on each year. IBM labs produced over 10,000 invention disclosures in 2000. Hewlett-Packard's Steve Fox says he receives thousands of disclosures from HP's R&D groups every year, but only files on half of them. Fox explains:

> There's a cost control aspect to this. We included in our patent review template a call for information that would help us control our costs in filing patent

applications. In fact the first usage of the template was to filter invention disclosures focusing on the strategically important things. We pushed back everything else.

HP has historically created a fairly tight screening criteria for its patent portfolio: one part focuses on filing on inventions that could be commercialized within the next five years. For HP, time to market is a critical factor, as the technology life cycle is continually shrinking. The second part is more futuristically oriented. To help business unit managers prioritize their technology goals, Fox created a Patenting Survey Form (see Exhibit 2.5).

In subsequent years, HP started using that same template to determine not only which patents to eliminate, but also which type of patents to encourage.

Using the template more on a "pull" basis rather than as a "push-back" filter, we're getting a whole lot more invention disclosures than we used to. Inventions

EXHIBIT 2.5 HP Patenting Survey Form		
Strategic Technologies/Products List the technologies or products that have the highest strategic importance over the next five years.	$100 Test Allocate $100 to pay for patenting activity among all listed.	Non-U.S. Protection Name non-U.S. countries where patents should be obtained.
1.		
2.		
3.		
4.		
5.		
New Technologies and Futuristic Patenting Opportunities (e.g., to preempt competitors or to fill technology gaps).	Rating Rate potential importance as "high," "likely," or "unknown."	
1.		
2.		
3.		

are strongly encouraged. When our new CEO, Carly Fiorina, came on board in July 1999, one of the first things she did was rebadge the company. She changed the logo, so underneath the HP logo where it used to say Hewlett-Packard Company, it now says "Invent." This meant inventing and reinventing everything under the sun, whether it was marketing approaches, e-Services, customer support, or technology.

Best Practice 4: Set Detailed Guidelines for Patent Filing and Renewal

Even when an innovation meets the general criteria a company sets for its patents, it is not always necessary to patent the innovation in every major country, or to renew it continuously in those countries. Uncontrolled filing and renewal can lead to excessive costs. For many companies, filing and maintenance fees can soak up over 50 percent of a company's patent-related budget. It goes without saying that substantial savings can be achieved by knowing what these costs are and making deliberate decisions on where to file. These companies recognize, for instance, that the costs of filing and maintaining a patent in some countries outweigh the minor benefits to be obtained there. They are aware that patent protection means little in certain countries of the world. They also carefully consider those locales where they intend to employ the technology and avoid pursuing legal protection in areas of the world where they do not expect to operate.

Techniques include setting country filing guidelines, consolidating patent agents, and aggregating renewal decisions.

Setting Country Filing Guidelines.   Companies that have progressed to Level Two consciously evaluate the countries in which to file each patent. Decisions and decision variables about country filings may differ in each case as they are affected by technology, by business unit, or by time frame. According to Bob Gruetzmacher, Director of Intellectual Property & Licensing at DuPont Intellectual Assets Business:

> Many years ago, DuPont had established guidelines as to what countries should be considered (and not considered) when filing for foreign patent protection. A key factor of course is the business need. Beyond that, issues center around a given country's patent law and history of respecting others' patents, as well as a patentee's ability to enforce the patent in the country where patent protection is being sought. Over the last 10 years many countries have modified, if not overhauled, their patent system to be in sync with the majority of the developed world. As a result, our guidelines have been modified accordingly. However, the "golden rule" remains, file and maintain patent protection only in those countries where it

makes economic sense to do so. When it comes to reducing patent costs, the foreign filings are the ones to receive early scrutiny.

John Raley describes in Exhibit 2.6 a process he has seen work successfully.

At IBM, both country filing and maintenance decisions are made on a globally integrated basis using IBM's WPT system, mentioned earlier.

EXHIBIT 2.6   A Successful Country Selection Filing Process

In obtaining a patent, the US may be "first to invent," but the rest of the world is by and large "first to file." Multinational companies need to consider both aspects. While it is important to be the "first to invent," it is critical that patent applications are filed as quickly as possible in order to protect the "first to file" rights that the rest of the world operates under. However, filing in a large number of countries can prove to be prohibitively expensive. Fortunately, there are strategies that can lessen the cost burden while preserving patent protection options.

In filing a patent application, it is natural to be optimistic that the invention is going to be big and broadly valuable. But, as time goes by, it is often learned that the invention is not as big as originally envisioned or as broadly valuable. So the challenge is to preserve options for broad geographic patent protection while not going bankrupt doing so. Examining the fees associated with patent filings identifies opportunities to defer major filing spending, for a modest fee, while more is learned about the invention and its viability.

Initially, a patent application can be filed in the US. With the exception of a few countries (and these are getting fewer and fewer as time goes by), foreign patent filings and their associated costs can be deferred until one year after the initial US filing.

At that time, it becomes necessary to make the foreign patent filing decisions. A very cost-effective option can be to file a PCT (Patent Cooperation Treaty) application and elect all PCT countries as the filing option. For a modest PCT fee, this strategy defers making any filing decisions (and their associated costs) for PCT member countries for up to another 18 months. Companies can use this yet additional year and a half to learn more about the invention and its viability without losing their "place in line" in the PCT countries. For countries that are not PCT members, patent applications will have to be filed at this "one year point" but these countries are becoming fewer in number as more countries join the PCT ranks.

(continues)

EXHIBIT 2.6   Continued

Eighteen months after the PCT filing, it becomes necessary to decide in which PCT countries to file patent applications. However, by this time, a company has had up to two and a half years after the initial US patent filing to learn more about the invention's business value. If the invention has proven to be significant, a large number of countries can be selected for patent applications. However, if the invention has proven to be not as grand as originally thought, filing can be in a smaller number of countries or not at all. Paying the modest PCT fee to reserve a "place in line" is much cheaper than initially paying patent filing fees in a large number of PCT countries.

Yet another opportunity at the 18 month PCT country selection point is to select the EPC (European Patent Convention) option. This further defers the need to file patent applications in EPC member countries (most European countries) for several additional years, sometimes as much as six years. Again, more time for the company to learn about the business value of an invention without needing to commit to the significant expense of filing patent applications in EPC member countries.

Deferring as long as possible the need to decide in which individual countries to file patent applications is good cash flow management as well as good R&D management as developers work to learn more about the invention.

Equally important is also having a good strategy for determining exactly which countries in which to file patent applications. At all of the above decision points, companies need to have a pragmatic decision template for selecting those countries in which to file patent applications. Without a good country selection strategy, companies risk having patents filed in too many countries (and paying for them) or not having patents filed in the right countries (spending less money but with questionable benefit). A good country selection strategy will guide obtaining patent protection where it matters most, thereby maximizing patent protection while minimizing the associated costs.

With many companies, the number of countries selected for patent filings varies by how valuable the patent is seen by the company. At first, natural optimism results in thinking that the invention is big, broad, and highly valuable. But as time goes by companies might learn that the invention is applicable only to a small set of countries—for example, developed countries only.

A good country selection decision-making template will integrate the business and technical assessment of the invention with an analysis of markets and competitors to determine the specific countries that are part of a filing strategy. Through time and experience the country selection list can be tailored to even further minimize patent application spending while not compromising protection of the company's intellectual property.

John Raley

With or without such advanced technology, it is a good idea to review all the countries where the company has filed patents to assess whether the patents are still appropriate. Criteria for this phase of the pruning may include location of manufacturing facilities, markets where products are sold, activities of competitors, local customs and attitudes regarding enforcement, and—last but not least—the cost of filing for patent renewal. Trademark filing guidelines are also worthy of consideration, according to Mark Radcliffe, senior partner of the Gray Cary law firm:

> Every time I talk to people on trademark issues, I tell them to think about them in both defensive and offensive ways. On the defensive, you want to register not just in countries where you think you will have a big market for the product but also in countries where there are trademark pirates whose businesses are registering third-party trademarks and selling them back to the original owner. Additionally companies should think of registering in jurisdictions where you may not sell anything but where there is a high degree of piracy for your particular product. For example, in the clothing industry, Panama is a big transshipment place where pirates exist and so you may register there even though you don't anticipate having dramatic sales. In the computer industry, the People's Republic of China and Thailand are well known for piracy problems.
>
> In some countries the patent protection is so weak or difficult to get effective enforcement that you rely on trademarks rather than patents as your primary form of protection. Trying to explain a semiconductor to somebody in Chinese can be very difficult. It is much easier to say here is the trademark and here is the thing they made and it is the same. The failure to do so can result in a real mess. If someone owns your trademark for clothing in Panama and they are manufacturing it, you have to chase them down all over the world instead of strangling it at its source, which would be in Panama.
>
> When we advise on trademarks, we tell people to divide countries into three categories. Group One countries are countries where they will have significant sales in a year or year-and-a-half, or where there are significant piracy problems. You want to file in all these countries. Examples of this would be if you have a computer product you would register in the U.K., France, Germany, Japan, etc. but countries to register in to avoid piracy would be Taiwan, Thailand, and the People's Republic of China. Group Two countries would be smaller markets like Denmark or Finland. There is not a big risk of piracy there and their legal systems are pretty good. You may decide to save some money and put those registrations off. Other examples would be New Zealand and Australia. Group Three countries would be Liberia and Chad, where there is the risk of piracy and/or no chance of a market for your product.

Consolidating Patent Agents. While they focus on setting country guidelines, companies should also consider consolidating patent agents retained to translate, prosecute, and make maintenance payments on patents in other countries. Many companies have been shocked to learn that over time they have developed a network of hundreds of such agents throughout the world, all of whom operate independently, price their services at retail, and provide little accountability for the fees they are paid. One *Fortune* 50 company has achieved significant savings by consolidating those relationships from over 300 individual agents across Europe to one or two per country. By doing so, it has exercised increased buying power, negotiated more favorable fee schedules, and reduced the bookkeeping required to keep track of the hundreds of agents' bills received from around the world. Working with fewer agents in larger markets can help a company to obtain better fee schedules and to require less administrative time and oversight.

IBM's very large portfolio generates equally large maintenance fees. IBM uses selective pruning to control maintenance expenses and ensure that its portfolio is maximally tuned to the marketplace. IBM's pruning takes the form of intentionally permitting patents to lapse once their licensing value has diminished. IBM patent attorneys designated as Patent Portfolio Managers evaluate the licensing potential for each patent, and select those to be maintained. Thus, based on input from the portfolio size planning process, a given patent may be separately scheduled for maintenance in some countries but not in others, creating a "checker-board" coverage model designed to produce broad but not exhaustive coverage in every relevant technology in every relevant country.

Aggregating Renewal Decisions.   Yet another way to save is to group patent decisions by size. No one wants to spend time making a "nickel and dime" decision. There are several ways to avoid doing so—and to concentrate instead on "big-ticket" items. One way is to put high-cost renewals on a separate track prompting an extra level of review. For example, cluster all European patent renewals (which are more likely to cost $250 apiece than the domestic cost of $20) for review by a single decision-maker. This could help in order to make the decision a $250,000 decision vs. a $20,000 decision.

Another way to aggregate renewal decisions is to put patents on a periodic, multi-year decision track instead of an annual track. John Raley describes how this process works.

> Patents must be renewed in every country in which they are filed. Since filing dates and renewal periods can vary by country (see Exhibit 2.6), these renewal decisions do not come due all at the same time. Reviewing a patent for renewal each and every time the renewal trigger is pulled becomes a very tedious management

task. Also, this becomes a country-by-country decision process and human tendency will be to renew the patent since it involves only one country and the renewal cost per patent per country is fairly small. However, while each renewal transaction is a small cost, the aggregate can be a huge expense.

Putting patents on a multi-year renewal decision cycle will result in much better management decisions. Re-casting the patent renewal decision as a dollar amount to keep the patent in force in all countries in which it is filed for the next several years will yield a much higher dollar amount associated with the decision. It is the nature of management that higher dollar amounts are subject to more scrutiny regarding the business value being obtained/retained for the money being spent. When the dollar amount is bigger, people put more effort into the decision, and a better decision is typically the result.

The decision can be made to unilaterally not renew the patent, renew the patent in only selected countries, or unilaterally renew the patent. If the patent is renewed, the odds are low that business circumstances will change sufficiently to reverse that decision before the next renewal decision cycle. If a patent is not renewed (or renewed in a small number of countries) considerable cost savings can be realized. This is particularly true for older patents since renewal fees typically increase significantly as the patent gets older. If a patent is filed in several countries, it is not at all unusual for the aggregate renewal costs over a patent's 20-year lifetime to exceed the aggregate filing costs for that patent. The cost savings realized by dropping patents that no longer serve a business interest is money that can be re-invested into R&D and help pay for broader filing of new patent applications relevant to business strategy.

In addition to improved cost management, a more subtle, and perhaps more important benefit of a multi-year renewal decision cycle is that it shifts the decision-making process from one of being country-specific to one of being focused on how the patent supports business strategy and plans.

Critical to successful implementation of a multi-year renewal decision cycle strategy is a good information system that documents the business and/or technology logic behind the renewal decision. In this way, when the patent is again reviewed at the next renewal decision cycle, the information from several years before is there and the decision is less vulnerable to the risk that the people who know about the invention may not be working for the company anymore.

Ford Global Technologies has a formal renewal process that involves both the FGTI licensing office and the firm's patent attorneys. The renewal team identifies technology bundles, checks on their status periodically, and makes decisions in the aggregate, not just on individual patents.

IBM has a noteworthy practice in this regard as well. IBM's approach, discussed earlier, first groups decisions by technology and business, to enable efficiencies on the basis of claim overlap and country characteristics. WPTS captures the "why" behind decisions and retains it along with all other information pertaining to docket quality, for use in subsequent reviews. To obtain size efficiency, IBM uses a maintenance model that concentrates review and pruning around renewal periods. This exploits two points inherent in patent systems and patents: many countries increase maintenance cost with time, and most patents outlive their usefulness with time, thus patents in the second half of their term receive close scrutiny, and pruning is more intense for them.

Best Practice 5: Regularly and Systematically Review the Portfolio to Prune Patents Not Worth Maintaining

Pruning is important for companies with large numbers of patents. Most large, established companies, with thousands of patents on file, have a lot of room for pruning. Many executives are surprised to learn that their patent portfolios continue to include patents on technologies as obsolete as the eight-track tape player. Other patents may be holdovers from R&D projects where the technology was later found to be commercially unworkable, too expensive, or no longer strategic to the firm. As discussed in Chapter 6, The Dow Chemical Company saved over $40 million in patent maintenance fees over a five-year period, by its judicious but significant pruning of the portfolio. According to Jerry Rosenthal, Vice President of Intellectual Property and Licensing at IBM, "We prune our portfolio every year." Specifics of IBM's many pruning techniques have already been discussed.

Successful companies have found it helpful to set criteria for continual pruning. Many use the same criteria for pruning as they use for determining the characteristics of innovations they will patent. Dow, one of the leading best practices companies, created a decision process for its patenting process that required two different perspectives on the desirability of patenting. One perspective involved technical importance and interest, while the other involved business need and intended use. In deciding whether to patent an innovation, the participants in the process ranked each innovation on both technological and business dimensions. When culling the portfolio, Dow used both technological and business perspectives in arriving at its decision of which patents were to be culled.

On the other hand, IBM's pruning analysis differs from its filing analysis in that filing is heavily focused on future value, while pruning takes into account past and current demonstrated value.

Other best practices companies have created their own versions of criteria for patenting and pruning. One approach is to create a "value grid." This is nothing more than a graphic representation of the company's patenting criteria. For many companies, the criteria may include not only technology and business considerations but also legal and patenting considerations as well. A simple value grid might contain three dimensions of value. The first is often the intended use for the patented technology, while the second is how enforceable the patent would be in a court of law, and the third is how prepared the company itself is to enforce the patent (i.e., sue over it). Companies can define different levels or degrees for each dimension and potential patents can be graded as to which level or degree they may be scored. When pruning a portfolio that contains patents graded by such a scheme, the pruning can be done, in part, based on each patent's score.

Sharon Oriel, Director of the Global Intellectual Asset and Capital Management Technology Center of The Dow Chemical Company, found that even getting management and the scientists to agree to the pruning process was difficult at first.

> For many years, we had been rewarding inventors based on the number of patents they generated, and now suddenly we had classified those patents in the bucket called "no business interest." For many inventors, they felt as if we had called their baby ugly. Additionally, some managers were very conservative and wanted to hold on to excess technologies, in case we might want to use it someday in the future. So we had a lot of education to go through and get people comfortable with this. I remember one day talking to a business manager, who had a technology he was not using but refused to get rid of, and I said, "How would you like to save three million dollars?" This was a relatively small business, so three million was significant. He looked at me and he said, "Is it legal?" And I said, "Yes." And he said "OK, go do it." Once I was able to monetize the savings, the decision was easy.

CONCLUSION

As Sharon Oriel's closing words reveal, cost control brings clear benefits to organizations—including the benefit of decision-making clarity. But the journey to the boardroom does not end here. Dow and other companies have progressed beyond this level. Companies cannot concentrate only on the defensive and cost control levels of our Value Hierarchy. If they do, they may miss opportunities to derive maximum value from their IP. To seize such opportunities, companies need to progress to the next level: the Profit Center Level.

3

LEVEL THREE—PROFIT CENTER

COMPANIES THAT HAVE moved to Level Three have crossed the Rubicon. They now realize that their IP generates value that transcends the revenue from their products and services. Whereas companies at Levels One and Two are focused on the defensive use of IP, companies at Level Three realize that they possess two kinds of intellectual assets. The first are the company's innovations themselves—the ideas that yielded the products and services that generate the company's prime revenue stream. But in addition, Level Three companies realize that the IP itself has value— notably in tactical (rather than strategic) positioning, and in the profitable generation of revenues (see Exhibit 3.1).

What Level Three Companies Are Trying to Accomplish

Companies at Level Three see their IP as business assets, not just as legal documents. As business assets, the bits and pieces of a company's IP can become puzzle pieces in answering the great question: How can we succeed in building this company's value?

At this level, companies typically want to do two things:

1. Extract value directly from their IP as quickly and inexpensively as possible

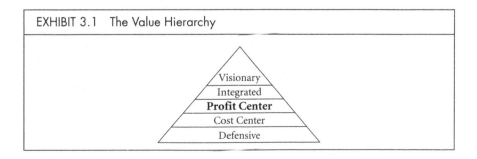

EXHIBIT 3.1   The Value Hierarchy

2. Focus on noncore, nonstrategic IP that has tactical (as opposed to strategic) value

Companies newly involved with Level Three tend to look, quite naturally, for what is often called "low hanging fruit," which are activities that will generate cash revenue quickly. For this reason they tend to focus on the IP that is already in the portfolio. They look for simple conversions of this IP into cash—typically through the mechanisms of licensing, donations, and royalty audits. Their view of the use of IP is most often tactical, leading them to create a capability for conducting simple assessments of their competitors and looking for marketplace opportunities within their immediate markets.

At Level Three, companies are concerned with more than the portions of the IP management decision system that are the province of the IP attorneys (see Exhibit 3.2).

The person in charge of IP management is now interested in converting into value the IP that is already in the portfolio. The focus of IP management activity shifts from what it was at Levels One and Two (IP as a legal asset) toward business activity that is concerned with the business use of the IP. At this level, IP managers examine the portfolio to identify its tactical use possibilities, as well as to identify what IP is marketable and what is not. We see companies creating the capability to value the individual pieces of IP as well as methods for linking it to the company's business and marketing strategies. Further, we

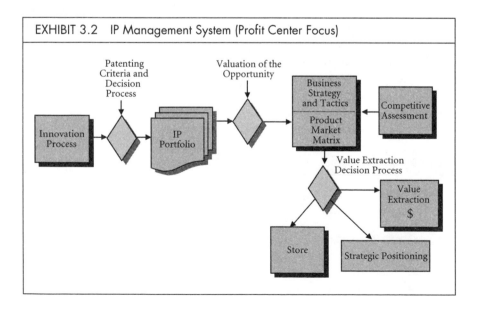

EXHIBIT 3.2   IP Management System (Profit Center Focus)

see companies at Level Three concerned about their competitors' uses of IP as well as with how they might use their own IP to best tactical business advantage—all for maximum profitability in the short term.

Setting a profit expectation for IP can be a self-fulfilling prophecy. It increases the likelihood of profits—if only because of the attention being paid to the function. The attention paid to the IP function is likely to increase the level of care with which IP finances are managed, and the aggressiveness with which IP managers seek additional revenues. If such initiatives achieve their goals, they increase profits—by reducing costs, increasing revenues, or both, as feasible.

BEST PRACTICES FOR THE IP PROFIT CENTER LEVEL

Best practices for creating a successful IP profit center will vary from company to company. However, some practices remain constant. For example, in almost every case, managers will have to obtain "buy-in" from senior management. The actual operation of the profit center will vary, however, based on its location within the firm. When the IP management activity is located in the legal or IP departments at the outset of implementing Level Three, the initial revenue generation process usually takes the form of infringement-based licensing. The legal staff, trained as it is in enforcement and in litigation channels, typically establishes methods and procedures to identify infringers and then to require the company to demand a royalty payment from them in lieu of costly litigation.

For many Level Three companies (particularly those who retain their IPM under the heading of the legal or IP departments) this is as far as their Level Three activity goes. Other companies—those that see their IP as business assets—tend to take a broader view of the cash generating alternatives available to them and begin to look at other revenue generation alternatives such as IP donations and royalty audits. They also begin to organize to extract value, and develop advanced screening criteria. (See Exhibit 3.3.)

EXHIBIT 3.3   IP Profit Center: Best Practices

Best Practice 1: Obtain management buy-in.
Best Practice 2: Start a proactive licensing organization.
Best Practice 3: Consider IP donations and royalty audits.
Best Practice 4: Organize to extract value.
Best Practice 5: Develop advanced screening criteria.

Best Practice 1: Obtain Management Buy-In

When companies approach us for help in extracting value from their intangibles, inevitably the first question they ask is, "How can I get management buy-in?" As is true for many of the mysteries of life, the answer is, "It depends!" In our many years of consulting, there are really only two ways to get management buy-in: You can appeal to greed or you can appeal to fear. There is not a CEO in the world who would pass up a sure chance to generate $1.5 billion a year in licensing revenue like IBM. The past 15 years has been a time where companies have been right-sized, downsized, reorganized, matrixed, realigned, and cost controlled to the point that the only unexploited assets left in the firm are its intangibles. CEOs are rapidly realizing that, to coin a phrase, "there is gold in them thar hills" and they are eager to have the newly found profits hit their bottom line.

As more and more companies tout their successes with intellectual asset management, it is becoming easier and easier for other companies to embark on programs to exploit their intellectual assets. Selling fear is much trickier, but more likely to result in immediate action. The road toward intellectual property failure is long and well worn by many Fortune 500 firms. Xerox PARC's inability to successfully commercialize many of the inventions that have revolutionized our lives in the past 20 years, most notably the personal computer, revealed an obvious deficit in intellectual property management. Apple Computer's unwillingness to license its operating system to software manufacturers cost the company the personal computer operating system standard. Other companies have spent many years and many millions of dollars on an R&D project only to watch it disappear as a competitor, only days earlier, filed patent applications that precluded their own project from ever reaching the marketplace. And yet others have found the costs of patent infringement so high that they are still paying to fund the patent owner many years after the fact.

Companies that have been at the wrong end of intellectual property management have the easiest time obtaining buy-in. According to Bill Frank, Chief Patent Counsel for SC Johnson,

> In speaking with other IP Counsel, they have only been able to get their management's attention after something really bad has happened. We looked at our situation, and noted some anecdotal things that led us to believe that if we didn't make some changes, we faced increased potential of something bad happening to us. We were fortunate to get management agreement that this was important. However, even with that commitment, things take longer to accomplish than you

might expect. From my experience, everything you think will take two months takes six. It takes time to build consensus and support. People may be willing to help but they also have many other projects and things to do all at the same time, which may have a higher priority than your project.

Regardless of whether you are using greed or fear as the motivator, the first thing to do is to find an ally or sponsor in upper management. Jane Tishman Robbins, former Director of Strategic Planning at Sprint Corporation, re-counts her efforts at obtaining management buy-in. (See Exhibit 3.4.)

Best Practice 2: Start a Proactive Licensing Organization

One of the most important steps a Level Three company can take will be to ini-tiate a proactive licensing program. A study sponsored by BTG, a global tech-nology transfer company, estimates that companies ignore more than $115 billion in technology assets that could be licensed. The study, conducted inde-pendently by the British-based Business Planning & Research International, showed that "companies ignore more than 35 percent of their patented tech-nologies because they don't fit into their 'core' business operations."[1] Ian Harvey, CEO of BTG, noted that for many companies, "selling or licensing their

---

EXHIBIT 3.4   Getting Buy-In at Sprint

I found that initially at Sprint, I had to get the support of senior management. To do so, I first had to make certain that we were all on the same page—that is, we were all speaking the same language (a common intellectual capital nomencla-ture) and understanding, or at least viewing, similar concepts in a similar way. Coming to this shared understanding of nomenclature and concepts was impor-tant given that the management audience represented a variety of functional areas within the company (technology planning, legal, tax, finance, business/cor-porate development, and strategic planning).

Very early on, we decided that we were going to focus our energy and effort on the area of intellectual property (a discrete subset of overall intellectual cap-ital) for two reasons. First, intellectual property is the most tangible of the in-tangible assets, so our senior managers could "get their heads around it in short order." Second, we already had in place systems and methods to both audit and inventory our intellectual property. So, we had a good sense of our current

(continues)

EXHIBIT 3.4   Continued

---

intellectual property assets; we knew what we were dealing with here. Thus, we quickly narrowed our intellectual capital management lens to focus on intellectual property.

Next, to give us perspective and a common analytical framework, I divided up the whole intellectual property management spectrum along three large component elements—IP value generation, IP protection and maintenance, and IP value extraction. Within each of these component elements, I identified current best practice work activities, decision-making processes, supporting systems and information, and organizational structures. Then, I used this IP value chain to do a deep-dive competitive analysis comparing Sprint and key competitors along this chain—examining available public information regarding the respective IP management organizations and activities while using the best practices criteria. Further, I employed the value chain to perform periodic updated competitive analyses to continue to apprise management of Sprint's IP management condition relative to that of our competitors.

Additionally, this IP management value chain was used for situation assessment purposes to size up our activities against current best practices, both within and outside the telecommunications industry. Here, I undertook a root cause analysis to better understand and explain Sprint's then-current IP management practices along the entire IP value chain, again from IP generation, to IP protection and maintenance, and finally to IP value extraction. So, the IP management value chain has been a helpful tool for us internally at Sprint.

We engaged in a comprehensive IP management competitive analysis and situation assessment (and sharing current best practices) but these efforts only went so far. To advance the ball, I had to make the case to management that Sprint had a business challenge that needed to be addressed. Thus, I had to convince them that there was an opportunity cost to maintaining the status quo, that we might be missing out on value—limiting our ability to extract maximum value from the IP portfolio in terms of cash, strategic position, enhanced supplier control, greater competitive protection, more design freedom, increased bargaining power, greater speed to market, etc. With these potential benefits of more active intellectual property management in mind, senior management had a much better sense of "what" the business challenge was and "why" it had to be addressed. Now, I just had to craft a "yes-able" proposal to address the lingering "how" questions—How much? How soon? How many people, support systems, and other resources will be needed? How do we organize and act to achieve our objectives? How do we fit this (if at all) within Sprint's current organizational structures and functional relationships?

Jane Tishman Robbins, formerly of Sprint

technologies could significantly bolster profits and maximize their return on R&D investment."

In the Profit Center mode, the culture of the company shifts to become more patent focused. Business unit heads and corporate executives are willing to consider the previously unthinkable—licensing patents previously thought to be most valuable if held exclusively. This process usually starts with baby steps—finding opportunities to generate revenues without forfeiting competitive advantage. The company begins licensing noncore technologies, or licensing outside the company's current field of services or products. All this is very different from the licensing activities of companies operating at Level Two or lower. Companies focused on cost control tend to have a "one-off" approach. They view any licensing income as a pure windfall rather than as part of a profit strategy. Understanding the specifics of its patent portfolio can help corporations know which patents are ripe for licensing, sale, abandonment, or enforcement.

Such a process can contribute a great deal to company value. Worldwide revenues from patent licensing have grown from $15 billion in 1990 to over $100 billion in 2000. Some experts estimate that companies are sitting on $1 trillion a year in unexploited licensing fees.

"I believe when properly done, IP licensing has the most compelling business model I have ever seen in my business experience," said Dave Kline, Vice President of Technology & Licensing for Litton Systems. Licensing revenue can mean big dollars for companies. As we have mentioned earlier, IBM generates $1.5 billion a year from licensing income. Dow Chemical increased its licensing income from $25 million to over $125 million in less than five years. Some experts believe that a well-managed patent portfolio should generate licensing revenues equivalent to roughly one percent of the firm's total revenues and five percent of its profits.[3] Licensing is a particularly cost-effective way to generate profits. Unlike patent-based revenues achieved through product sales, no additional volume in sales (and related expenses) is required to generate additional profits.

Before companies create a licensing organization, there are several things they should think about:

- What kind of technology is the firm willing to license?
- What type of licensing is the firm interested in?
- Into what markets is the firm interested in licensing?
- What kind of resource commitment is the firm willing to make?
- What level of revenue is the firm looking to generate?

From Levels One and Two, a company should have a fairly good idea of the existing intellectual assets it owns and is willing to license. Many companies we talk with who are interested in mining their patent portfolio for licensing opportunities are only interested in "naked patent" licensing. That is, patents with no associated know-how. This is often the case because CEOs do not want licensing to interfere with the core business of the company: selling products that have legally protected ideas in them. If companies are interested in revenue generation from licensing, they will not be happy with naked patent licensing only. It has been our experience that patent-only licenses are few and far between—and have relatively low revenue-generating potential. If companies are willing to add know-how into the licensing transaction, the amount of revenue generated will rise dramatically.

Licensing should not only be considered for patents. Trademark licensing is also a very lucrative business. Firms such as Coca-Cola and Sara Lee extract the bulk of their IP value (and even their corporate value) from their trademarks. Neither of them is a classic "manufacturer." Instead, they license their brand to selected companies who make the actual Coca-Cola or Sara Lee products. Harley-Davidson has indicated that it receives over $300 million annually from trademark licensing. According to Jeff Weedman, Vice President of External Business Development and Corporate Licensing at Procter & Gamble, trademark licenses are about more than generating cash.

> If I look at the amount of effort I put into a trademark license, it's comparable to what I put into a technology; yet the direct revenue stream is a lot less for the trademark licensing project. So why would we make such an investment? It's because when we license the Pampers name for baby clothes, for example, that's important for our baby-care business unit because it builds brand equity and ultimately total revenue. Consumers walking into retail aisles see the Pampers name not just on diapers and wipes, but also on a whole new line of baby merchandise. In effect, Pampers is fully meeting those consumers' need to care for their babies. Without a doubt, these types of licensing efforts support and strengthen the established brand. The company manufacturing the licensed products creates advertisements using the same Pampers graphics and visuals we use, so the impact on the consumer is much, much greater. It's a strategic play.

IBM's experience is similar to P&G's. IBM licenses its trademarks under carefully controlled programs to high-quality manufacturers of products complementary to IBM's own products, including printer paper, mouse pads, computer cabling, and laptop computer carrying cases, to name a few. The program generates significant revenues, and increases the visibility of IBM's major trademarks through the advertising conducted by IBM's licensees. By taking its program global, IBM has built brand loyalty in countries where it otherwise does not have a significant consumer presence.

Licensing transactions come in two varieties—carrot and stick—as explained by Bob Bramson, President of VAI Patent Management Corp., a technology brokerage and licensing firm:

> There are two kinds of licensing of patents and technology in a broader sense. One is what we call "stick licensing," which is about licensing patents against infringers who violate the patent by making products covered by one or more claims of the patent. Infringement-type stick licensing tends to be litigious, unfriendly, and aggressive, because nobody voluntarily takes out the checkbook and says how many millions of dollars do you want for your piece of paper (patent)? As I've often said, no chief patent counsel ever got a raise, a promotion, a bonus, or a pat on the back from the CEO for being the first one to sign up and write multimillion-dollar checks to somebody else who owns a patent.
>
> You can also generate revenue (without litigation) by selling (rather than licensing) stick patents. This is common in the computer, electronics, and telecommunications industry, thanks to companies like Texas Instruments, IBM, Lucent, and Xerox. They have been aggressive in asserting their patents against infringers in that those companies are sought out by the TIs and Lucents and IBMs and Xeroxes to take royalty-bearing licenses under the licensor's patents. Often the alleged infringer will seek to expand its own patent portfolio to get more patents, which are infringed by the TIs and Lucents and IBMs of the world. And so, if you have a patent that is or may be infringed by any of these companies or other companies in the computer electronics/communications industry, you might find one of those potential licensee companies, or even a company in litigation that would be interested in purchasing the patent.
>
> Carrot licensing is often called technology transfer. In carrot licensing, the principal licensed value is a new, better, or cheaper product. It's the technology that's being licensed. And the patent, although important, is of secondary significance. Nobody is going to take a license if they aren't convinced that you're giving them the ability to manufacture a newer, better, cheaper product. And then once you cross that hurdle, the issue of how well protected that newer, better, cheaper product is (by the patent) comes into play.
>
> Whether you're doing stick licensing or carrot licensing, the process has three components. The first is the identification of a licensable opportunity, which may require the patent owner to sue people, or threaten to sue people, or to license the technology. The second element is the strategy of how you're going to realize value from the patents. And the third element is the implementation. Keep in mind that it's a lot easier to identify the dollar potential of a technology than to identify when licensing revenue is going to come in. And there are a lot of

unrealistic expectations among patent-owning companies that are creating enormous pressures on the licensing executives' teams.

Companies new to licensing are usually interested in licensing noncore IP only, or else core IP into noncore markets. Using the Pampers story above as an example, infant clothing (noncore market) is not really related to the diaper market (core market). When deciding whether to license into core markets, Ford's Henry Fradkin relates four reasons why he thinks licensing into core markets is useful:

First, everything else being equal, our competitor pays more than Ford does because the competitor has to pay the royalty. Second, it is a lot better to have our competitor get hooked onto your technology than be refused and try to design around and perhaps come up with an even better design. Third, if our technical people know that the competitor is using the first generation or current generation of a particular technology or process usually that motivates the Ford engineers to go ahead and design the next generation so that we can create a new competitive advantage. Finally, selected technologies sometimes become industry standards. Isn't it a lot better to have the industry standard based on our technology rather than someone else's?

A secondary related advantage is that this can make our technology a "commodity," resulting in lower prices Ford must pay to a supplier.

Many companies ask us, how do we get started? Our answer is, "Go back and talk to your technology people, they are probably being contacted daily by potential licensees."

We have found that the best source of our deals come via referrals from our technical people, particularly when they are working with someone outside of Ford. It means that our engineers may be working with a supplier and the supplier is going to make parts or do a process for Ford Motor Company based on Ford intellectual property. The supplier and the engineer may realize, "This could be good technology to make parts or something for other companies, both inside and outside of the automotive industry." But they realize that the supplier needs a license, and what will happen is that the engineer or the scientist or even the business person will call up one of us in the Technology Commercialization office, usually me, and say, "Such and such company would like to get a license to use our technology." That's how it all starts. Every now and then we will get unsolicited requests from companies saying, "I saw your patent," or "I saw a paper from SAE (Society of Automotive Engineers)" or "I heard about the technology that you have" and they are interested in licensing the technology. And probably the final way that we do get hold of people is we make cold calls. If we know that we have a certain technology and we read about something in the paper or we may do a citation analysis, we'll make a cold call on a company and say, "Have we got the technology for you!"

It is one thing to identify a few opportunistic licenses, and another entirely to create a licensing business. Most companies we speak with are interested in some kind of portfolio mining exercise. Portfolio mining is the systematic review of an intellectual property (usually patent) portfolio to determine opportunities for carrot and/or stick revenue generation. Most IP consulting firms offer portfolio mining services, and not all use the same methodologies. How is a company to know which is the correct methodology? On pages 78–80 (in Exhibit 3.5) is the experience of Litton's Dave Kline.

For a more detailed discussion of portfolio mining and how it is performed, please see Appendix A.

IBM is considered a leader in the generation of licensing revenue, and many companies want to emulate Big Blue. But many executives do not realize the resource commitment that IBM has made in order to generate over a billion dollars annually from licensing as described in Exhibit 3.6. For companies that want to duplicate IBM's commercial success from licensing, we ask, "Are you willing to hire large numbers of attorneys to place near your technology to capture all new ideas in order to patent them? Are you willing to license *all* technologies in your portfolio, regardless of whether they are core or noncore? Are you willing to license your competitors and force your technical folks to continuously innovate?" The answer of course is almost universally, "No."

Clearly, the licensing activities of a Level Three company are quite strategic. Gone are the ad hoc characteristics of the Level Two company. In their place is a formal, written licensing policy and standardized license agreements. No patent is off-limits, regardless of how precious it may seem to its owner. Every patent has a price. Granted, that price may be quite high, but if a licensee is willing to pay, the Level Three patent owner is willing to license, even to a competitor. The Level Three company no longer waits for potential licensees to come knocking. Instead it has put in place a team to go in search of the right licensee candidates.

Best Practice 3: Consider IP Donations and Royalty Audits

Once management has authorized value extraction initiatives within the firm, the IPM team must find a quick success to help build momentum. Two of the easiest ways to do so are either an IP donation or an IP royalty audit. From Level 2, companies create a relationship between intellectual property and business use. The companies place nonstrategic assets in the "excess category."

EXHIBIT 3.5 How Do Companies Create a Licensing Organization?

About a year and a half ago at Litton Industries we undertook a baseline benchmarking effort to try to understand what was actually going on in the commercial licensing area with some of our contemporaries and in some of the other industries that had undertaken it as a formal business endeavor. Our objective was to see what had been accomplished, who was in the business and what their business models were, as well as what tools and processes were available for this kind of activity. Our objective was to adopt "best business practices" in developing a business plan which would give us the maximum opportunity to leverage off the technologies that we have across all Litton divisions. This consists of four very technologically diverse businesses: Information Technology, Ships and Associated Systems and Services, Advanced Aerospace Systems and Electronics Components and Materials.

The benchmarking effort carved out a representative subset of the total corporate patent portfolio, of approximately 1,000 domestic patents. Contracts were placed with several different organizations each of which had a different approach to front-end patent mining and marketing. The activities fell into three categories: technology profiling/assessment, mining/valuation and pure marketing.

At one end of the spectrum is an approach that is highly technology oriented. It involves performing in-depth technical assessment of the various patented technologies and how they might relate to use by others. This included assessing fields of use and the problems and solutions they map into. The output includes identification of the industries and key companies involved in this technology space. This last element was added by Litton to assist in identifying potential licensing sources.

The second approach involved more conventional patent mining activity. The portfolio is structured into clusters of technologies which can be one or many patents. The clusters are assessed using automated patent search and other automated tools to establish current patenting organizations and potentially interested industries. This results in the ability to assess potential licensing interest in a particular technical commodity consisting of either individual patents or clusters of technology. For this approach we employed two different teams each employing its unique set of tools and processes.

The third approach involved heavy-duty marketing, which revolved around documenting and representing the technologies to communicate their benefits to others and getting it to a very broad group of potential users. This involved a great deal more follow up with many potentially interested parties.

The total benchmarking effort was carried out over a six-month period with the same subset of patents given to each organization. The patents selected were about 5 percent of the total portfolio representing a broad cross section of the types of technologies that we have across our businesses.

(continues)

EXHIBIT 3.5   Continued

In parallel with this look at our patents, we attempted to understand the experiences of others. We found that a number of companies got heavily and aggressively into licensing activity only to find, after engaging potential licensing candidates, that there were internal issues and barriers within the business units which prevented moving quickly and continuously toward closing deals. This basically killed the whole process.

At Litton we have attempted to address some of these issues by combining the Chief Technology Officer role and patent licensing responsibilities under one organization. Working with all the divisions on technology planning as well as licensing, helps to eliminate unforeseen conflict between our business and licensing objectives. As indicated earlier, we have found that there are technologies that have been developed for a specific project years ago that were never fully exploited because they were not within the core business or long-term interest of a particular business unit—yet they represent a potentially valuable business asset to others. We were able to find a number of commodities that were not being exploited, which had been sitting dormant for some time. We found others that were being used by business units focused on their fixed customer market and were not being exploited in other concurrent non-Litton businesses.

We have some world-class information technology that is a number of years old but appears to be leading edge even against today's state of the art for knowledge-based search and network control. We have leading-edge technology in applying optics to the medical field that hasn't been exploited. We have some very interesting technologies used within our infrastructure for manufacturing processes and electronic/optical packaging that have uses outside of our normal business structure. We have some unique product-packaging technology that helps to protect and minimize the cost of items shipped. What we have found is technology that ranges from enabling new and innovative products, to improving the distribution and processing of information, to improved packaging and shipping of goods. It covers areas never contemplated or recognized for potential value beyond our own businesses.

Permit an observation and comment on the intellectual capital management (ICM) process. It was presented to us as a tool to be incorporated at the outset of our activity along with patent mining. I believe it is an important tool downstream for the realization of the fullest value and then ultimately the highest leveraging potential for your technology. However, it overwhelms the complexity of getting on with the basic business. I believe it is something that should be folded into the business process after you get a licensing operation rolling. In the long run, application of ICM will create much greater awareness of the potential value and applications of unexploited technologies. As a final note, it is clear that our early efforts and our implementation processes are likely to produce applications, interactions

(continues)

EXHIBIT 3.5   Continued

and relationships with new industries. It will very likely introduce our business units to new customers and lead them into new markets. It will help identify unused technologies that have commercial market value in other industries. It will also lead to the strengthening of our overall IP process, so that in the future we can expect to see growth in the quantity and commercial value of patents being generated. It will result in a much stronger management of the overall IP process across the Company. These are all very positive returns. Litton has had very positive licensing experiences to date.

David Kline, Litton Industries

EXHIBIT 3.6   The History of Licensing at IBM

We have been filing patents for about 100 years, literally since the company was founded. For most of our history we did not have a specific policy regarding cross-licensing. A major change in our approach came in 1956, when we were involved in antitrust litigation with the U.S. government. We agreed to license all our patents to any and all comers who respected our intellectual property. The last of the patents under the consent decree expired in 1991. Nevertheless, because cross-licensing has served us well, we have maintained our open licensing policy to this day.

Why do we cross-license? Speed. One of the reasons this industry moves so quickly—compared to almost any industry—is that companies in this industry cross-license their intellectual property to each other. Certainly for a fee to some, depending on who has more value, but the *willingness* to cross-license enables everyone in the business to continue to leapfrog technology. We started that way back in the '50s and it has helped get our industry on a path where competitors recognize value in licensing intellectual property.

Moving forward in time, the growth of the PC clone business in the mid-'80s caused us to ask: "What do we want to do now?" We invented the PC but other huge players grew the business around us. We had a choice to make at that time: Did we want to practice our monopoly and exclude others from the business? Or, did we want to license them and allow them to continue, to enable the industry to grow? We decided to allow licensing for the rest of the industry for what we considered very reasonable terms. At that time, the Dells and Compaqs weren't doing any R&D; they were living off our R&D. We agreed to license them for royalties, all of which went back to the operating divisions to further R&D in those divisions. We were able to lower our costs of doing business and further our R&D. We made that decision in 1987. By the 1988–89 timeframe, it was beginning to become a significant income opportunity for IBM.

(continues)

EXHIBIT 3.6   Continued

At that time, we were mostly interested in growing the portfolio and didn't worry about maintenance. There wasn't a lot of cost pressure at that time. We were getting about 700 patents a year, and for practically everything we filed in the United States and in the big five countries outside the U.S.

We probably have close to 1,000 licensees who are licensed to our patents either through royalty-bearing or cross-licensing agreements coming out of that phase of our development. We believed then and believe now it is an important way to keep progressing the information technology industry ahead.

In the mid-'90s, we moved into the next phase. We realized there was a new opportunity in licensing our technology and know-how in addition to patents. Given enough time, someone else would eventually duplicate our technology anyway. Therefore, they were going to catch up to us or get value from our technology one way or another. Why not license it out and enable others to avoid having to go through the expense of re-developing what we had already developed, at the same time open up a whole new revenue stream for IBM? We made that change in the 1995 time frame. In the years since then, technology licensing has become the biggest piece of our licensing business.

Once you license your technology, the only way you are going to win in the marketplace is move ahead and develop more new technology. Someone else now has the technology that was new yesterday.

To determine the value of our technology in a licensing opportunity, we look at what it cost us to develop the technology, as a proxy for what it would cost someone else to develop it. Then we ask how long would it take them to develop it. If it would take them three years as opposed to us making it available to them immediately, a time-to-market factor is added to the technology value. We go through a very rigorous methodology to figure out the value of it to the other party. We spend a lot of time doing that and we do it very closely with the division that developed the technology. They are the ones that have those answers.

Intellectual property licensing is not an operation we run from corporate in a vacuum. There is an extremely cooperative relationship between us and the operating divisions. We don't license know-how to a huge number of players. We look for players that will make a significant commitment to shorten the time we need to spend transferring the technology to them. We look for players that will be our partners, complementing our business. They may become a second source for others by using our technology. We help to create and maintain the standard of what we developed. We do not treat technology transfer merely as a way to unload intellectual property. For us it interlocks with and furthers other goals of IBM at the same time.

Jerry Rosenthal, IBM

Some of these excess assets will have no continuing value, so the company will stop paying maintenance fees and allow the patent to lapse. Some of them may still have value, but just not to the originating firm. Joe Daniele, Senior Vice President of IP and Technology Commercialization at SAIC, explains:

> SAIC is in its thirtieth year of existence and has never had a nonprofitable year. In a company that is consistently profitable, a process of regular, annual charitable donations of IP can be valuable. We have found that you can free up large amounts of cash in a short time with donations. In starting up an IP group at SAIC, one of the first things we did was an IP inventory (by an IP Task Force) to sort and evaluate the patents in our portfolio. We confirmed the existence of about 50 unused and non-strategic patents. Also, in most cases, the inventors had long since left the company, and so these were mostly naked patents, and they no longer had a strategic position in the portfolio. For the most part, they were representative of earlier times, projects and products that were no longer a part of the business. We could sell, license or donate them. We chose to set up a regular program of donation, so we were able to get the money upfront, via a tax deduction. This was a way to take unused assets that were no longer strategic to our operations, and turn them into free cash.
>
> This approach gets attention. It helps pay the bills and shows how a sophisticated approach to intellectual property can turn unused, but valuable assets into cash in a way that may not have been expected. In addition, the donations bring a societal benefit, in that the IP is now used to generate income and new jobs.

IP Donations.   It was The Dow Chemical Company that created the concept of donating intellectual property for a tax write-off. Dow managers reasoned that if you could get tax relief from donating a tangible asset, why not apply the same logic to an intangible? Sam Khoury, Dow's former Senior Intangible Asset Appraiser, headed up the IP donation concept within Dow, and by 1996, Dow had successfully donated its first intangible to a university.

There are several things to remember before embarking on an IP donation:

- Currently IP donations are only allowed as tax deductions in the United States.
- The donation value is the fair market value (FMV) of the technology.
- The FMV calculation must be conducted by an independent third party.
- The recipient, must be a registered nonprofit 501(c)(3) entity.
- The donor and recipient must agree on the FMV of the technology.
- Once completed, the FMV calculation has a limited life, so the transaction must be completed within six months of the valuation.

As part of its work with the IRS, Dow needed to show that donating IP was not an activity that was specific to Dow; other companies could do it as well. Not surprisingly other chemical companies were quick to pick up on the idea, as Bob Gruetzmacher of DuPont explains:

> Sam Khoury and I were having lunch back in the early nineties at one of the annual meetings of the Licensing Executives Society (LES). This was shortly after Dow completed its first donation. I was intrigued by what he had done and invited him to come to DuPont to describe the process to our Corporate Technology Transfer staff plus a few of our tax and finance people. Sam did pay us a visit and our audience really took a liking to the idea. Our tax and finance people wanted to spend time making sure that we established a consistent process (choice of donation candidates, valuation, etc.) which was in perfect compliance with the IRS guidelines. It took a little time given the size of our company and diversity of portfolios but eventually everything came together and we completed our first IP donation in late 1998. In this instance the technology gift was a textbook candidate for the ideal donation. It had recognized value and commercial viability, it was non-strategic to DuPont and had no ready buyers. Licensing was considered but DuPont no longer had the sufficient technical resources to effectively carry out the necessary know-how transfer to multiple licensees. In February 1999 we donated 23 more patents of significant value to three other universities.

Below are several more recent examples of donations:

- From December 1998 to September 1999, Ford Motor Company donated "bundles of technology" worth $40 million.
- In October 1999, the Procter & Gamble Company gave 40 patents to the Milwaukee School of Engineering. The value of the gift was not publicly disclosed, but the university called it the largest gift it had ever received, which means it was worth over $10 million.
- In January 2000, Eastman Chemical Company gave Clemson University a portfolio of U.S. and foreign patents worth $38 million.
- In January 2000, SAIC gave Woods Hole Oceanographic Institute hardware, software and a patent, valued at approximately $2 million, for a system for chemical analysis of the deep sea ocean bottom.

Companies donate IP for a number of reasons. Obviously there is a tax benefit. But surprisingly, most companies admit that they receive far more value in goodwill from universities and nonprofits than they do from a tax break. Jeff Weedman, of Procter & Gamble, explains:

The reason we donate technology is because we simply have too much of it to commercialize ourselves. Our donation candidates are technologies that have expensive technical challenges to solve before they can be effectively commercialized. It is a candidate for donation because we don't have the resources, capability, or desire to solve and develop it fully, particularly in light of the focus areas we've chosen to invest in and fully develop. However, the technology is regarded to be very robust, valuable, and potentially useful to many people. So, as part of our process, we donate that technology to a university, research, or not-for-profit institution we think is best equipped to solve those remaining technical challenges and successfully commercialize it. With the donation, recipients get full rights to the technology and they own it free and clear. If they can successfully solve the technical challenges, we'd even love to become a customer of the technology in some cases. Bottom line: A recipient can sell it or license it back to us—whatever they see fit to do.

Donating creates value from a technology which otherwise may not reach the marketplace in a useable form. Also, the donation forms a unique, interactive bond between the business and academic community. That's great for both of us. It's also good for the economy if the technology can be successfully commercialized; it will create jobs, build new companies, and, overall, improve the lives of consumers. Quite often, this is a situation that the universities could not have implemented or even dreamed of on their own. Clearly, our technology donation program is a winning proposition for all parties involved.

Royalty Audits.   Level Three companies track their fees from licensing, typically paid as a stream of royalty payments. This activity does not typically occur at Level One and Level Two firms. Licensing occurs there, but it is often haphazard and very opportunistic. Many companies license when it is easy, for example when a potential licensee approaches them with an interest in a particular technology. While it is true that technology licensing creates royalty income, agreements need to be audited to ensure that the full amount owed to the licensor is paid. Profit-minded companies operating at Level Three, unlike purely defensive or purely cost-conscious companies operating at lower levels, realize that they may not always "reap what they sow" when it comes to royalties from licensing agreements. The most astute companies conduct what might be called a *royalty audit*—a review of license records to determine whether royalty payments have been correct. This is generally a matter of paying too little, too late. Some licensees even hold the royalty payments in an accrual account until the licensor asks to be paid.

The typical royalty audit includes documenting the licensee's compliance with the license terms. One component of this is a periodic monitoring of the licensee's business activities through publicly available information. A more powerful component, though, is the ability to conduct formal royalty audits of licensees. Most standardized licensing arrangements permit the licensor to send an independent auditor to inspect the books of the licensee. Additionally, the licensee is often required to pay the cost of the royalty audit if there is a discrepancy in royalty payments above 10 or 15 percent. Studies have shown that such audits surface an average underreporting of 12 percent, but the range is wide. While some companies find very little underreporting, others find it to be far greater. In our consulting work we have found underpayments as high as 50 percent.

Stanford University has a royalty audit program, as do Dolby Laboratories and Ford Global Technologies. In 1997, when Ford instituted its program, it found many cases of royalty nonpayment. One such case stands out for FGTI's Henry Fradkin:

> One of my licensing managers called up a licensee and said, do you realize you haven't paid us royalties in 10 years and there is an annual minimum? The fellow was absolutely shocked. He went back to his license agreement and found that it was true. It turns out that his managers thought the license agreement had expired, since they were not using the technology and never received any notices. He offered to settle for ten cents on the dollar. When my manager responded, "You mean you willfully are saying you don't want to pay the royalties you owe us?" he decided to pay 100 percent.

In that case, the licensor was not using the technology, Fradkin emphasizes. In other cases, the licensee is in fact using the technology, in which case Ford may ask not only for back payment, but also may consider suing for infringement. Settlement payments in these cases can be quite significant.

Such discrepancies usually do not reflect a lack of integrity on the part of the licensee. Our experience suggests that the underreporting may be the result of changes in the licensee's product codes or model numbers or personnel. For example, as model numbers change, the person responsible for preparing the licensee's royalty reports may not be aware of new products that embody the licensed technology. When the old model numbers are phased out, the royalty checks dwindle to nothing.

Some licensors may be concerned about the effect that a planned royalty audit will have on the company's relationship with its licensees. Licensees, though, have come to expect royalty audits as normal business practice. You can be sure that their other licensors are also conducting royalty audits and that the licensees have grown accustomed to the practice. Auditing licensees is simply good business. After all, what other aspect of today's business world is conducted on the honor system?

As Jerry Rosenthal, Vice President of Intellectual Property and Licensing at IBM, the company with the most fully licensed IP portfolio, explains:

> We have a pretty good handle on where most of our licensees are. We are in a lot of businesses. The money goes back to the divisions from which they came. The businesses know if the amount of royalties are vastly different than the published size of that business, we will write a letter to the licensee stating that we think we have a discrepancy here between what they published and the amount of their checks. We think they ought to take a second look at it. The problem gets fixed right then and there, 99 percent of the time.

At a minimum, royalty audits help clear up misunderstandings and discrepancies between the two parties about the meaning or interpretation of vague terms or conditions. We've even learned that licensees can find it beneficial to conduct a royalty audit as well. Such was the case when two large pharmaceutical companies had a dispute about the amount owed on a patent license. A royalty audit conducted by the licensee highlighted a $300 million difference between what the licensor claimed was owed and what the licensee's own royalty audit revealed. An arbitrator later selected the lower amount.

Having made the decision to engage in all these value-extracting activities, what form should that take? This now leads us to our next best practice.

Best Practice 4: Organize to Extract Value

At Level Three, intellectual property management is now an activity that is larger than just the legal group. The activities that support IPM cut across a variety of functions: legal, R&D, marketing, finance, and strategic planning. How do companies decide what decisions are made at the business unit level and which ones are made at the corporate level? What activities are conducted at the business unit level and at the corporate level? And finally, does the revenue that is generated flow back to the corporation or business unit? These are all valid questions. To help us sort through these issues, we created an Authority and Activity Matrix which you can see in Exhibit 3.7.

The matrix results from a series of questions and answers that the people in a company's IP organization must pursue. Initial elements in this series are questions about what is the company's long-term vision, and where is it going. The answers to these questions trigger the next question in the series: What is the company's strategy for achieving this vision? Following the answer to this question, one must ask: What role(s) could intellectual property play in helping the company enable its strategy? The roles, once known, allow the company to determine which functions (see Exhibit 3.2) must be performed. Once the functions to be performed are known, the company can then ask itself how it wishes to organize in order to perform these functions.

In creating an organization, one of the frequently asked set of questions concerns the degree to which companies should centralize IP activities or decentralize them. Centrists argue that only by bringing IP management activities under one roof can one expect to control and direct the most effective uses of IP. Decentralizationists, by way of contrast, argue that the innovations at issue, along with their corresponding pieces of IP, were created by and for the business divisions and are rightfully "owned" and used by the business divisions. For this reason, the business divisions ought to be the home of any activity that manages and focuses the uses to which IP will be placed.

In our experience, there are two areas of consideration when companies debate the question of centralization vs. decentralization. The first concerns the authority to release any IP documents or matters outside of the company; the second concerns the activities associated with the IP management functions themselves. The following list includes these generally agreed-upon functions in business units (BUs):

- IP generation, protection, maintenance, and enforcement
- Portfolio inventory, management, and administration
- Portfolio mining and opportunity identification
- IP training, education, and process design
- Brand management
- IP transactions
- Competitive assessment
- Innovation
- Relationship management (customers, suppliers, others)
- Marketing

As the first page of Exhibit 3.7 shows, there are at least nine different possibilities we have identified for centralizing or decentralizing the IP management authority and activity within a firm. The second page contains our judgments of where companies we know about might fit on the matrix. The third page of the exhibit highlights the very central cell in the matrix, because its "mixed" approach is arguably the most frequently occurring situation. The exhibit highlights the functions that are centralized as well as those that are decentralized in this popular organizational mode.

EXHIBIT 3.7 Degrees of Activity and Authority Centralization

Activity

Authority	Decentralized	Mixed	Centralized
Centralized	• Value extraction may or may not be strategic to the firm. • IP activity fully dispersed throughout the BUs. • All value extraction efforts are approved centrally.	• Value extraction is not entirely strategic to the firm. • Value extraction activities are shared: legal and licensing tend to be centralized, other functions are decentralized. • All value extraction efforts are approved centrally.	• Value extraction important to corporate strategy. • All IP activities are under one roof (business & legal). • All value extraction efforts are approved centrally.
Mixed	• Value extraction is probably not strategic to the firm. • IP activity fully dispersed throughout the BUs. • Some forms of authority given to BUs, others reside within corporation.	• Value extraction is not entirely strategic to the firm. • Value extraction activities are shared: legal and licensing tend to be centralized, other functions are decentralized. • Some authority given to BUs, other resides with Corporate Staff.	• Value extraction is not entirely strategic to the firm. • All IP activities are under one roof (business & legal). • Some authority given to BUs, other resides with corporate staff.
Decentralized	• Value extraction is not strategic to the firm. • IP activity fully dispersed throughout the BUs. • Value extraction is approved and released by BUs.	• Value extraction is not entirely strategic to the firm. • Value extraction activities are shared: legal and licensing tend to be centralized, other functions are decentralized. • Value extraction is controlled and approved by BUs.	• Value extraction may or may not be strategic to the firm. • All IP activities are under one roof (business & legal). • Value extraction is controlled by BUs. All value extraction is approved by BUs.

(continues)

EXHIBIT 3.7 Continued

Activity

Increased Speed of Response →

Authority	Decentralized	Mixed	Centralized
Centralized	[No Gathering Company is in this category] *Minimize Central Staff*	Xerox Roche Holding AG *Shared Decision-Making*	IBM FGTI Litton *Efficiency and Rapid Response*
Mixed	Skandia *Minimize Central Staff Shared Resources*	Boeing HP Eastman SAIC *Shared Decision-Making Shared Resources*	Fortum *Efficiency and Moderate-Speed Response*
Decentralized	[No Gathering Company is in this category]	Dow Dupont *BU-Centric Decision-Making*	Lockheed *Efficiency but Slow Response*

Value Extraction (Cash/Non-Cash)

(continues)

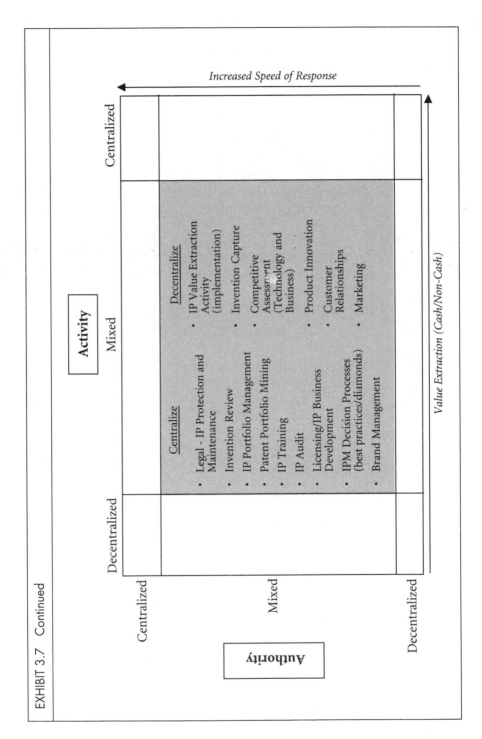

EXHIBIT 3.7 Continued

90

Litton recently centralized its IP function after many years of allowing the business units to pursue licenses opportunistically, in support of their unique business interests. Dave Kline recalls the many decisions the company had to make as it centralized. (See Exhibit 3.8.)

For DuPont, decentralizing authority made much more sense. As Bob Gruetzmacher explains:

> In DuPont only a licensed patent attorney may actually file a patent application with the PTO or an analogous agency in a foreign country. Notwithstanding that all DuPont patents are assigned to the DuPont Company, the actual responsibility of intellectual property management resides within the respective businesses. Each business pays for, controls, and nurtures its own intellectual property. It makes decisions regarding when and where to file, how to protect (trade secret vs. patent), whether or not to license, or whether or not to abandon. Most IP management groups within business units carry out periodic docket reviews, but not always at the same time frequency. We have a corporate philosophy around filing in countries where there are poor patent enforcement practices. But the ultimate responsibility regarding decisions around intellectual property resides largely within the businesses. This has worked pretty well for us because when you have the businesses paying for the patents, they have the tendency to be a little more discerning when deciding on what to file on, where to file, and what to maintain. Economics and budgets govern the process.

For each company, the decision of how best to organize to extract value will depend on a number of factors, but most importantly the corporate culture and organizational culture.

Best Practice 5: Develop Advanced Screening Criteria

In Level Two, companies began to screen their intellectual property in conjunction with the strategy of the firm. This initial screening was to allow companies to move from patenting everything to patenting things that were strategic to the firm. For Level Two companies, "strategic to the firm" usually related to creating products and services for sale. Now at Level Three, companies have expanded their value extraction horizons beyond the products and services of the firm to include the technologies and know-how of the firm. Here intellectual property has value in the piece of paper or the know-how that can be licensed, sold, or donated. So at Level Three, companies need to widen their screening criteria to include technologies or intellectual assets that may not have a direct value to the firm (i.e., be useful in current or future products or services) but

---

EXHIBIT 3.8   Centralizing the IP Function

Once we decided to centralize the IP function at Litton, we faced a number of issues. Some of the current issues are: what is the appropriate organization, to whom will it report, and who will report to it; what are the associated functions that will reside within its structure; will it be staffed in-house, outsourced or be a blend of internal and external support; and what business processes and tools will be used? There are a wide variety of new automated tools that perform relatively the same functions but vary considerably in the cost of implementation. The indirect costs need to be carefully considered—i.e., staffing, training, maintenance, etc. Patent search tools such as Aurigin, MAPIT and others, all have considerably different business requirements and arrangements. Which, if any, is right for you depends on your business structure and the way you intend to deploy them.

Other issues to be considered are the initial size and budget and the metrics or "success criteria" established when you start up. Do you want to go "instant on" and immediately address your entire portfolio, or do you want to phase into the business? We all know that the front end of licensing new commodities or technologies doesn't necessarily produce instant financial results as some would lead you to believe. It takes time. What is your business plan and what cash flow profile do you expect to see? What do you have to commit to?

Coming back to the issue of organizational structure and where it will report, this is basically driven by the business objectives and philosophy of the Executive Staff and Board. It is a cultural issue, unique to each corporation, that is governed by the attitudes, mindset and the experience base of those running the show. However, based on many conversations with others, it must report to the highest possible executive level within the company and have the full support of the finance and legal departments. In most companies, "legal" has historically managed this function and, in this new business process, it now becomes an essential support function to the "licensing operation." In that regard you must have an intimate blend of business and the legal support to provide focus on licensing as the primary business objective rather than protection, which is historically what patents have provided. I quite often meet with the management of other companies that don't have an appreciation for patent licensing vs. patent protection. When engaged in discussion, they find this business approach to be something quite foreign to their normal business thinking.

Some final, but no less critical issues are how existing internal organizations will interface with the licensing operation. These organizations historically generate the IP. Up to this point they have had sole use of the IP and have done the associated licensing. How do you interface these operations into a centralized licensing organization so that they understand their new role and are responsible for its success? This is a major challenge for all companies. It is essential to

(continues)

EXHIBIT 3.8   Continued

have the strong continuous support of the operating units and technologists. To accomplish this, these operations should be properly incentivized. This must include inventors and those personnel directly involved in the licensing processes. There are many ways to accomplish this and again it varies from company to company.

They also need to know that this new business has the full support of Corporate Executive management. This can and should be accomplished through directives and formal policy guidance which defines their roles and responsibilities and how the organization will operate. The message needs to be clear and unequivocal from the highest possible level within a company.

David Kline, Litton Industries

---

may have indirect value (i.e., can be directly licensed or sold) without having to be embedded in a product or service. Rockwell's Jim O' Shaughnessy, explains:

Intellectual capital can and must be leveraged. You can create a fund of intellectual capital for about one-tenth the cost of the problem it is solving. In the past at Rockwell, if we had a million-dollar problem to solve, we passed the hat to find one million dollars. It had to come from somewhere so somewhere suffered the loss of one million dollars in capital it could use to support its business or function. We were robbing Peter to pay Paul. We might have solved a problem, but we also denied ourselves an opportunity that may have had greater potential.

Today, if we do the right things, we can actually *create*, say, a half a million dollars of intellectual capital, and we can substitute that for half a million dollars in financial capital. And in any given transaction, as long as the other party agrees that it's a million dollars in value, it doesn't really matter what the components are: you have accomplished what you needed to accomplish.

But the rabbit in the hat is that you can create half a million in intellectual capital if you're really good for less than $50 thousand. Now, what we've done is taken $450 thousand of pressure off the balance sheet. We can put it someplace else. What's really interesting is that that half a million dollars in value can be used many times over. Because it is intangible, its use doesn't dissipate its intrinsic value.

So when you're through, you may actually get millions of dollars worth of value, transactional value, over the life of the intellectual capital for that same investment of $50 thousand plus perhaps something from the investment.

Conclusion: Building beyond Profits

With such aggressive attempts to increase revenues while reducing costs, IP-rich companies can emulate Thomas Edison's slow but sure journey to the boardroom. But we still have farther to go. Profits are not everything. We have not yet arrived at the boardroom door. More stages are ahead—including the Integrated Level, the next tier in the IP Value Hierarchy.

4

LEVEL FOUR—INTEGRATED

COMPANIES THAT HAVE achieved the fourth level have come to understand the strategic implications of intellectual property for their firm. They look beyond defense, costs, and profits. (See Exhibit 4.1.) They realize that IP can be used to position them broadly in their marketplace as well as providing tactical positioning. They also see that IP may be used as an effective weapon against competitors. While profits may be made directly from their IP, companies at Level Four realize there are still greater opportunities. IP is now viewed as an integrated business asset that can be used in a broad range of ways: as a negotiating tool, as a way of positioning the company strategically, or even as a way of affecting stock price.

In addition, the Integrated Level marks a shift in the nature of the IP function. At this level, the IP function starts looking outside its own walls to integrate its expertise and resources with those of the rest of the company. It becomes more innovative and looks for ways to help other parts of the organization reach their goals.

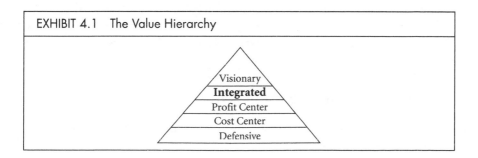

EXHIBIT 4.1   The Value Hierarchy

Visionary
Integrated
Profit Center
Cost Center
Defensive

What Level Four Companies Are Trying to Accomplish

Companies at Level Four see their IP as a set of strategic as well as tactical assets. At this level, companies are usually interested in IP as a set of business assets. Their IP management objectives include:

- Extracting strategic value from their IP
- Integrating IP awareness and operations throughout all functions of the company
- Becoming more sophisticated and innovative in managing and extracting value from the firm's IP

With these objectives in mind, Level Four companies are now interested in adding IP to their portfolio so that it can be used more strategically. In part, the selection of what to include in the portfolio is heavily influenced by a more sophisticated and complex understanding of competitor IP strategies and portfolios. As a result, Level Four companies often invest in developing comprehensive IP competitive assessment capabilities.

Whereas Level Three companies are focused on learning the tactical possibilities that IP makes available to them, Level Four companies are more intrigued with the strategic possibilities. By Level Four, companies have come to understand the fundamental importance of knowledge and information to their long-term benefit. With this in mind, Level Four companies begin to change the ways in which they deal with their human capital and tacit knowledge. At this level, company managers realize that they don't own the tacit knowledge of their employees and that they should be finding ways of codifying and developing ownership of this important resource.

At Level Four, companies are concerned with more than the portions of the IP management decision system that are the province of the IP attorneys (see Exhibit 4.2). IP is now critical to deciphering competitive actions and the firms' reactions as well as finding ways to maneuver strategically in the market. No longer is the firm dependent on its own IP creation, now the company begins actively seeking outside innovations wherever possible in order to save time to market and fill in portfolio gaps. Thus the technical, marketing, and finance functions become more actively involved in the business decisions involving IP.

Best Practices for the Integrated Level

As in other levels, solutions abound. Exhibit 4.3 contains five best practices for better IP integration in corporations.

EXHIBIT 4.2   IP Management System (Integrated Focus)

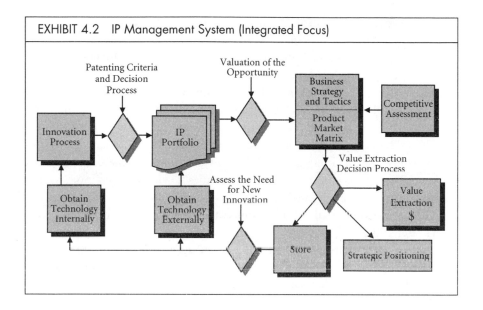

Best Practice 1: Align IP Strategy with Corporate Strategy

The basic strategy guiding IP integration can be described in one word: connection.

First, and most fundamentally, there is a connection between IP and the very direction the company is headed. At the risk of overusing the word strategy, we would say that in a company operating at Level Four, *the IP strategy must be fully aligned with the corporate strategy*. At Level Three, we learned how to monetize intellectual property that already existed in our patent portfolio. The next question is obvious. "What new intellectual property do we want to create?" To answer that question it is important to understand where

---

EXHIBIT 4.3   IP Integration—Best Practices

Best Practice 1: Align IP strategy with corporate strategy.

Best Practice 2: Manage IP and intellectual assets across multiple functions.

Best Practice 3: Conduct competitive assessment.

Best Practice 4: Codify IP knowledge and share it with all business units.

Best Practice 5: Focus on strategic value extraction.

the company is going strategically and what are its corporate goals, in order to understand the roles that IP can play in enabling those goals.

We cannot stress enough that the value of a firm's intellectual property depends not only upon the kind of value desired but also upon the company's context. In fact, we have learned that the company's context provides a new and very useful measuring stick that can be used to determine the relative importance of innovations to the firm or to calculate the value of the firm's intangibles. The value companies place on their innovative ideas largely depends on the firm's view of itself, and on the reality of its marketplace. Put another way, each firm exists within a context that shapes its view of what is or is not of value. Context may be defined as the firm's internal and external realities. Internal realities concern direction, resources, and constraints. They define the firm's strengths and weaknesses as well as its capabilities for competing in its external world. The external realities concern opportunities and threats and focus on the fundamental forces affecting the long-term viability of the industry as well as the immediate opportunities available to the firm.

For most firms, their context is expressed through the firm's vision of what it wishes to become and the strategy it selects for achieving that vision. Companies that have defined a vision and outlined the strategy for achieving it, are in a position to now determine the roles their intellectual property can play in leveraging the strategy and in achieving the vision.

Different companies will determine different roles for their intellectual property. Indeed, it is unusual to find two companies with exactly the same roles for their intellectual property simply because no two companies have exactly the same context (vision and strategy). For example, for some product design and manufacturing companies the role for intellectual property may be to create the innovations that will become the firm's products and services of the future. In other manufacturing companies, where the firm's value added involves assembly and integration of components to create products and services, the intellectual property may focus on integrating the innovations of others and adding value through low-cost manufacturing or distribution. In still other companies, the intellectual property may be integral to creating a reputation or image that the company uses to differentiate itself in its marketplace. IBM fits this last profile. It is at its core a technology company. Year after year it ranks number one in U.S. patent acquisition as well as patent and technology licensing. This ranking builds and supports the company's reputation for technology leadership, which in turn adds to the demand for IBM's products and services embodying that technology.

The set of roles any one company selects for its intellectual capital depends largely on the kind of firm it is, its vision for itself, and the strategy it has chosen. The flow of thought for aligning the vision, strategy, and intellectual capital are displayed in Exhibit 4.4.

EXHIBIT 4.4 Alignment of Vision, Strategy, and Intellectual Capital

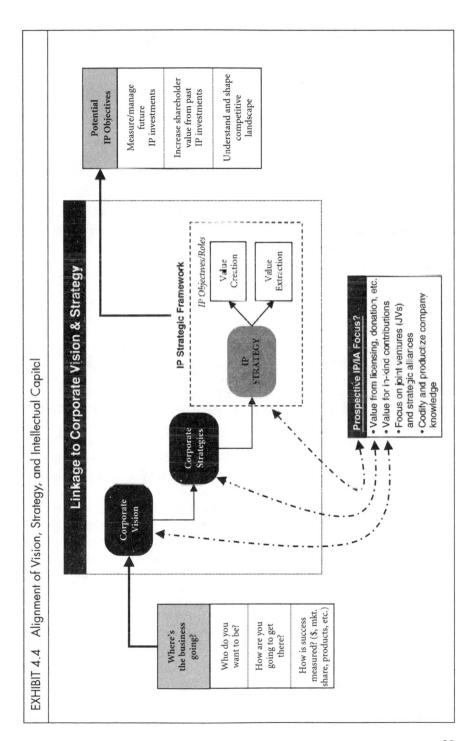

Linkage to Corporate Vision & Strategy

Potential IP Objectives

Measure/manage future IP investments

Increase shareholder value from past IP investments

Understand and shape competitive landscape

IP Strategic Framework

IP Objectives/Roles

Value Creation

Value Extraction

IP STRATEGY

Corporate Strategies

Corporate Vision

Prospective IP/IA Focus?

- Value from licensing, donation, etc.
- Value for in-kind contributions
- Focus on joint ventures (JVs) and strategic alliances
- Codify and productize company knowledge

Where's the business going?

Who do you want to be?

How are you going to get there?

How is success measured? ($, mkt. share, products, etc.)

Roles for Intellectual Property.   Companies ascribe a range of roles for value extraction from their intellectual property. While most people tend to think quickly of the revenue-generating role, there is a range of others that are employed. Exhibit 4.5 represent some of the most often mentioned ones.

But how do companies actually align their IP strategy and corporate strategies? Joe Daniele discussed how this is done. (See Exhibit 4.6.)

If a company has multiple units, then each unit may have its own unit strategy. The IP strategy for each unit will differ accordingly. SC Johnson operates this way (see Exhibit 4.7).

Few line managers like to create strategy documents. Most of our clients want to leap immediately into actionable things relating to IPM, not create a strategy and align it with the corporate goals. And yet, there is perhaps no other best practice as important as this one. If the IP strategy is not aligned with the corporate strategy and goals, then you will have wasted time, money, and resources. *Ad hoc* IP systems without a view to the needs of the entire enterprise are likely to fail miserably, as Jim O'Shaughnessy of Rockwell explains:

> The day I showed up, we were targeted as a defendant in a number of different patent infringement lawsuits. If you aggregated all of the claims for all of these lawsuits, the financial demands on our company considerably exceeded $1 billion. It's difficult to achieve this kind of result without a nearly total systemic breakdown.
>
> In particular, people throughout the company didn't regard IP very highly in terms of using it as a business tool or lever. There was little connection between the patent department and the business unit. And there was a fairly large disconnect between the patent department and the rest of the law department. Very little articulation of goals and objectives means that common strategies cannot be developed, let alone implemented.
>
> But, beneath the turmoil, we had a lot of people who were very creative. Keep in mind, we pioneered the Space Shuttle program and brought some fantastic technology to American society. But then there was a slip between the lip and cup when it came to capitalizing on the technology as a basis for real competitiveness. It became apparent that we had to transition, and think more strategically.

S.C. Johnson's Bill Frank makes a key point:

> It is important to look closely at the relationship between IP and the businesses. IP activities should be aligned with your strategic plan both overall and for each of the businesses within an organization. Accordingly, each business should have its own intellectual property strategy.

Exhibit 4.7 shows our view of the IPM creation context, process, and people.

EXHIBIT 4.5 Roles for Value Extraction

Defensive	Patents	Trademarks	Know-how	Relationships
Conflict Avoidance/ Resolution	• Protection (exclude others) • Design Freedom • Cross-licensing (defensive) • Litigation Bargaining Power	• Protection (exclude others)	• Protection (trade secret)	• N/A

Offensive	Patents	Trademarks	Know-how	Relationships
Cost Reduction	• Litigation Avoidance • Access to Technology of Others • Improved Knowledge Transfer • Reduced Knowledge Gaps	• Litigation Avoidance • Access to Technology of Others	• Litigation Avoidance • Improved Knowledge Transfer	• Reduced Marketing Costs
Revenue Generation	• Products and Services: Sales, Licensing, JV, Strategic Alliance, Optimization of Core Technology, Value Extraction from Non-Core Technology, Integration, Donations • Patents: Sales, Licenses, Donations, Infringement Policing • Increased Bargaining Power (e.g., suppliers, customers, affiliates, JV/alliance partners) • Market Penetration • Increased Speed to Market	• Products and Services: Sales, JV, Strategic Alliance • TM: Sales, Licenses, Co-branding, Infringement Policing	• Sales • Licenses • JV • Strategic Alliance • Integration • Increased Speed to Market	• Products and Services: Sales
Strategic Position	• Reputation/Image • Competitive Blocking (exclusivity) • Barrier to Competition • Supplier Control • Customer Control • Optimization of Core Technology	• Name Recognition • Customer Loyalty • Barrier to Competition • JV • Strategic Alliance	• Reputation/Image • Barrier to Entry	• Reputation/Image • Customer Loyalty • Barrier to Entry

EXHIBIT 4.6   Aligning Corporate and IP Strategies

How does one develop an intellectual property strategy that is consistent and aligned with the strategy of the corporation so as to support the corporation's goals? First thing you've got to do is know what the corporation's goals are. Where is the corporation going and what is the technical strategy of the corporation, because intellectual property tends to be primarily technical, at least in the sorts of firms we're talking about here. Then you break this technology strategy up into various technical categories in order to reflect what the market is calling for in these various categories. These are technical categories that related to the company's products or services. You want to understand how well aligned your current portfolio is with the products you're looking to deliver over the next five or ten years, because most intellectual property, patents in particular, have a pretty long lifetime. It's around for 20 years. So everything you've got now is going to be supporting the future for roughly the next ten years, (if you take the average life of a portfolio).

It's obviously going to vary if you've been doing something strange like sitting on a portfolio and not doing anything strategic for the last 10 years. For example, if you have a portfolio that is heavily into optics and your future is in digital electronic network areas, you might find that you don't have that close an alignment, in which case you might have a desired state that's pretty high. You might have 2 percent of your portfolio in networks and yet 30 percent or 40 percent of your future products are in networks, just to give an extreme example. You look out five years to your best guess of where your products are going. You lay out what your product strategy is. Then your portfolio should reflect that product and technical strategy.

Next you look at a basic gap analysis. What have you got today? And where do you need to be? You do that in your major product lines. At Xerox when we looked at the technical strategy, there were a number of areas that reflected the technology supporting our products. We did a gap analysis. We looked at what our current portfolio was. We reflected percentage-wise what the portfolio should look like in the future. We included a growth factor assuming we would grow the portfolio at a certain rate per year. Growth of the portfolio is mainly a financial decision because it costs a lot of money to invent, do the filings and maintain the patents. So you need to understand how much you want to spend. It can get very expensive.

In summary, you look at where your portfolio is today, and where you expect to be tomorrow. Then you've got to go out and go into the various technical groups and set goals and targets—and make inventory and filing of patents in specific areas part of their goals for the next year and the next five years.

Joe Daniele, SAIC, formerly of Xerox

EXHIBIT 4.7

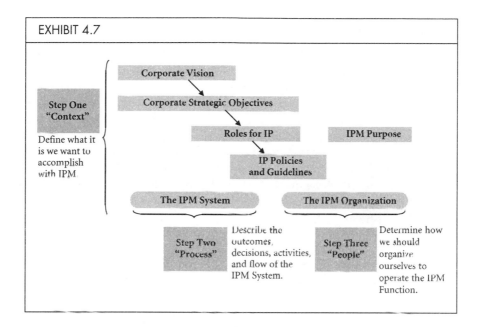

The first step is to define the context, determine what it is the company wants to accomplish with IPM. Once you understand what you want to accomplish, then it is helpful to look at where you are today and determine what elements need to be created, reorganized, or redefined. The next step is to create the process that involves describing the activities, decisions, outcomes, and flow of the IPM system. And finally, the last step relates to people, determining how best to organize to achieve the above two objectives. It is at this stage that executives begin to understand how IP connects with every important operating *function* of the company.

In Exhibit 4.8, Jane Robbins of Sprint Communications Corporation describes how Sprint executives began to understand this.

Best Practice 2: Manage IP and Intellectual Assets Across Multiple Functions

So how can the IP be leveraged across the enterprise? The following discussion shows how this works in a number of areas.

"It all started with candles," says Jeff Weedman, Vice President of Global Licensing and External Ventures for Procter & Gamble. "That's when we began connecting sciences." Connecting sciences?

EXHIBIT 4.8   Strategy Link at Sprint

At an important point in our company's history, an inflection point of sorts, we took a critical look inward at our intellectual property management function and asked: How and where does this strategically fit into Sprint? Why does this fit? And why now? At that time, we wanted to find an executive to head up a comprehensive intellectual property management function at Sprint with responsibility across the entire intellectual property value chain—from IP creation/generation to IP protection and maintenance, and IP value extraction. But this wasn't just an HR hiring issue: we first needed restated, actionable, strategic objectives for the intellectual property management function. As well, these restated strategic objectives had to align with and support our larger corporate strategic objectives and underlying vision. Further, these restated strategic objectives had to be linked with a redefined intellectual property role as to value creation and extraction. We wondered whether all of this should be accomplished before we ever hired this executive?

However, we wanted to give the person charged with heading up a redesigned IP management function at Sprint the opportunity to make his or her mark on the function, to mark a course for the future. It was a Catch-22 situation. Also, there were lingering questions about where this person would fit organizationally within Sprint given the multifunctional nature of the position. What kind of reporting relationships would this individual have and how would he or she be linked to the leaders of other impacted organizations at Sprint? We quickly realized we weren't just hiring another vice president in the Law Department with intellectual property authority. We knew the redesigned intellectual property management function would involve our network engineering and planning groups, our tax and finance organizations, our various business development groups, as well as our larger corporate development and strategic planning organization.

Indeed, it didn't take long before we realized that, to move forward, we had to back up from the tactical hiring decision-making. Thus, we first had to broaden our focus to encompass the preliminary strategic planning work. Then, we could propose a redesigned intellectual property management function to enable execution of our reformulated strategic objectives. Finally, with the revised objectives and redesigned function in mind, we could concentrate on hiring the right personnel and best organizing them to realize maximum value from Sprint's intellectual property portfolio. Pursuing this more strategic approach, in our view, would position Sprint to build an intellectual property function and portfolio that best reflects the company we are today and strive to be in the future.

Jane Tishman Robbins, formerly of Sprint

Weedman explains that candles, P&G's original business in 1837, provided the technology base for making soap. "That brought us fundamental expertise in fats and oils, which led to the creation of Crisco shortening."

Crushing oilseeds gave P&G researchers expertise in plant fibers, which led to insights into paper and absorbent products, like disposable diapers (Pampers) and bathroom tissue (Charmin).

"Fats and oils are also a fundamental base for surfactants, the technology used to produce detergents, like Tide," Weedman says. "Making detergents, in turn, gave us experience with hard water and calcium. That helped us understand how to improve oral health, through products like Crest, and overall bone health, through products like Actonel, our new prescription drug for preventing and treating osteoporosis."

Most people may think about P&G as a premier products marketer. "At our core, though, we're a technology company," Weedman says. "Connecting technologies to create products to better meet consumers' needs is both our history and our future. It's what we're all about."

Weedman refers to the Swiffer Wet Jet as one of P&G's most recent examples of integrating their IP strategies across multiple functions. (See Exhibit 4.9.)

Research and Development. It goes without saying that the IP function should be linked to R&D. Yet many companies could benefit from strengthening this link. One way to do so is to provide mechanisms to share knowledge across business unit boundaries so that R & D does not have to waste time solving problems already solved elsewhere in the company. This can be done with cross functional and organizational patent committees, interlinked planning processes, or as in the case of Avery Dennison, making the same Director responsible for strategic planning and intellectual property management.

- Avoid spending time and money on projects where IP protection will not be available or, worse yet, where a competitor already holds a blocking patent.
- Monitor competitors' patent filings to provide a window into competitors' strategies and new product developments. A case in point is Avery Dennison. In 1994, one of its units developed a new film that could be used to label products. Procter & Gamble had granted the company a contract to provide the product for its shampoo bottles. But Avery knew that Dow had its eye on this market as well. Rather than compete, sue, and countersue, Avery went to Dow, showed its patent filings, and asked Dow not to enter the market. Dow saw the writing on the wall, and wisely redirected its R&D into other areas.[1]

EXHIBIT 4.9   Product Development at P&G

Swiffer WetJet fuses the best of Procter & Gamble's technologies to alleviate one of consumers' most detested chores—mopping. This idea first took shape at the "Seminar of Dreams," a session which brought together the company's best technologists to "cross-fertilize" many of the company's core competencies. Combining the insight from HomeCare, that the mop can do as much cleaning as the cleaning chemistry we provide to the consumer, with the competency we have in the Paper Division, to create disposable, absorbent cleaning structures, was the seminal moment. From there, Corporate New Ventures picked up the idea, learning that mopping is one of the most despised household tasks, and it has not changed for generations. Corporate New Ventures completed an Attractiveness Assessment in which the consumer, technical, and business model began to take shape. Ultimately, the Fabric & HomeCare GBU took the lead to complete the consumer-technical-business model and then to commercialize this idea as the "Swiffer WetJet."

The product development required the floor cleaning understanding of the HomeCare group combined with the best technologies of the Paper Divisions—Tissue & Towel, Diapers and Feminine Protection sectors—to make this big idea a reality. The HomeCare group led the consumer research efforts to understand today's habits & practices and to develop the conceptual positioning: "Swiffer WetJet revolutionizes the wet floor cleaning process reducing the time, mess and effort." To jump start the technical development process, Paper Technologists were actually transferred into the HomeCare organization to lead this work. These technologists were able to design the product from the ground up to best meet the consumer need. The final cleaning pad re-applied some of the best materials and design thinking from Diapers, Tissue-Towel, and Feminine Protection. For example, the pad's super-absorbency is based on the same super-absorbent polymers used in diapers, the stay-clean topsheet re-applies aperture, formed films from FemPro. Meanwhile the cleaning solution was developed, building upon cleaning models and chemistry familiar to the team in HomeCare.

The implement design and sourcing required that we look outside, to learn and to create new competencies. We sought out expertise for the design and manufacturing of the implement, since we had never made such a durable good before. The final implement design uses a battery-powered pump to dispense cleaning solution onto the floor where the absorbent cleaning pad can then remove the dirt from the floor. The design and quality of this implement are best-in-class.

As a result of connecting technologies, along with exceptional marketing and branding strategies, Swiffer WetJet was recognized as one of the most innovative new products in 2000.

Jeff Weedman, Procter & Gamble

- Assist in gap analysis providing insight as to what technologies the company is weak in and how or where it might obtain such technologies without building its own capability. S-3, a small chip design firm, acquired a key patent from Exponential Technologies in order to stall its largest competitor, Intel. The acquired patent predated Intel's Merced chip patent, and could have prevented Intel from using it. S-3 used its patent position to negotiate a lucrative cross-licensing agreement.[2]

"We've been around since 1837," says Jeff Weedman, Vice President of Global Licensing and External Ventures for Procter & Gamble. "In that time, we've probably made billions of business decisions. But we've made only a handful that have been so visionary, so revolutionary, that they've dramatically changed our company and our culture."

One of those decisions, Weedman says, was made in 1998. P&G decided to break with its long tradition of holding its patented technologies close—in some cases, even long after the patents themselves had expired.

Instead, P&G adopted a new policy: all of its technologies could be sold or licensed five years after the initial patent was granted or three years after market introduction—whichever comes first.

"This may not seem like such a big deal," Weedman says. "But, at P&G, it's nothing short of a revolution. Now, instead of locking up our 27,000 patents in a vault, we're making them available to others, even our competitors."

Weedman says the impact within P&G has been striking. "Suddenly, our R&D community realized that we really do need continuous innovation if we want to stay ahead of competitors. And our commercial folks knew they needed to get our best technologies in the marketplace and around the world fast if they want to maintain a competitive edge. It also made these groups realize that they'd better work closely together."

As for Weedman's organization: "It created an inventory of valuable technologies unmatched by even the most advanced technology companies. In an instant, it also said, 'We're open for business.'"

For IBM, a continued emphasis on IPM has created a need for the R&D group to continually innovate to stay ahead of the competition. Fred Boehm and Jerry Rosenthal of IBM elaborate:

> We feel IP is the core of our business. We exist because we make great inventions that customers have a need for. We think the heart of any company in this industry is to be making and protecting the inventions they make. We also believe that because of our willingness to license patents to others at reasonable terms, the IT industry has grown to the size it has as fast as it has. We did it earlier than anybody else. There are industries that don't license at all. But in our industry and in

our company, licensing provides the challenge for us to stay one step ahead of competition and that is what drives our engineers to do the great things they do.

Finance and Tax.   The finance department also benefits from the efforts of a Level Four IP function. Properly handled, IP can also be used to create important tax benefits for the organization, potentially putting millions of dollars into after-tax income. A popular tactic for lessening the tax liabilities associated with licensing revenues has been to create domestic or foreign holding companies for a company's intellectual property and intellectual assets, as Ford Global Technologies Inc. has done. Often it is the finance function of the organization that is best positioned to evaluate the need for IP insurance. Several carriers now offer different products in the two broad areas of "pursuit" insurance and "defense" insurance. Pursuit insurance is offered to companies who wish to cover the out-of-pocket costs associated with enforcing their intellectual property. Defense insurance is offered for those companies who fear that intellectual property infringement actions may be filed against them. In both cases, the insurers conduct a complete evaluation of the risks before taking on the company as an insured. Also, as mentioned in Level Three, a company can use IP donations as charitable contributions to achieve tax savings. Forward-thinking companies are starting to utilize IP information more strategically in M&A transactions, divestitures, and as collateral for borrowings. (See Best Practice 5, on page 119.)

Human Resources.   HR benefits from integration with the IP function by building awareness of the technology gaps that need to be filled in the IP portfolio, so that they can be on the lookout to recruit talented scientists or engineers to add to the company's breadth of technical expertise. The HR function also benefits from training about IP for employees throughout the company. Such training is typically designed to familiarize employees with the policies and procedures used to protect corporate trade secrets and codify ideas. The training should also help explain the importance of knowledge so that it is not inadvertently squandered or given to suppliers, customers, or, worse yet, competitors.[3]

Having an integrated HR function enables identification and retention of key inventors through revised compensation and other award systems. This increased focus on IP by the human resources personnel helps prevent unplanned "brain drain" caused when such inventors are offered early retirement or other severance packages in connection with downsizings or mergers.

The HR function may also be responsible for putting in place programs to motivate and reward new discoveries. Motivational tools include formal "innovation initiatives," innovation training programs, innovation work groups, and inclusion of innovation in all major aspects of company life, including the company's communication, job design, performance appraisal, and compensation programs. Andersen regularly details these best practices in its annual publication, *HR Director.*

Marketing. In the marketing arena, companies can generate significant revenue once they understand how to market their intellectual assets to the right buyer. Dave Kline of Litton emphasizes the connection between marketing and IP. He says it goes far beyond mere patent mining:

> There is a great deal of focus on the front end of the process, i.e., patent mining. Many managers are caught up in the patent "churning" process, but as with any other business, marketing is the toughest part of this business. Many people in this business have appeared to underestimate this at the start and have had difficulty. Identifying the customer, getting to the right people or organizations and getting them engaged is "where it's at." The real payback in this goes right back to basic business: how do you find a customer and generate deals?

Alternatively, a company can gather both business and technical information about its competitors to predict future products, markets, and technology platforms planned by competitors—and either get there first or throw a wrench in their plans. Bill Frank, Chief Patent Counsel of S.C. Johnson, uses this external focus as a kind of early alert system.

> All of a sudden competitor "x" is starting to pick up patents in your area. This can be a scary or interesting proposition, depending on how you react to it. It is scary if you learn about it too late. It is interesting if you find out about it early through competitive assessment. Of course, competitive assessment is not easy. It is like looking for golden needles in big haystacks. But the effort is worth it—and it is better than hindsight, which is easy but worthless. They are pretty good-sized needles sometimes. You just have to look for them. You can do something about competitive threats if you have a year or two advance warning before a product hits the shelves.

Information Technology. At the integration-minded company, operating at Level Four or above, the information management system (or systems) devoted to IP tend to be more user-friendly because it must be accessible and useful to numerous constituents outside the IP function—including managers, engineers, scientists, and other employees. The system now offers access to information about the company's competitors' products and IP, not just its own.

Such access is on an as-needed basis, with careful attention to appropriate security.

The systems used by the Level Three company can be used as the starting point for the Level Four system we are describing here. However, whereas the typical Level Three system would only contain information about the company's own patents and products, the Level Four system would contain further information traditionally considered to be well beyond the scope of a Level Three system. Such information might include data on worldwide markets, products, and related technologies. Also, unlike the Level Three system, the Level Four system likely contains information about *competitors'* patents, products, and technologies. Such information is particularly useful in a company that emphasizes market share in its corporate strategy.

Having a widely shared IP information system can save time and money. Recently, a division manager of a Fortune 50 company with several thousand patents was asked how his engineers and product development people avoided recreating the wheel in their efforts to develop new technologies. After all, wasn't it possible that their particular problem had been solved previously, somewhere else in the company? His answer was that they had to walk down the hall and inquire, hoping that someone was either around at the time or happened to remember seeing it in the patent portfolio. How many millions of dollars are wasted in today's corporations in an effort to locate what should be readily accessible information?

Rockwell has designed an extensive *portfolio database*. The database has numerous uses at all levels of the Value Hierarchy (for example, cost reduction), but one important use is the ability of the database to group patents by class of product, and by competitive impact. For details on the database, see Exhibit 4.10.

Best Practice 3: Conduct Competitive Assessment

Until now, the company has been focused on an inward view of intellectual property management. How can the company better utilize its existing IP for value? At Level 4, however, the IP focus shifts to an external view: what IP should we create for additional value? Now, the company is focused on looking outward at its current and future competitors to determine where they are currently positioned and where they are likely to move in the future. Once this information is known, the company is in a better position to create and utilize its intellectual assets to stop or preempt a competitor. We call this external viewpoint Competitive Assessment.

Many companies are already practicing competitive intelligence—collecting information about their business competitors. Competitive assessment now

EXHIBIT 4.10   Designing an Intellectual Property Data Base—
Rockwell's Guidelines

Perhaps the most difficult aspect of developing a database is determining where to start: should the databases be built from existing databases, or should the company make a clean start? Before making this decision begin by focusing on the end uses of the database. Here are the objectives we set forth at Rockwell when we were building our database.

1. The database should readily identify patents that have value but that are not being used by the corporation (i.e., good licensing candidates).
2. The database should allow its administrators to easily identify nonperforming assets so that they can be sold or abandoned.
3. The database should be designed so that it can dynamically reflect and accommodate the strategic direction of the company.
4. The database should provide access to the costs associated with maintaining the portfolio and individual assets.
5. The database should provide the users with the ability to easily group patents comprising similar technologies.
6. Within a technology area, patents should be easily grouped and identified as being fundamental versus iterative in nature.
7. Where a particular asset is iterative in nature, it should be easily grouped with patents that are fundamental within the same technology group.
8. The database should have a mechanism to allow its users to group patents that might be applied to a particular product or class of products.
9. The database should identify competitors and potential competitors for each patent.
10. The database should be designed so that it is easily (if not automatically) appended with new information from a variety of sources.
11. The database must be designed with hierarchical access control, so that only those with a "need to know" have access to sensitive information.
12. Each patent should identify alternatives to itself and the associated costs (advantages and disadvantages) of each.
13. The database should be a constantly updated (interactive) source of information on individual assets.
14. Procuring the information required for the database must add little or no extra burden to inventors or to their management.

Kelly Hale, Rockwell International. Reprinted with permission from *Profiting from Intellectual Capital: Extracting Value from Innovation*, by Patrick Sullivan (New York: John Wiley & Sons, 1998).

adds technology competitors into the mix, because today with the increase of individual inventors and start-ups, technology competitors are more difficult to detect and ignorance of who they are can have devastating results.

Avery Dennison was once precluded from a significant market because it was unable to detect a small technology competitor who was able to patent a key technology first, thereby rendering millions of dollars of R&D useless. Joe Daniele of SAIC notes that this inward focus can be a large problem for many companies:

> A big mistake companies make in this area is to overly focus themselves inward and a lot of them do it. They are looking at protecting what they have and may not be aware of what their competition is doing and often they don't know why they are creating these patent rights. They don't know what they will do with them. It is not until companies start looking at what their competitors are doing and what direction they are going that they are playing the patent game the way it should be played.

Exhibit 4.11 highlights many uses for competitive assessment. When thinking defensively, companies want to understand where their competitors are currently strong and where they are likely to move in the future. More importantly, it is important to know where their competitors are currently *not* inventing, which we call "white space." One of our clients related a story where an inventor approached the patent attorney and asked him to tell the inventor where to invent: "It would be a whole lot easier if you would just tell me where the white space is so I can focus there."

When a company is looking to use its IP offensively, competitive assessment can help identify possible targets for IP monetization; determine the technology trajectory of a competitor and determine whether the company or its competitor is likely to patent first; and finally identify in-licensing and M&A opportunities. Dow believes very strongly in competitive assessment and Bruce Story, Intellectual Asset Director for the Dow Polyolefins and Elastomers business group, describes how competitive assessment provided a significant competitive advantage for Dow. (See Exhibit 4.12.)

Best Practice 4: Codify IP Knowledge and Share It with All Business Units

To date this book has been focused on extracting value from IP. However, in order to legally protect an idea, it must first be codified. How do companies determine which knowledge to codify? Lew Platt, former CEO of Hewlett-Packard, once said, "If HP knew what HP knows we would be three times as

EXHIBIT 4.11 Possible Direction Provided by Competitive Assessment

Offensive

GOAL	Identify acquisition targets	Surface possible opportunities for licensing your technology	Identify future technology trends
APPLICATION	Search patent data for companies holding technologies that compliment the acquisition objectives	Search patent data for companies that are using similar or complimentary technologies	Analyze patent trends of entities within or entering your market space
USAGE	Capitalize on existing technology resident in other companies; surface candidates that might otherwise be off the radar screen	Identify potential demand for developed technologies	Establish leadership position within the market; proactively react to potential competitive threats
BENEFIT	Rapid, less risky entry into a market through buying versus building	Opportunity to generate alternate sources of revenue without jeopardizing current market position	Protection of existing and possible enhancement of market share

Defensive

GOAL	Profile competitors' areas of technology competence	Analyze action in your company's core technology areas	Isolate white space opportunities
APPLICATION	Analyze technology trends, compare portfolios, identify key inventors, isolate filing practices	Search worldwide patent data to find companies and technologies that have the potential to impact the markets for your technology	Use theme mapping to identify patent activity by detailed technology area
USAGE	Gain knowledge of what competitors are doing in the market, including direction of technology, patenting velocity, hiring of key inventors, etc.	Understand players in the area that may not have been considered competitors, but might be so in the future	Identify heavily and not so heavily patented areas
BENEFIT	Ability to focus own competitive positioning based on improved knowledge about your competitors' strengths and trends	Proactively react to companies moving into your competitive space—acquire, joint venture, strategic alliance, exclusive arrangements, etc.	Knowledge of where there are hidden opportunities for patenting

Source: Jill Rusk and James Ewing, Andersen

EXHIBIT 4.12   Competitive Assessment Case Study

I'm the Intellectual Asset Director for the Polyolefins and Elastomers business group, which is one of the largest business groups within Dow. That includes products like polyethylene and polypropylene and SARAN* and a number of other related packaging-type resins. It's a global business with manufacturing and sales and development people in every area of the globe. There are R&D people, as well, in most areas of the globe. The intellectual asset strategy became an integral part of the business strategy from the very beginning of this project. Our strategy has been largely driven by the competitive assessment that we did.

Recently, new catalyst technology has revolutionized this business, and our competitors had a lot of activity in the intellectual property front in this area. So we were going to have to make sure that we also had both intellectual property as well as the right to practice, so that we could commercialize and extract all the value possible from this new technology. Not only Dow but a number of our competitors were racing along the same or a similar development path to come up with these new kinds of catalysts for the polyolefin industry.

We were able to jump ahead of everyone else when we had our first patent and technology published, back in 1989. So it's only been 11 years since the first patent was filed. Now we have hundreds of patents in that field. We have introduced one new product per year for the last eight years, based upon this new technology. In addition, we have formed a billion-dollar joint venture and have licensed this technology to several world-class companies.

That very first patent was filed 14 days before a very similar patent by Exxon was filed. The patented technology is called INSITE*. Now you have to realize that we had spent over twenty years and several hundred million dollars in R&D to create the Insite technology, so I can only imagine that Exxon had a similar development cost, and clearly the design around cost was not insignificant.

For us the key was focusing on intellectual asset management principles and being able to clearly articulate the white space within which we wanted to innovate. By looking outward we had a good sense of who was going where and what they were doing, and that enabled us to craft broad patent protection for INSITE to maximize value for Dow. At Dow the competitive assessment process is a combination of patent and technology information combined with individual knowledge and publicly available information from press releases and articles in the trade press. Being able to collect all of that in one place and being able to analyze it was very, very helpful to us. That process has allowed Dow to develop a pretty significant business.

Bruce Story, Dow

---
*Trademark of The Dow Chemical Company.

profitable." As Daniele of SAIC points out; "Knowledge is continuously created in an organization, and if not sorted and captured in some way, whether by formal or informal processes, or by the nature of groups or organizational dynamics, this knowledge simply dissipates into the ether."

Many people confuse knowledge, information, and data. Karl Eric Sveiby, who has authored numerous books on managing tacit knowledge, explains: "Data when compiled can become information. Information, when combined with experience, becomes knowledge. On their own, data and information do not represent knowledge. It is the internalization of information that turns it into knowledge." For example, parents always tell children not to play with fire because they will get hurt. Children generally do not understand this warning until they have in fact gotten burned.

Here experience combined with information generates knowledge. When companies and consultants speak of Knowledge Management, they are talking about the codification of data and information, not of knowledge. H.B. Fuller realized that its employees were knowledge-rich and sought to create a way to capture and leverage that tacit knowledge, as Exhibit 4.13 explains.

An Integrated company will make knowledge about its IP portfolio available to other company functions. In the Level Four culture, knowledge sharing is encouraged. Examples of companies practicing knowledge-sharing abound. Xerox and S.C. Johnson have systems to share knowledge. The Dow Chemical Company, as shown in the case at the back of this book, also provides an example.

H.B. Fuller exemplifies the Integrated practice. If individuals or groups need more knowledge in a particular area, H.B. Fuller encourages apprenticeship and mentoring. It has formal programs for both these activities. It also believes strongly in the value of educational workshops, external, internal, and "hybrid." In the last case, the company has used a strategy to merge external symposia with internal symposia to create a highly practical learning opportunity. Paul Rothweiler explains:

Like many companies we often send several people from around the world to trade association meetings. While there, Fuller's employees use the opportunity to learn from colleagues from other parts of industry. They also take advantage of having a number of Fuller people together in the same place, who may not normally meet because they work in various parts of the world. This then becomes an opportunity to have an internal symposium right then and there. Sure, they're not within the physical confines of the H.B. Fuller Company, but why should that stop us? We have the opportunity, for no additional cost, to come together at these external symposia and share what we've learned at the symposia and what we are working on back home. This exercise also allows the employees

EXHIBIT 4.13   Balancing Innovation and Profits

An Interview with Paul Rothweiler at H.B. Fuller

Q: How would you describe the management of IP at H.B. Fuller?

A: H.B. Fuller is a specialty chemical company and historically our primary focus was on selling adhesives, sealants and coatings. Our understanding has changed and we now see that we are a provider of not only a material, but also a provider of knowledge around materials, manufacturing, and processing. We have come to realize that what we *know* has great value.

Several years ago our then CEO, Walter Kissling, decided to put together a project called P2K, which was short for Project 2000. One part of P2K was a project we called TKS, which is an acronym for Technical Knowledge System. It was during the design of TKS that I became aware of all the areas that are involved in managing intellectual capital. (See graphic at the end of this chart.) You might say that while working on the project, I codified what we were attempting to codify.

Every company has knowledge about customers, competitors, its products, and projects. These items typically fit on the right side of the chart because what is known about these topics is usually codified so that it can be shared amongst other communities. On the left side of the chart we have tacit knowledge, that is rich in texture and can't easily be codified so that it can be shared with others in the corporation and/or the company can't 'afford' to codify. Many companies shy away from attempting to formally manage tacit knowledge because we're now talking about things that rely on human dynamics, human relationships in order to be managed. There is also a tendency for some to deny that it is possible to influence/manage tacit knowledge because they just haven't taken the time to think about how to go about it. It's much easier to conceptualize and deal with the things on the right (codified knowledge), because we are familiar with how to manage it through computer systems and documents. It's easy to populate and its distribution does not rely on human dynamics.

From the very beginning we had a three-word phrase, 'capture, distill, distribute.' At the heart of it all was the commitment to generating and leveraging knowledge. Because the system is a loop, there must be a balance between managing tacit and explicit knowledge in order for a knowledge management program to perpetually create value. You can also think of it as a balance sheet, with an investment in time and resources to create 'potential value' in the form of tacit knowledge's innovation, with activities for turning the potential into kinetic value and revenues.

Once H.B. Fuller addressed its need to design a global system for codifying knowledge, we then started to pursue ways to improve the management of our tacit knowledge. A team was put together with representatives from various parts of the company to determine H.B. Fuller's needs and propose a series of programs, starting with the introduction of a 'yellow pages' of tacit knowledge. The intent of building a yellow pages was to make it possible for people to find other people who have common interests; somebody who would have experience on a particular topic regardless of what division or country they were in. From

(continues)

EXHIBIT 4.13   Continued

this discovery process communities of practice would then naturally be allowed to form, resulting in increased efficiencies in problem-solving abilities and an increase in the quality and rate of innovation.

Taking all this into consideration, Fuller decided to pursue the codification of knowledge. While I support the decision, there is a part of me that would have preferred to shift the balance of our efforts a little more toward augmenting existing tacit exchange programs, and introducing new ones. The reason I feel this way is because it is the rich, tacit knowledge that has the large return on investment, whereas the codification of information and data. At best, it creates incremental improvements. Innovation is going to happen more often while managing tacit knowledge.

The balance is going to be different in every company and each needs to find the right balance for their situation. The fulcrum point will also change over time due to external and internal forces. Seeking that balance is the ultimate journey.

Q: Once Fuller made the investment, how did you put the product in place?

A: TKS was designed in modules which included training on how to use the tools, the 'dance steps' people were to perform in the form of work instructions, the definitions in the form of standards, metrics, and additional behavioral information in the form of 'best practices.' Each of the divisions was given essentially the same package to implement and each assigned an Implementation Manager to assist them in the preparation and implementation of the modules.

The Implementation Managers were very important throughout; they provided input during the design phase, tested the tools and processes, provided counsel to the divisions' management team, delivered training and closed the feedback loop to the design team. The Implementation Managers made sure there was a handshake between the design team, line management, and the users.

Q: So is it safe to say that a company has to decide ahead of time why it wants to codify knowledge?

A: Yes, to make sure there's a return on the investment. Before starting the codification process, the business needs to decide what value the codification will bring and to fully understand the intentional and unintentional outcomes from the proposed processes. Reasons for codifying knowledge include creating a broader understanding of new and existing products/services that the company sells in order to improve overall performance. The intention may be to improve learning, to increase the speed and/or reduce the cost of delivery. A company may also decide to codify for revenue generation purposes, to sell the know-how. All three things have very different returns on the investment.

In H.B. Fuller's case we used a corporate strategy to guide us in what we would codify in addition to an internal team of subject matter experts from various parts of the company to verify our decisions. If we hadn't used this process we could have superseded the corporate strategy with our own unintended strategy, which would have lengthened the time to implement the corporate strategy.

(continues)

EXHIBIT 4.13   Continued

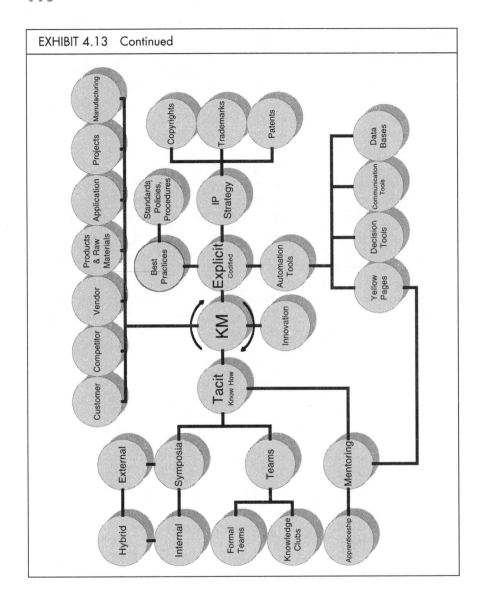

to reinforce and validate what they have learned at the symposia before returning home to share with others. Finally, these symposia are a great opportunity to meet and share with customers and vendors because many of them attend the same symposia.

We can all relate to the fact that by meeting with someone in person, we can exchange the equivalent amount of information contained in a small book in about twenty minutes. Getting together is still by far the most efficient method for exchanging knowledge. Even though we can justify this strategy based solely on what is gained, we can also see how it reduces the travel time and cost that would otherwise have to be incurred to achieve the same outcome. This is an example of where people need to look around and take the opportunities presented to them. We have gotten a lot of mileage from these "hybrid" external/internal experiences.

Best Practice 5: Focus on Strategic Value Extraction

Having a truly integrated Level Four IP function can also help in the merger, acquisition, divestiture, and joint venture activities of the company. It can also help with commercialization.

When companies at the Integrated Level acquire assets or entire companies, the IP function is equipped to value the intellectual property included in the transaction. The well-integrated company can identify potential acquisition candidates by studying their IP portfolios. Texas Instruments' acquisition of Amati is a case in point. TI paid $400 million for a company with $40 million balance sheet value in order to gain access to valuable DSL patents. Similarly, in the mid-1980s, SGS Thomson purchased a company called Mostek from United Technologies for $71 million, and within seven years generated $450 million in licensing revenues.[4]

Jim O'Shaughnessy of Rockwell observes:

In buying and selling companies, we do a strength/weakness analysis. 'I have these complementary assets over here. What do I need in order to create intellectual assets that are optimal for the mix I have and for the way I see it evolving?' We ask these questions when we start to do an acquisition. 'What are we going to get? What is the new company going to look like when we're through?' We're buying human capital. 'How do we keep it here?' Our corporate development team has adopted an analytical way to look at innovation, and is seeking to develop complementary assets of the right type.

Often we are just given a portfolio of patents and maybe copyrighted information, and we'll go back and try and understand what else are we getting or what else should we be looking for? For example if it were a small company, what's the real critical nexus of knowledge in that company? If you find out it is in two scientists, the patents are nice but they are not worth anything without those two scientists. Then the deal better include some way of keeping these two scientists.

In addition to its ordinary acquisitions, a well-managed Level Four IP function is constantly alert for opportunities to acquire IP from troubled companies or bankruptcy trustees at a fraction of original cost.

The Level Four IP function is also integrally involved in the divestiture of corporate assets or divisions. It can be the responsibility of the IP function to be sure that all IP assets are properly linked with the appropriate business units. When there is an overlap of patent use between divisions or business units, the IP function can ensure that valuable assets are not mistakenly sold with the divestiture.

Here are some cases in point:

- One well-known consumer products company accidentally sold one of its patents as part of a divestiture, only to learn after the fact that the same patent protected an important product line within the core business of the company. To its dismay, it had to license the patent back from its new owner. Had the IP function of that company been fully integrated into the rest of the company's operations, that unfortunate event would likely not have happened.
- Another consumer products company spun off a paint brand without realizing the trademark they were giving away was more valuable than the entire purchase price they'd negotiated.

All these tales can be warnings to acquirers and sellers of company units.

The Level Four company also relies upon its IPM function to assist in the identification and design of joint venture activities. Many of today's largest companies are entering into joint venture arrangements with each other and with much smaller organizations. Often the most important contribution to the assets of the joint venture is the IP and know-how provided by one or more of the partners. Procter & Gamble recently announced its joint venture Emmperative—an online company that would enable multinational corporations to manage their global marketing campaigns through the Net. Emmperative estimates that the market demand for these services might be worth two to five billion dollars over the next few years. P&G's contribution to the joint venture is its substantial marketing know-how. P&G estimates that the venture's online format could enable a firm to launch a brand from scratch 30 percent faster. P&G has spent the last 160 years honing its marketing expertise across a product line that now contains about 300 household brands, including Tide, Pampers, and Pringles.[5] The Level Four company counts on its IPM function to help minimize the investment and maximize the return on those joint venture contributions.

As O'Shaughnessy from Rockwell elaborates:

> The one thing that I did was work with our senior executives to convert them in small steps. The idea that ultimately resonated was that value is now a function of both intellectual capital and financial capital. If we don't build a fund of intellectual capital, all we're doing is putting a lot of pressure on our balance sheet and making financial capital carry all the water. It's unwise. You can create a fund of intellectual capital for about one-tenth the cost in the same sense that I used in our earlier example of a million-dollar problem to solve, or a million-dollar opportunity to seize. In the past at Rockwell, you passed the hat in order to find a million dollars to solve your problem or seize your opportunity.

Level Four companies look beyond IP to IA to extract more from their IP revenues. They are interested in directly commercializing their know-how. For example, DuPont for many years has had a stellar safety reputation and expertise. Many companies interested in having world-class safety processes would go and benchmark with DuPont. In 1999, DuPont spun-out its safety knowledge into a free-standing business. Now it is generating revenue directly from its know-how. Daniele of SAIC explains his views on know-how commercialization.

> At SAIC, I have tried to create a framework for how management should think about know-how commercialization and the risk/reward trade-off. The goal is to reduce risk and add value at each stage or event. By so doing, your options open up. We always convince people who come to us with a technology commercialization idea, to put together a business plan, and we help them do it. As a precursor to every technology commercialization activity, the questions we ask are very simple. First, does the technology work, and second, does anyone want to buy it now? We ask these questions until we understand the answers. Given a business plan, even a short, simple one, you can then go out and speak to customers and get some feedback on your products, markets and approach. If you can't get some initial customer interest, the market may be telling you something. Maybe you are going in the wrong direction. Maybe the packaging is wrong, or it is ahead or behind its time, or it adds insufficient value. If you have some customer interest, then you have choices. You can sell it yourself, spin it out, license, or partner.
>
> You sometimes need to start thinking about complimentary assets. You have to understand what is missing. When we go visit with customers we always try to

learn something. Most don't buy initially, but you always try and find out why. You always ask their opinion of the technology or product or its downsides and problems. We use the feedback that we get.

We had a case of a B2B start-up where we got customer and VC feedback early on, and it substantially changed the plan and created a much more valuable business as a result. At each decision point, moving ahead with customer feedback adds value to the bottom line and it also opens up options. The key is to add value through every commercialization event from business planning through customer feedback and product delivery.

CONCLUSION: ON THE BRINK OF VISION

Journeying forward with Thomas Edison, we have covered four of the five levels of the Value Hierarchy. If you have read this book thoroughly to this point, you now know how to move your IP function from the Defensive Level, up to the Cost Control Level, on to the Profit Center Level, and to the Integrated Level. You have also seen some of the best practices used at all these levels.

Are you ready for the Visionary Level—the fifth, and most valuable level?

5

LEVEL FIVE—VISIONARY

THE TOP LEVEL of the Value Hierarchy is the Visionary Level. (See Exhibit 5.1.) Companies at Level Five, like those at Level Four, have proven they can fully integrate their IP strategies with their business strategies, creating a broad range of intellectual assets. But beyond that, at Level Five, companies look outside themselves and into the future. Companies at this level use their IA to stake a *claim* to the future, defining and protecting both their current products and markets as well as those to come.

WHAT LEVEL FIVE COMPANIES ARE TRYING TO ACCOMPLISH

Companies at Level Five continue to view their IP as strategic assets, but see them from a different perspective than do companies at the lower levels. At this level, companies become interested in using IP as a tool for creating the future of the firm as well as defining the technology future of their particular industry. Their IP management objectives include:

- Staking a claim on the future
- Encouraging disruptive technologies
- Embedding intellectual assets and IA management into the company culture

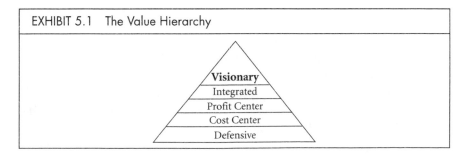

EXHIBIT 5.1 The Value Hierarchy

Visionary
Integrated
Profit Center
Cost Center
Defensive

With these objectives in mind, it becomes clear that at Level Five companies have become more interested in thinking about their IA as a way of creating and managing their evolution into the future. This includes new and more far-thinking criteria for selecting what is to be included in the portfolio as well as more visionary ways of using the portfolio's contents. Further, Level Five companies have become aware of the power that measuring the management of their IA has, both within the firm and for investors outside of the firm.

Level Five companies, building on their Level Four foundation, find they have an increased awareness of the rule-changing implications of the firm's IA. Indeed, different from their colleagues at other levels of the IP Value Hierarchy, companies at this top level have come to realize that the future is theirs to create and that its creation is made easier through the use and leverage of the firm's IA. In this regard, IA may be used in several ways and Level Five companies tend to use all of these. The first involves thinking about the company's business and industry in future terms. Where is the industry moving and how is it evolving toward that future? What kinds of technologies will evolve from the current ones and where might one expect to find disruptive technologies exploding onto the scene? Level Five companies have come to realize that it is possible to determine how the future will evolve and to determine how to position themselves in the path of that evolution.

The successful company of tomorrow will be the one that most accurately anticipates the trends in products, customer preferences, and technologies. The IA strategy must be to not only attempt to *anticipate* those trends, but also to help *create them,* and ultimately to find a way to legally protect the company's interests and innovations related to those trends.

The market leaders of today are those companies that have successfully anticipated, and in some cases, even created the demand for products that didn't previously exist. As an example, Bill Gates and Microsoft are creating our futures for us. They are envisioning what our lives could and should be like using computers in ways that most of us have not yet even dreamed about. In the process of creating that future, Microsoft is also staking out its claim to the intellectual property rights which will protect those innovations.

Level Five companies tend to realize one more "truth" about the power of their position. That is, by measuring not only the amount (the stock) of their IA but also the management of the flows, they can achieve two very important results. First, they can dramatically affect the performance of IA management within the firm and produce even greater levels of focused IA and market benefits. Second, they have an opportunity to provide information that the capital markets desperately seek: how and how well does the firm leverage its IA to create new and improved revenue streams on a renewable and sustainable basis?

At Level Five, just as at Level Four, companies are concerned with all aspects of the IP Management Decision System (see Exhibit 5.2).

- Identifying gaps to create trends in one's own industry-setting "new rules of the game"
- Patenting strategically—creating patents that position the company in the path of industry evolution
- IAM performance measurement and reporting

Best Practices for the Visionary Level

At the opening of this chapter, we tried to capture the essence of the Visionary Level by describing a number of actions and attitudes. These, in fact, are the best practices adopted by companies that operate at the highest level of the Value Hierarchy. With lower levels, the best practices may change: there always will be new ways to defend intellectual property, to save costs, to increase profits, and to integrate innovation throughout a company. But when it comes to the Visionary Level, the Best Practices are the Vision, and the Vision is the set of Best Practices. (See Exhibit 5.3.) Without these best practices, Vision is only a slogan. With them, it can be a reality. Although we have identified only two best practices at the Visionary Level, many more are beginning to emerge. (If you are pioneering those best practices, let us hear from you.)

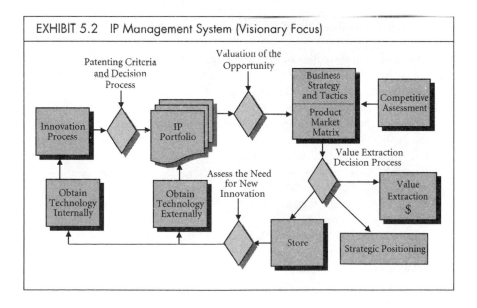

EXHIBIT 5.2   IP Management System (Visionary Focus)

EXHIBIT 5.3   Best Practices for Level Five—Visionary

Best Practice 1: Patent strategically—Identify and exploit trends in one's own industry to create new rules of the game.

Best Practice 2: Institute a performance measurement and reporting system.

Best Practice 1: Identify and Exploit Trends in One's Own Industry to Create New Rules of the Game

As George Pake, founder of Xerox PARC, once said, "The best way to predict the future is to invent it." Visionary companies literally create a future trend by identifying the sources of dissatisfaction among their customers and other stakeholders. The gap between what the customer presently has versus what he or she would *like* to have creates opportunities for the company to improve existing products or services or develop completely new ones.

Consider the telecommunications industry. Most of us ten years ago would never have predicted the surging popularity of personal fax machines, cell phones, pagers, and videoconferencing. This was an industry that not only anticipated trends in consumer preferences, but also actively identified the sources of consumer dissatisfaction related to communications and set out to fill those gaps. Along the way, those same companies blanketed themselves with patents and other intellectual property rights to be sure they were adequately protected.

Hewlett-Packard is very future-focused, as Steve Fox explains:

"We're looking more futuristically and there are two ways to view it: If the world is a big jigsaw puzzle and you've got it almost all put together but there are a few missing pieces and you can't find the pieces because technology has not moved yet to the point where they're easily identifiable, what you should do is futuristically think about the pieces that would fit into the spots where there are currently gaps, then discover the missing pieces, and patent them now. Another aspect occurs when a business is on a certain strategic path, and another company is on a seemingly different strategic business path. They may not be the same path at this point in time, but downstream there is a good chance that those two paths are going to converge and there is going to be an intersection point. When they get to that intersection point they become direct competitors. So what is it that they can patent now that will cover what their competitor does five years from now?"

O'Shaughnessy of Rockwell notes, "You draw a boundary and say this is our market, every piece of it can be influenced by a properly constructed intellectual property portfolio. Some pieces are more important than others, but the idea is to pick out pieces that are important, concentrate on them, and then think, "How do I build intellectual capital that is important to my ability to influence the way this market unfolds in the future."

Not all such examples are so recent. For example, years ago, when cable TV was first introduced, set top converters were needed to receive the cable frequencies and convert them to frequencies that the TV itself could handle. Zenith, a successful company at the time, foresaw the day when people would become dissatisfied with the extra wiring and other complications caused by the set top converters and would demand direct hook-up capability. Many years before the market demanded this feature, Zenith had patented the cable-ready technology and was prepared to license it to the rest of the industry when the idea became popular. In that way, Zenith was assured of a role—at least for a time—as one of the technology leaders of its industry.

Even though most of us probably look to the high-tech industries for examples of companies anticipating or creating trends in consumer preferences, we need not overlook the more basic products and markets.

Consider food companies, which have set out to address the dissatisfactions customers had with their food choices. After all, most great-tasting foods had always been high in calories and high in fat. Customers wanted to be able to enjoy their favorite foods without the corresponding effect on their waistlines. (Perhaps this is the proverbial "having their cake and eating it too!") To respond to those dissatisfactions the food companies created low-fat versions of the most common diet-busters, such as ice cream and potato chips. Let there be no doubt that where there are such innovations there is also patent and trademark protection. Those companies have successfully used their proprietary innovations to "lock in" their place in the market, a market that they in effect created.

The process of gap insight should be ongoing. By striving to continually identify the sources of unmet customer needs, a company will lay the foundation of a new market for yet to be developed technology. According to Mark Radcliffe of Gray Cary Ware & Freidenrich:

> The more sophisticated companies are the ones that do this and think about where they want to go. It is very easy to do your business and not look very far ahead and protect what you have. The problem is that if companies are not looking ahead and thinking strategically they will run into a wall of problems that they didn't see. I think that more and more companies are going to be thinking ahead. There has been an enormous shift between the value of capital and financial resources to intellectual property resources. We saw that back with the Polaroid case where

Kodak thought they would enter the instant marketplace and they did a fairly extensive patent analysis and they were wrong. It was a billion-dollar mistake.

The role of a true Level Five IP function is to help lead the company into consciously and proactively identifying the sources of customer need. It is no longer adequate for the IP function to simply maintain databases of patents, trademarks, and technologies. The Level Five IP function sees the value of the intellectual assets associated with knowing your customers' sources of dissatisfaction. In fact it takes the lead in creating such intellectual assets to provide competitive advantage in the marketplace. In essence, this is a three-step process.

1. The company, with the participation of the IP function, proactively seeks "gap insight;" that is, it looks for sources of dissatisfaction among its customers and other stakeholders. The key is to execute this step consciously and proactively, not simply leaving it to chance with a "seat-of-the-pants" approach. As we've seen, such gap insight provides the window to economically viable innovation.
2. Once such insight is gained, the IP function must then work with R&D to develop the technologies and products to fill such gaps.
3. The IP function carries out its more traditional role of protecting those new technologies with the appropriate intellectual property rights—be they patents, trademarks, or otherwise.

IBM's approach is to use linkage with its Research Division, Solutions Laboratories, and Global Services Innovation Centers. All three are constantly working with customers to understand their problems and unmet needs, but at three different levels. The Research Division is focused on very long-term opportunities. This approach has led to the invention of the scanning-tunneling electron microscope, high-temperature superconductivity, laser-based surgery, and the disk drive, to name a few—discoveries that have created entire new industries. Current Research Division work includes wearable PCs and voice-controlled hand-held devices. These innovations are heavily protected, sometimes within days of fundamental discoveries. Resulting patents have become the basic teachings of the industries they spawned. Hand-in-hand linkage between the IP function and the research function is mandatory to achieve such results.

IBM Solutions Laboratories work in the medium-term product horizon, focusing on current strategic problems of customers in industries such as banking, finance, energy, and transportation. Strategic developments such as the Sabre airlines reservation system have come from these efforts. Finally, IBM Global Services Innovation Centers work in the services space, generally with focus on specific customer challenges in emerging marketplaces such as e-business. IBM's electronic exchanges, for example, have come from these efforts. Designed both to identify and create market trends at their own levels, the Solutions Laboratories and Innovation Centers require close interlock between the IP function and the business to identify the right problems and protect the solutions to these problems.

Strategic patenting is integral to the Visionary company. Some Visionary companies use outside advisors to help them with strategic patenting, such as Lanny Vincent, partner, Vincent & Associates, who rediscovered a process for collaborative (or invention-on-demand) in a structured way. (See Exhibit 5.4.)

At Rockwell, managers use a process called "TRIZ," based on a Russian phrase. The inventor of the process was a patent examiner who broke inventions down to their component parts. Another term for this is "directed evolution" (a term coined by Ideation International).

Jim O'Shaughnessy of Rockwell explains: "If you take sort of the molecular approach, you atomize a problem into individual components, and then look and see how each individual element of the problem was solved by some one else. Then you take out all of the redundancy and rebuild." The process helps companies prepare to patent an invention before the invention is reduced to practice. This can help at every level of the Value Hierarchy, starting with the Defensive Level, but it is also important at the level of Vision because the process of practicing TRIZ can help an enterprise become more aware of its knowledge base.

Rockwell holds Innovation Workshops to get ideas going, and then makes sure these permeate the mindset of the organization. (See Exhibit 5.5.)

Today, part of that future involves business processes. Business process patents exemplify the shift toward knowledge-based companies. The USPTO is taking this area very seriously, and has begun an action plan to keep ahead of the curve. On March 29, 2000, the agency announced a "Business Methods Patent Initiative" to deal with this development.

Once again, an appreciation of history can help. Historically, most patents have been granted only for technological and scientific discoveries (including discoveries in biotechnology, where patents emerged in the 1930s).

The only major exception to this science-only rule historically was the hard lesson learned by the French in the years 1791–1792, when the national French legislature passed, lived with, and then revoked a new patent act that provided protection for various financial innovations. Protected inventions included certain types of banking systems, credit plans, exchange controls, life insurance, life annuities, mortgages, and tariff systems. Legislators saw that they had opened up a Pandora's box when multitudes of financial inventors

---

EXHIBIT 5.4   Innovation Workshops: Key to Strategic Patenting

We hold innovation workshops at various companies. The workshops typically grow out of a need to define a path of technical or market development that is attractive to the company. Adopting language from one of our clients, we call it a Strategic Patent Initiative. A full-blown SPI doesn't start with a workshop; it actually starts with a survey of the white space. We gather a group of people—both technical and business people. We ask, where are we headed and where do we need some protection? That's defining the white space. Our clients go through a formal process. The group produces a list of opportunity statements.

Interestingly enough, in the semiconductor industry, that white space is really clear. It is all about miniaturization. Chips are getting so small that the traditional techniques of mask and etching are getting more and more difficult, so they have to reinvent the tools to help them do that—hence huge opportunities for invention.

In other areas like consumer electronics or automotive areas or medical instruments, the white space is not as clear. Now, typically we join up with companies at a point when they have already been working on the white space, either from an advanced R&D program or through corporate planning and scanning kind of activities.

Frequently executives are now starting to realize that there is a powerful tool called patents. There are patents that we can file for and hopefully receive without initiating too much innovation or product development work.

Most of our clients are using the workshops to see into the future. They see an area emerging, there's an issue going on with the business, and they need to go after it, so they'll run an innovation workshop because of the content. That is, they need inventions in that area, they need intellectual property, they need to beef up their portfolio there.

For instance, we did a workshop on automotive suspensions, and there's nothing new in suspensions. We had a group that was just totally de-motivated, they were saying there's so much art here and what are you going to do with a coil spring? Yet we ended up after the workshop with about 25 invention disclosures there.

Lanny Vincent, Vincent & Associates

---

suddenly materialized, all begging for protection. On September 20, 1792, the French national assembly voted to stop granting such patents, and to rescind those already granted. Many then, as today, expressed fear that granting patents in such areas would stifle creativity.

During the past century, however, there has been a *reappearance* of such patents on nontechnical, nonscientific inventions. Business method patents have been around in the U.S. since the 1800s. According to Rosenthal of IBM,

EXHIBIT 5.5   Building a Innovation-Based Culture through Workshops

We are in the process of changing the whole culture. We have developed what we call the virtuous *cycle of innovation*. This is not the same as invention. I am trying to stamp that word—"invention"—out of our lexicon. "Invention" has a lot of baggage. When you think of an invention, you think of scientist and engineer laboring over a bench coming up with a Eureka, and that's the invention. What's the metaphor? It's a light bulb—a new awakening. Innovation doesn't have all of that baggage. Innovation is just a new way of looking at things. So the bar is lowered. However, we're not looking for random acts of innovation, but very focused acts of innovation.

It is not difficult to get an engineer to agree that ideas have value, and that patents on ideas are good things. Line managers are very different. They are driven by numbers. Before we founded Rockwell Technologies as a business with P&L responsibility, almost uniformly people were told, "You do patents on your own time, not on company time."

But now we are building a knowledge culture. We're also incentivizing that new culture. We see this as a way to involve both individual contributors and their managers in a team-oriented approach to developing the necessary funds of intellectual capital that will sustain Rockwell in the future. We have incorporated into our innovation practices the use of thought experiments performed in workshop settings.

Thought experiments are valid ways to solve problems. An experiment may be conducted on a bench, looking at dials and gauges, but what are you doing? You're looking at those dials and gauges, but you're analyzing the inputs they represent based on what you know. You're bringing all of your life experiences into that bench environment and then adding new experiences to them. But you don't solve the problem on the bench, you solve it in your mind. You're adding new impulses, new sources of information, then you're analyzing it and coming up with a solution.

The real value of the human capital of an organization is the ability to be imaginative, and the ability to harvest the value of the imagination. As Einstein said, imagination is more important than intelligence. Albert Einstein is a hero of mine for one simple reason. Not because he used to examine patents, but because he was able to construct in his mind the general and special theories of relativity. He didn't have a big laboratory compared to all the modern equipment people now have. He wandered around the Alps thinking big thoughts! He came up with his general theory without a single piece of equipment. It took 15 years for confirmation. Scientists later were able to look at the so-called gravitational lens and confirm the theory: it was perfect.

So when we hold our Innovation Workshops, we don't need a bench. We gather eight or so people and sit in a conference room, and later we post ideas on our intranet site. Our thought experiment is more akin to Albert Einstein than a lab experiment—although our thoughts may not be as lofty as the general theory of relativity.

Jim O'Shaughnessy, Rockwell

"Fifty years ago IBM understood the value of intellectual property. We were patenting what are today called business methods before they were known as such. We're not sure whether business-method patents are good or bad for the economy and IBM in the long run. Until the effects become clear, we're working with others in our industry and with government to improve prior art sources as well as the laws. We're also patenting aggressively, because we know the best defense is a good offense."

In the 1990s, Amazon.com patented the one-click ordering, enabling businesses to take orders from online customers without asking them to repeat key information. In the same decade, Signature Financial received a patent on its "hub and spoke" system, which allows a single portfolio fund (the hub) to pool assets from many mutual funds (the spokes). In 2000, priceline.com secured a patent on reverse auctions (for the lowest bidder), and has already used it to sue Microsoft.

All of these events have broadened the concept of patentable property beyond the realm of science and technology. Wise men and women differ on the question of what should and should not be patented. Some believe the patenting of business processes sets a dangerous precedent. They predict that we may have to undo this type of patent, just as the French did more than two centuries ago. Others believe that granting protection to business process inventions will stimulate creativity.

Whatever one believes on this score, it is clearly now more imperative than ever for companies to seek to be Visionary—to identify all their patentable assets (including business processes), and to mine them for value.

Best Practice 2: Institute a Performance Measurement and Reporting System

Besides creating trends in the marketplace, Level Five companies must also become leaders in measuring and reporting on the linkages between their intangibles and cash flow.

We think of innovation as value in waiting. No one would disagree that innovation has value, but how do we measure and report on it? For many years some in the investment community have claimed to have the answer to this question. Indeed company analysts have created proprietary models that attempted to evaluate a company's ability to extract value from its intangibles.

Several years ago, when Steve Wallman was a member of the Securities and Exchange Commission (SEC), he became interested in the problem. Once he left the SEC he began to focus on these very claims. If in fact they were true, then

Wallman feared that investment analysts had access to company information that individual investors did not have. Wallman worked with the Brookings Institution to sponsor an intangibles research initiative to evaluate the public policy implications of disclosures relating to intangibles. (See Exhibit 5.6.)

For the past several years around the globe, accounting professionals and others have debated on whether and how to incorporate intellectual capital into the financial statements. Today the general consensus (certainly among most accounting professionals we know) is that intellectual capital is important, but that it should not be "forced" into the current financial statements, which are intended to reflect transactions, not value. Instead of lobbying for changes in accounting rules, companies and accountants are now exploring alternative ways to measure and report on value creation and value realization. A handful of companies today, notably Skandia and Dow Chemical, have developed methods to report on intellectual capital. These metrics help corporate management and shareholders to measure the value of the typical company's intangible assets.

Some of the most innovative thinking in this area has originated in Canada. The Canadian Institute of Chartered Accountants (CICA) has been exploring ways to report on the value of intellectual capital. After some discussion, the CICA did not recommend including pre-transactional capital in traditional financial statements. The CICA began to ask, "How then should we measure and report on all value—including value not yet realized through a transaction?" See Exhibit 5.7 and 5.8 and Appendix C for a more detailed discussion.

How will the Level Five company set about measuring the performance of its intellectual assets? Well, if the IA function and strategy are to be fully integrated with the business strategy of the company, that company must be able to value its IA in the same way it values its other assets. One measure of value (albeit a narrow one) is return on investment. To bring IP into the company's overall strategic picture, a company must be able to measure the return on its IP investment for comparison with returns in other parts of the company. Obviously, to begin with, it must understand and be able to measure what that investment is. So far, few companies have valued their patent portfolio on any basis and even fewer have attempted to place a value on the more elusive intellectual property assets such as trade secrets and brands.

A firm can establish internal metrics that can be used to measure improvement (both qualitative and quantitative) in the productivity, processes, and values related to IP. For example, it can measure the return on investment for training by tracking the activities covered by training courses to results in departments involved in those activities.

EXHIBIT 5.6   The Brookings Intangibles Project

Unseen Wealth: Report of the Brookings Task Force on Intangibles (Washington, D.C.: Brookings, 2001), a report I coauthored with Steven M. H. Wallman, grew out of a project that we put together about two years ago at Brookings. We tried to systemically review the implications of the growth and importance of intangibles for a number of different kinds of policy questions. When we started, we weren't even sure what the relevant policy questions were, but it was increasingly obvious to us that intangibles were becoming the most important source of value in the corporate sector.

In a broad sense, we do not have available a consistent language, a consistent taxonomy of how to understand how these things fit together or a set of metrics that allows us to measure them in a way that we all agree upon, even in broad terms, let alone at the level of the details. So we don't have measures that are comparable from one firm to the next.

We suspected that this has enormous implications on public policy. We also suspected that it might be that public policy had implications for the efforts going on in the business community to solve the problem. There might be ways in which the public rules, everything from tax rules, reporting requirements, to the threat of lawsuits or the need to respond to regulators and fill out forms, were having an effect on the way businesses think about their own internal assets and how they would think about measuring and quantifying them.

First, are there policies that are getting in the way of efforts by the private sector to solve this information problem themselves where that policy may need tweaking? Secondly, are there areas where government assistance or government engagement at some level could be useful in helping the private sector solve that problem? And thirdly, are there ways in which government policy biases resource allocation decisions because those policies were put in place to influence the investment in hard assets and have a biased effect in their implications for investments in soft assets? In the end what we came up with was a document that reviews the evidence that we have of the growing importance of intangible assets in the economy. It also reviewed what we think the problems are, the public policy problems that result from not knowing or having better information. What we specifically propose is a public/private collaboration on a pilot study, perhaps housed at the Bureau of Census which has been in the business of collecting data for decades. Over a period of a couple of years, the study would collect on a very systematic basis a substantial amount of data that could then be fed into models that people are testing and trying out and over a period of time they would begin to identify maybe 15 or 20 indicators that really count.

Second, we propose changes at the SEC. Specifically we argue that the Securities and Exchange Commission (SEC) needs to begin encouraging companies to discuss these issues in the management discussion analysis section of their financial reports. Tell people what the company thinks its value drivers are and what they're doing to manage them. We also think the SEC might need to expand its safe harbor protections for companies that do report forward-looking information.

(continues)

EXHIBIT 5.6   Continued

There would be a requirement that the information be developed in good faith and be couched in a lot of language that says look, this is experimental. It's not verifiable. It hasn't been audited. This is our best estimate of what we think is going on and what we're trying to do is see if we can find metrics that provide our investors with better information. So put appropriate cautionary language around it and firms could add that information if they so chose.

And the third area of policy reform that we think should be explored involves systemically reviewing a variety of different areas of intellectual property right law to clarify exactly what the law is and how much protection firms have particularly in areas where there's enormous uncertainty.

So we propose a variety of different ways that we could begin moving toward a rationalization of the intellectual property right laws in such a way that would create a higher level of certainty around what protection firms really do have over their intellectual property.

Margaret Blair, Brookings Institution

EXHIBIT 5.7   A Framework for Integrated Performance Reporting Practices and Capabilities

© MatrixLinks, CVIC, CICA, 1998. This chart is excerpted from a longer report featured as Appendix C of this book.

(continues)

EXHIBIT 5.7   Continued

The CICA in Canada has for the last five years been sponsoring a fair bit of work in the area of performance reporting. It has created a specific initiative to support that work, which has been called the Canadian Performance Reporting Initiative or CPRI. CPRI looked at things as a continuum and recognized that organizations are at different places along that continuum. In that sense the thinking is very parallel to the value hierarchy where you are trying to provide a way for people to visualize where they are and where they might like to go. It is the same idea with this.

We recognized that financial reporting as the first circle is a base case. Everybody does it. Having said that, some people do it better than others. Within each of these circles there are different levels of proficiency or different practices that might be important.

The second circle, operational performance reporting, might capture the reporting related to manufacturing or quality management, or whatever the nature of the operation is.

In the third circle, integrated indicators reporting, we include the phenomenon of the balanced scorecard. This circle would also incorporate performance reporting systems like the Skandia Navigator, because the Skandia Navigator isn't just about intellectual capital.

The fourth circle we called comparative performance reporting. More sophisticated organizations tend to engage in some form of benchmarking or comparison of their performance because they are just measuring themselves against themselves we may be missing the boat in terms of what is going on out there.

The final circle we called value creation reporting. It is where we have been focusing our efforts more recently and includes practices relating to shareholder value. But our approach, which we call Total Value Creation (TVC)™ goes beyond looking at shareholder value to a whole variety of techniques that are attempting to not simply look at historical performance, but to look at the future value-creation potential of the enterprise and provide a way of measuring progress toward that future.

One of the reasons that we developed the 'five circle' approach is simply to reflect the fact that when it comes to internal performance reporting, Generally Accepted Accounting Principles (GAAP) is really the lowest common denominator. There are two fundamental approaches that people are working on to try and address the shortcomings of GAAP. Some people are trying to address them through what we call the intangibles approach. They try to get intellectual capital into the traditional financial statements. Other people are working on developing a whole new framework focused on value creation. They believe that no amount of trying to capitalize intangibles will actually solve the problem. And of course we are in the latter camp.

Rob McLean, MatrixLinks International Limited

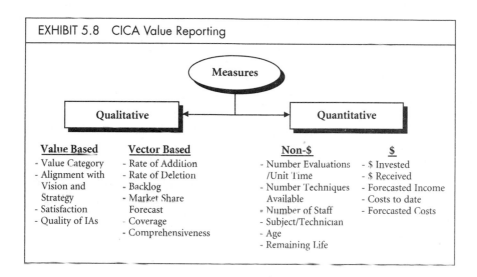

EXHIBIT 5.8   CICA Value Reporting

Qualitative		Quantitative	
Value Based	**Vector Based**	**Non-$**	**$**
- Value Category	- Rate of Addition	- Number Evaluations	- $ Invested
- Alignment with	- Rate of Deletion	/Unit Time	- $ Received
Vision and	- Backlog	- Number Techniques	- Forecasted Income
Strategy	- Market Share	Available	- Costs to date
- Satisfaction	Forecast	- Number of Staff	- Forecasted Costs
- Quality of IAs	- Coverage	- Subject/Technician	
	- Comprehensiveness	- Age	
		- Remaining Life	

Any reader with corporate experience already knows the many ways to measure financial value. But in the company achieving the Visionary Level of the Value Hierarchy, there is a deeper awareness of nonfinancial value as well. Such companies use qualitative measures of value.

Measures may be either qualitative or quantitative. We often use qualitative measures when the item to be measured cannot be measured in quantitative terms. Qualitative measures are judgment-based, and use descriptive adjectives rather than numbers.

Quantitative measures may be indirect or direct. Sometimes, when it is difficult to measure an IC activity directly, companies have found that they can use indirect indicators rather than direct tallies. Direct measurement often requires that something be completed before it can be counted, there are times when we need to measure work-in-progress. Indicators are helpful under these circumstances. Although they can be fuzzy, they do provide some information on amount. Vectors are another form of measurement that works well when measuring intellectual capital activities. Vectors are helpful because they provide information on where a trend is headed as well as how big it is. In geometry, vectors are directed line segments (arrows) that measure both direction and magnitude.

When most of us think of measurement, we immediately think of quantitative measures such as feet, time, weight, dollars, and so on. These measures allow us to determine where we have been, where we are going (in terms of distance and time), and where we are today in a physical sense. In the past, when companies were largely concerned with physical assets, measurement traditionally centered around quantitative outputs—in particular amounts of product, dollars, and sometimes time. Quantitative measures provide a precise snapshot of the firm's activities and in doing so, quantitative measurement requires that there be points at which measurement may be taken.

While quantitative measurements tell us what *has* happened, qualitative measurement tells us what *is* happening. Exhibit 5.8 highlights sample measures under each of these two headings.

IBM is an example. It has measured the *defensive* value of its portfolios—the value delivered through access to others' patents. This form of measurement combines aspects of qualitative and quantitative analysis, yielding an estimate associated with the many cross-licenses the company has been able to negotiate based on the overwhelming size and scope of its portfolio.

Some companies have begun qualitatively measuring their patent portfolio for example. To do this, they have created a scoring mechanism that tries to assess the quality of the individual patents in the portfolio. The value of a patent, for example, may include:

- The intended use of the patent (commercial vs. protection vs. anticompetition vs. litigation avoidance)
- The patent's ability to exclude others from taking certain actions, such as infringement
- The company's ability to detect infringement

The actual value of a patent can and should be valued based on these factors, in combination with other, more easily quantifiable ways. (See Exhibit 5.9.)

Another approach to expressing the value of individual patents and patent portfolios, developed by Paul Germeraad, CKO for Aurigin Systems, Inc., recognizes two key elements. First, the attributes of intellectual property value are like apples and oranges. They are both fruits, but different. Second, a powerful visual tool to show apple and orange relationships are star maps. This visual form of looking at a patent portfolio is especially powerful when comparing portfolio strengths across competitors. Using software developed by Aurigin Systems, Inc. intellectual property professionals can construct such graphs for strategic planning and management team review.

Companies operating at the Visionary Level depart from the usual forms of measurement. One such initiative is captured in an initiative called Total Value Creation™ (TVC™), sponsored by the Canadian Institute of Chartered Accountants. Although its name is trademarked, TVC™ is not just another privately owned consulting company model. Rather, it is a worldwide shared initiative of

---

EXHIBIT 5.9   New Ways to Measure Value

At Rockwell Technologies, we have a measurement system that links the creation of invention to the extraction of its value. We link innovations to revenues, and say, for example: "Well, you know, we made $50,000 off this. X shares ought to be contributed to the stock account of Mary Jones because she is the one who developed this." We cannot track all the linkages, but we try to track the ones that are the most important. We also rely on input from innovators and managers to help us keep our eyes on the right balls.

This new way of measuring invention value breeds a sense of interest in the success of technology. It helps senior management realize that innovators contribute the technology that underlies the long-term success of Rockwell. What's most important, it gives contributors, and especially teams of contributors, a stake in the outcome of the technology they develop. Through that, we encourage their participation in the entire value extraction process because they will gain when the company benefits from the use of their innovations.

Jim O'Shaughnessy, Rockwell Technologies

---

accountants and others to agree on a way to go beyond traditional financial accounting (generally accepted accounting principles) and standard management accounting (such as cost control and budgeting).

TVC™ strives to overcome the limitations of traditional accounting. According to Rob McLean, President, MatrixLinks International, and TVC Project Director, CICA, traditional accounting:

- Measures and reports on the realization of value based on third-party transactions (vs. *pretransactional value creation*)
- Focuses on assets and liabilities (vs. *future value streams*)
- Focuses on value realization from the perspective of shareholders (vs. *value creation for stakeholders*)
- Is limited to measuring financial results (vs. *financial and nonfinancial value streams*)
- Is limited to periodic reporting of historical performance (vs. *continuous reporting of future value streams*)
- Focuses on entity performance (vs. *value chain/network*)
- Does not integrate financial performance with other performance information (vs. *integration of financial and nonfinancial information*)
- Provides one-way communication to shareholders (vs. *interactive with all stakeholders*)
- Provides single reporting format (vs. *multiple simultaneous formats*)[1]

Of these nine points, the first may well be the most significant when it comes to intellectual assets. Ever since the invention of our double-entry accounting system in the late medieval period, financial reporting has been transaction-based. An exchange occurs—for example, a company buys a conveyor belt—an accounting entry is made: credit cash, debit plant, and equipment. But if no event with a third party occurs, no financial entry is made. So, for example, if someone discovers a new technology, nothing happens on the company's financial statements initially—until the impact of the discovery begins to take the form of transactions leading to higher sales, licensing fees, and the like. Companies wishing to gain a greater vision of their intellectual capital can benefit from a reporting process that gets away from an exclusive focus on third-party transactions and recognizes other types of events. Visionary companies work in that direction.

Many IP professionals have heard of Skandia and its Intellectual Capital Supplement. In the United States Dow Chemical released a triple bottom line report in 1999 and 2000 which consists of financial, environmental, and social progress within the company. As you will learn in the Dow case study (see Chapter 6), reporting on IC is not far behind. For U.S. companies, the issue relating to external reporting on intellectual capital is the need for a "safe harbor" from litigation. It is difficult for firms to release forward-looking information on a trial basis unless they are sheltered from class-action litigation. Through the Brookings intangibles project and continued exposure at the SEC, there appears some hope that "safe harbor" can be granted for the first few pioneers in this movement.

CONCLUSION

Visionary organizations like the ones described here truly carry on the Edison legacy, and so can you. As a leader or advisor working with a technology-rich company, it is your job to be sure that the company's shareholders reap the value of its investments in intellectual property. The IP Value Hierarchy can help you determine how your company measures up with others, both within and outside your industry. It also gives you a road map for how to get to where you'd really like to be. Remember that two-thirds of your company's value is related to its intangible assets. You are the one minding that store, so mind it as well as possible.

Few companies today have completely mastered Level Three, let alone Level Four. There may not yet be any that are completely satisfied that they have reached the ultimate peak of success—Level Five, the Visionary Level. It is entirely possible for a company to be performing at different levels in this hierarchy at the same time. The differentiating factor, however, is the degree to which a company views, develops, and monetizes its intellectual assets. As a company reaches the highest level of engagement, its focus on IA permeates the company and extends beyond the organization itself and into the future.

The following case study shows how one company has traveled through all the levels of the Value Hierarchy. The Dow Chemical Company, profiled in Chapter 6, first started managing its intellectual property in the late 1920s, and has since become the envy of IP and IA managers worldwide. Following the story of Dow, we have included three appendices that will provide further details on mining your portfolio, conducting competitive assessments, and developing reporting metrics.

We hope that our book gives you the tools you need to improve your position in the Value Hierarchy and, like the companies we have profiled, realize greater value from your intellectual assets. We wish you every success.

6

THE DOW CHEMICAL COMPANY: A CASE STUDY

You can't easily see it, touch it, or put a dollar value on it. But intellectual capital is a key strength that is vital to Dow's future, driving our vision to be the best at applying chemistry in ways that deliver greater value to our customers, shareholders, employees, and society. Effective management and use of intellectual capital will go a long way in helping Dow achieve that vision.[1]

William S. Stavropoulos
Chairman, Board of Directors
The Dow Chemical Company

THE PRECEDING CHAPTERS have described the best practices used by today's companies in realizing value from their intellectual assets.

Thomas Alva Edison's spirit lives in the boardroom of leading companies around the world. One such company—a true model of the Edisonian path traveled throughout this book—is The Dow Chemical Company. Dow exemplifies all aspects of the Value Hierarchy described in this book—from defense of valuable inventions, to cost-saving, to profit-making, to integration, and, finally, to using intellectual capital to change the future direction of the company. To understand how, let us begin by considering the origins of this global enterprise.

THE DOW CHEMICAL COMPANY: BUILT ON INVENTIONS

The Dow Chemical Company was incorporated on May 18, 1897, by Herbert H. Dow, to begin the first commercial production of bleach. The first bleach was made in November and the first sale by The Dow Chemical Company was made in January 1898. Today, Dow is a leading science and technology company that provides innovative chemical, plastic and agricultural products and services to many markets. With annual sales of $30 billion, Dow serves customers in 170 countries and a wide range of markets that are vital to human progress, including food, transportation, health and medicine, personal and home care, and building and construction, among others. Committed to the principles of sustainable development, Dow and its 50,000 employees seek to balance economic, environmental, and social responsibilities.

Throughout its first century, Dow has created, patented, and generated significant revenue from products that are industry standards today such as STYROFOAM™ brand plastic foam, METHOCEL™ multifunctional food gums, Drytech™ superabsorbent polymers, to name a few. The company continues to introduce new products, such as SiLK™ semiconductor dielectric resins. As Richard M. Gross, Corporate Vice President of Research and Development notes, "Dow has been and always will be a science and technology company. In fact—and I believe this is true for the entire chemical industry— we provide enabling technology that is the foundation of tremendous value and progress for other industries. Our scientists and researchers work to create new and innovative solutions to both unmet and latent needs of our customers. Our goal is to continuously create products that make life better while moving forward on our corporate commitment to the triple bottom line of environmental, social and financial progress."

How did Dow become a pioneer in managing its knowledge capital? Let's take a look at the knowledge capital management journey at Dow: from Intellectual Property Management in the 1930s and 1940s, to Intellectual Asset Management in the 1980s and 1990s to Intellectual Capital Management in the 21st Century.

THE JOURNEY FROM PATENTS TO INTELLECTUAL ASSETS

From the beginning, the company managed its patent portfolio. New inventions were reviewed by the Chief Engineer, Thomas Griswold, and filed by a Cleveland law firm. In about 1928, Griswold organized the Dow Patent Department and started with a portfolio of more than 350 patent applications.

In 1939 Dow continued to build on the legacy of managing patents. The company moved from having the Chief Engineer review patents to having a Patent Committee review patents. Dow named its first Director of Inventions Management in 1947.

Dow established a formal group in 1958 to manage inventions and technical agreements. The group became part of Corporate R&D in 1968. Starting in 1990, Dow R&D management began focusing on how to improve "the patenting process." Dr. Fred Corson, then-vice president of R&D and a member of the Board of Directors, named Ron Glomski Director of Inventions Management to identify and implement improvements in how Dow managed its inventions.

A multi-functional team (R&D, business, patent and licensing) developed a "should" map for managing Dow innovations. Two key gaps emerged:

1. There was no patent strategy in place.
2. Measurement of success for inventors, patent attorneys, and departments was based on quantity of inventions, not quality.

Dow addressed these gaps by not only process improvements but also the human dimensions. Managers at the company recognized the need to start developing and populating an Inventions Management Group with people who had business and product management experience in addition to technical competence. They also recognized the need for improved communication and teamwork. Dow really started with the innovation end and added the business piece.

Because Dow had a long history of patenting, it already had processes in place for patent prosecution. In fact, Dow had developed a comprehensive electronic database to view and manage its large portfolio of more than 20,000 patents and hundreds of technical agreements. During 1992, the Inventions Management Group worked with the business-aligned Patent Task Forces to assign primary ownership of each property in the corporate patent portfolio to one of the active business units based on technology, business use, and strategy focus. The vast array of active agreements were assigned ownership as well. This alignment then catalyzed the development of patent strategies for each business unit, which became an integral part of the business strategies.

To begin the process of aligning the patent portfolio with the businesses and assign ownership, the Inventions Management Group created a framework for these teams to review and assess each patent. The three main classification categories were:

1. Current Business Use (practice, defense, license)
2. Potential Business Use (practice, defense, license)
3. No Business Interest (available for licensing, allow to expire, abandon)

As you can see in Exhibit 6.1, at the end of 1993 (a year and a half after they started the classification process), Dow found that roughly 25 percent of its patent portfolio was of no business use. As a result of the classification process, Dow downsized its patent portfolio by more than 10,000 patents, generating cost savings of over $40 million over a five-year period. Dow was proud of this alignment effort, and when Gordon Petrash assumed responsibility for the Inventions Management Group in 1993, the company began talking externally about its efforts and realized what a significant step it had just taken toward world-class intellectual property management.

EXHIBIT 6.1   The Dow Chemical Company Patent Portfolio*

	Current Business Use 43%/53%			Potential Business Use 32%/33%		No Business Interest 25%/15%		
	Practice	Defensive	License	Practice/ Use Def.	License	Avail. For Corp. Lic.	Allow To Expire	Abandon
12/93	19%	11%	13%	22%	10%	7%	14%	4%
5/99	17%	13%	23%	16%	16%	1%	11%	3%

* These numbers are always in a state of change.

Dow's portfolio alignment efforts coincided with the USPTO's tripling of patent fees. This fee was not large on a per-patent basis, but when multiplied by thousands of patents, it added significant costs to the bottom line. Not surprisingly, Dow began to ask the businesses to absorb the now-rising patent costs.

Cost-saving in intellectual property was part of a larger transformation at Dow. This transformation began in 1993 with the introduction of the company's Strategic Blueprint, a strategic roadmap emphasizing four key elements of success: setting the competitive standard business-by-business, productivity, value growth, and culture. Dow was returning to its innovative roots and seeking to change the way shareholders and employees viewed the chemical business. "The chemical industry is a knowledge industry," notes Gross. "Dow is moving from being perceived as a great manufacturing company—with focus on capacity and hard capital assets—to being known for great manufacturing AND great science and technology, with strength in innovation. The 'knowledge industry' perspective helps provide a more solid direction to our innovation, with focus on identifying customer and marketplace needs, adopting new business models, and reaching for fast commercialization."

Why did Dow focus first on intellectual property? "Patents were the most tangible of the intangibles. Everyone in Dow understood what patents were," reports Sharon Oriel, the current Director of Dow's Global Intellectual Asset and Capital Management Technology Center. The corporation realized these innovations could become corporate assets, now that they were aligned with a business and strategies were being developed to manage the portfolio. As a result, in 1993 the group changed its name from Inventions Management to Intellectual Asset Management, and the businesses now had Intellectual Asset

Management Teams (IAMTs) not Patent Task Forces. IAMTs are cross-functional teams sponsored by the business leadership and representing a key technology area and/or value center of the business. Team members come from business, patent law, R&D, and IAM. The teams are chartered to drive value creation and extraction via the appropriate identification, acquisition, maintenance, utilization, and leveraging of intellectual assets. Today there are well over 100 such active teams throughout the company. Intangible assets at Dow were well on their way to being managed like Dow's tangible assets.

As a result of the patent alignment and classification effort, Dow identified an opportunity to move further up the value pyramid. Not only were the businesses starting to see that they could create revenue from their intangibles, but an opportunity was identified to significantly grow Dow's licensing income. Dow's patent portfolio contained valuable innovations which were not being used. The Intellectual Asset Management leaders challenged management in 1994 to grow Dow's annual $20–25 million licensing income to more than $100 million by 2000. Management stepped up to the challenge and established a Technology Licensing and Catalyst Business to actively extract value from the total intellectual asset portfolio. According to Dow's 2000 10-K the company had revenue related to patent and technology royalties totaling $61 million in 2000.

The patent lawyers at Dow have played a key role in this IAM partnership. "The attorneys are well integrated in the process," says Associate General Counsel Graham Taylor. "Many of them are on the Intellectual Asset Management Teams, so their voice is being sought out as managers make decisions on strategy." Taylor admits that business people, not lawyers, should make strategic decisions. "You don't want a bunch of patent lawyers driving your intellectual capital strategy," he acknowledges. On the other hand, he believes that a strong IAM/ICM program hinges on a dedicated force of inside patent counsel who are experts in the technology and the law, and who are in tune and aligned with the company's business goals. After all, he says, patent protection is an important bedrock of progress. "The pyramid of progress rests on a strong bedrock of intellectual property and on the ability and willingness to enforce that intellectual property. Without strong intellectual property laws, there would be little incentive to innovate, and the pyramid would crumble. Maximizing innovation within an organization requires knowing and operating within those laws to bring value to the organization. By definition, intellectual asset management requires a highly skilled and proactive group of intellectual property lawyers," Taylor states.

As businesses began to more proactively and strategically patent and to truly manage their intangibles, the Intellectual Asset Management group recognized that it was important to have Intellectual Asset Managers residing within and reporting directly to the business rather than as part of a corporate function. A look at the Dow Performance Chemicals business shows these principles in action (see Exhibit 6.2).

As the businesses began to more proactively manage their intellectual assets, Dow needed to create a central group to focus on identifying and developing better IA practices, and corporate measures, and driving consistent use of these tools across the company. In 1995, Dow created the Global IAM Technology Center to support the network of business-aligned intellectual asset managers. "The role of the Tech Center," says Sharon Oriel, Director of the center, "is to provide a centralized effort to develop and identify IA better practices for the company and to assist in the consistent implementation of these best practices through partnering with the business aligned Intellectual Asset Managers." The Tech Center has created and sponsored the development of the IAM management model, developed tools for patent and technology mapping and valuation techniques, and become the center for knowledge sharing for the IAM Global network.

Dow continued to look for ways to create value from intangibles. Through partnership with the Tax Department, IAM established a process that complies with the Internal Revenue Service guidelines to donate unused intellectual assets to nonprofit institutions. Dow completed its first donations in 1995. Donations have been made to numerous institutions including Case Western

---

EXHIBIT 6.2 Performance Chemicals Case Study

An Interview with IAM Director Randy Stauffer

Q: Can you tell us a little bit about how IAM works in the Performance Chemicals Business?

A: Performance Chemicals is probably the most complicated business in Dow. It is made up of about 25 different value centers (or businesses) ranging in size from less than $50 million to more than $700 million in annual sales. I am responsible for ensuring that our intellectual property is aligned with the business objectives. In the mid 1990s, we had many patents that were not being leveraged, and we decided that we must get additional value from our patents. With a variety of different businesses, the types of value you extract from IP will be different. Some will look to cut patent costs, some will try to leverage (license, sell, trade, etc.), some will realign R&D, etc. In some of the businesses we abandoned as much as 75 percent of the portfolio.

(continues)

EXHIBIT 6.2   Continued

Q: So once you had cleaned up your existing portfolio, did you go back into R&D and point out the gaps in the patent portfolio?

A: Absolutely! We went back to each of the 25 businesses and asked, 'What is your business plan?' Once we better understood the objectives of the business, we were able to look in the patent portfolio and find the technology gaps (if any) where we did not have a legally protected position based on the future objectives for the business. In some cases we cut R&D entirely, because based on the business plan— for example, to be the lowest-cost commodity chemical supplier, there was no further R&D investment required, so we eliminated cost. Other businesses— Antimicrobials, for example—said, 'Our business has little to do with manufacturing; it is strictly an intellectual asset-based business, comprising government registrations, composition-of-matter patents and application patents. For those businesses, we picked the area where we felt we could best compete and then directed the R&D toward those technology areas. We aligned research to get patentable technology, which you can leverage into the marketplace.'

Q: What would you tell people who are just embarking on intellectual asset management?

A: First and foremost, this is not a program of the day, it is a commitment. This is not something that happens once and it's done. To do this right, it must become embedded at the cellular level of your organization. This has to be part of what you do; it is not something that someone does for you once. Top management must be committed. A corporate organization needs to be in place to ensure leveraged work processes, standard measurements, and adequate investment returns on the entire process.

You can't say 'I'll do this for a couple years, then I'll go do something else.' Once you get support and commitment from the top management, you have to have the discipline to carry out these processes. It is a culture-changing operation. When we first cleaned up our patent portfolio and got rid of all those costs, some people thought, 'Well this is great, this is fantastic, now we're way ahead.' But rather than rest on your laurels, you need to keep pushing forward and asking additional questions: 'Can we donate it? Can we license it? Can we trade it? How else can we make additional revenue?' It's not a breakthrough technology, but in today's marketplace, you really make the difference by some of these incremental processes that you do just a little bit better, and the sum-total of those activities can make you very successful. Be aware of it; build it in, because it does give you a sustainable competitive advantage, probably more than the product life cycle. If you ignore IP, you do so at your peril, because someone else won't, and you'll find that there's been a shift in the marketplace and you're out. And you're not only out but you can't get back in. And then you're out of business.

Randy Stauffer, Dow

Reserve University (H.H. Dow's alma mater) as well as Penn State, the University of Missouri, the University of Washington, and Texas A&M.

Dow launched a dedicated Knowledge Management (KM) effort in 1995 to further enhance its ability to leverage its knowledge assets. This effort quickly evolved to a structure much the same as the IAM effort with a corporate best-practices center and a network of Information Stewards. According to Jim Allen, Director of Knowledge Management for Dow, the mission of KM at Dow is "to turn information into knowledge, to make better decisions, faster, in support of growth, productivity and governance." This is a true enterprise-wide effort, cutting across business unit and function. It also goes well beyond just documenting knowledge, as it includes utilizing the knowledge in people's heads. Allen goes on to say, "This means we have to capture what we know, share what is known and use what is shared." Effectively integrating this world-class KM program with the Dow IAM effort was a key milestone in Dow's intangibles management evolution.

After the focus on cost cutting, Dow leadership added the goal of aggressive growth. In 1998, the company turned its attention to value growth. According to Oriel, R&D set a stretch goal in 1995 of having 15 percent of revenue generated from truly new products (not line extensions) less than five years old. "We are very close to meeting that goal in 2001." The company plans to increase earnings per share by an average of 10 percent per year. Effective management of all knowledge assets is a critical factor in Dow's ability to achieve this target.

With the emphasis now on growth, the Dow IAM Tech Center, in partnership with the business IAM network, the Technology Licensing & Catalyst Business, the Knowledge Management Tech Center, the Tax Department, and the Intellectual Property Law Group, began developing processes and tools to stimulate company growth by more effectively leveraging knowledge assets. The company began to both extract value and create value from intangibles. "In the early 1990s," notes Gross, "we were successful in leveraging low-hanging IP fruit. From 1998 onward, it has taken, and will continue to take, effort and commitment to continue to develop intellectual capital management to meet our growth expectations."

One example of the effort and commitment to accelerate growth is the creation of technology platforms. Tony Torres, Business Director for the Fibers Platform, explains:

> With the Fibers Platform, Dow is trying to establish two things, speed to market and leverage of technologies that aren't being utilized to their full extent. So we have created market-facing platforms, for example Fibers, to leverage capabilities

from the technology in order to deliver market solutions first and products second. One of the things we have noticed in the markets today is that short life cycles are creating a bigger need to get to market faster than ever. Historically, we would build a plant and then provide products and services. That just takes too long in today's rapidly evolving markets. We have decided that to get to market quickly we don't need brick and mortar to have a competitive differentiation and established barriers to entry. What we need instead are three things: People, Partners, and Patents. People meaning internal know-how. Partners are the companies that give us access to the markets where we want to go; and Patents you need because you can't go talk to any potential partners unless you know you are protected. Now, in essence what we are trying to accomplish with the Fibers Platform is taking Dow assets and looking outward and trying to figure out how we can best put them to use, and then contacting a potential partner and bringing them a complete package of People and Patents to combine with their tangible assets. Let me give you an example. Say a business division has created a glue and has patented an automotive application for the glue. There could be 25 other possible applications outside the automotive field, but since the business is only focused on automotive applications, they aren't going to pursue any other application. This is where I come in. My job is to find those 25 applications, create the necessary intellectual property, find the appropriate partners who can utilize our know-how and intellectual property with their plant or manufacturing capabilities, and *voila*, we have just leveraged our intellectual assets for value!

Exhibit 6.3 highlights Dow's growing emphasis on leveraging its assets through the Value Web approach. The technology platforms need to identify what they bring to a given marketplace, and what are they lacking, in order to find the best partners for success.

THE JOURNEY CONTINUES: INTELLECTUAL CAPITAL MANAGEMENT FOR THE 21ST CENTURY

With the creation of new platforms built on technology, people and relationships with customers and suppliers, Dow was truly moving beyond the management of just intellectual property and standard IAM practices to more proactive management of all its knowledge assets. Dow was one of the first companies to recognize that effectively managing ALL your intangible assets was a critical element in gaining and sustaining future value. The Dow IAM Network was one of the original pioneers of the concept of Intellectual Capital Management (ICM), and first introduced the concept to Dow management in 1997. The initial impact was the recognition that Dow was a knowledge company and that it did indeed require knowledge and the effective application of

EXHIBIT 6.3   The Value Web

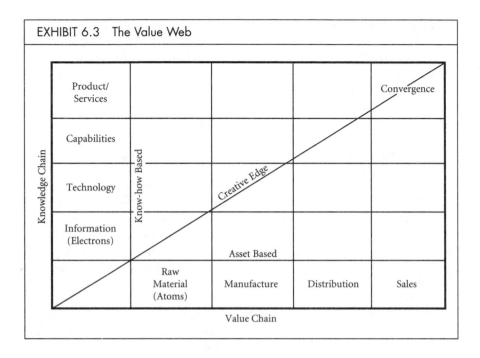

it to drive the future value of the company. "While Dow didn't immediately start using the term intellectual capital management, the concept was beginning to take root," Oriel says. The focus in the late 90s was on identifying and measuring the key value drivers of growth (a mix of both tangible and intangible assets) then on proactively managing all knowledge assets. The company began using a "balanced score card" approach to measure and track its accomplishments. In 1999, Dow published one of the first "triple bottom line" reports, called "The Public Report." The report reviews financial, environmental, and social progress and challenges.

It's clear that Dow is operating at all five levels of the Value Hierarchy described in this book. But the story doesn't end here. The significant value-enhancing component of IAM had been proven, world-class IAM had become part of the corporate culture at Dow, upper management was fully supportive and committed, and the new ICM seed had been planted. Dow was now poised to take the next evolutionary step in the management of its knowledge assets. In 2000, Dow launched its first official comprehensive Intellectual Capital Management program in the Polyurethanes business.

To better understand the significance of this next evolutionary step let's begin by reviewing some company-specific terminology that Dow has developed to broadly apply to how it managed its knowledge assets as it moved into ICM. First, the basic Dow intangibles definitions:

Intellectual Property: Codified knowledge with legal ownership
Intellectual Asset: Codified knowledge providing value to the company
Intellectual Capital: All knowledge with the potential for value

Now let's review the Dow definitions for the key intangibles management processes:

Knowledge Management: The systematic and disciplined management of knowledge and the associated processes of creating, gathering, organizing, disseminating, leveraging and using knowledge to make decisions, cause action and generate value.

Intellectual Asset Management: The proactive management of Dow's Intellectual Assets including patents, trade secrets, trademarks, copyrights, know-how, technical and business reports and technology related agreements.

Intellectual Capital Management: The process of proactively managing, protecting, leveraging and reporting ALL knowledge assets to assist in gaining/sustaining competitive advantage and maximizing future value growth.

The ICM Pilot Program

This first comprehensive ICM effort was in the form of a pilot program in one of Dow's major business units, the Polyurethanes business. The primary reason the ICM effort started in this business was that the Polyurethanes business has a very aggressive growth strategy, and business management knew that the only way to achieve its growth goals was to more effectively leverage all its assets, both tangible and intangible. David Near, the Intellectual Capital Director for this business, says, "Senior management in the Polyurethanes business realized they weren't effectively protecting and leveraging all the knowledge assets owned by the business, and therefore knew that there was a significant amount of yet untapped equity hidden in those assets." Securing commitment from upper management is a prerequisite of any successful IAM or ICM program. The leadership of the Polyurethanes business at Dow is completely on board, as evidenced by comments from David Fischer, Vice President of Dow Polyurethanes: "A world-class ICM program, effectively aligned with the business strategy, provides a road map to successful and sustainable future value growth for the business."

The Polyurethane ICM pilot was officially launched in early 2000.

The ICM model[2] that Dow is using corporately is a slightly modified version of the model developed by ICM pioneers Petrash, St. Onge, Edvinsson and

Armstrong. Dow uses "Knowledge Management" rather than "Knowledge Flow" as the enabling link across the three ICM components, because it was a more accurate depiction of the ICM-KM structure at Dow. The Dow ICM model has three primary components (which you can see in Exhibit 6.4 below).

- **Organizational Capital** (structural capital) encompasses the hardware, software, databases, systems, work processes, business models, organizational structure, patents, trademarks, trade secrets, and all other "codified" knowledge. It is everything left behind when the human capital walks out the door at the end of the day. It can be owned by the company and it represents organizational knowledge.
- **Human Capital** is the combined capabilities, knowledge, skills, experience, innovativeness, and problem-solving abilities of each individual in the organization. It is not owned by the company. It represents individual knowledge.
- **External Capital** includes alliances and relationships with customers, strategic partners, suppliers, investors and the community. It can be

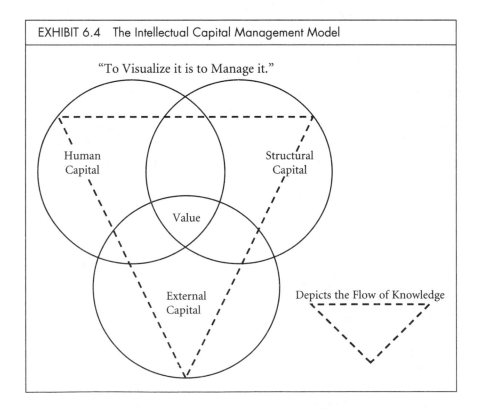

EXHIBIT 6.4   The Intellectual Capital Management Model

"To Visualize it is to Manage it."

Human Capital

Structural Capital

Value

External Capital

Depicts the Flow of Knowledge

leveraged (to some extent) by the company and it represents enterprise-wide knowledge.

To Near, the distinction between "Intellectual Asset Management" and "Intellectual Capital Management" is far from academic. "When people asked me the difference between IAM and ICM, I say it's a matter of scope both in terms of the range of intangible assets you're trying to manage and the number of people, capabilities and functions required to make it happen. ICM and IAM are not synonymous terms at Dow," says Near. "Rather ICM represents all value-adding knowledge embodied in our people, processes, IP, and external relationships, and IAM is the value-creating and extracting component. ICM is simply the next logical step in intangibles management beyond IAM for Dow."

The primary focus of the Polyurethane pilot was to drive ICM through the business-decision process on a project-by-project basis. According to Near, "Effective ICM is an issue of structure. A successful, comprehensive ICM program needs to employ capabilities beyond what we've historically utilized to drive our IAM program here at Dow. These include robust business portfolio management, best-in-class project management practices, and an even more integrated relationship with Knowledge Management to build the necessary learning and sharing culture."

The ICM pilot program has a number of key objectives—many of them already realized as benefits:

- Develop and implement comprehensive ICM strategies for all growth projects.
- Effectively measure and manage the return on human capital.
- Enhance the utilization of customer and other relational capital.
- Efficiently acquire rights to new, emerging complementary technologies.
- Secure protected entry into new markets with "disruptive technology."[3]
- Significantly enhance licensing revenues.
- Quantitatively define the full enterprise value of the business (tangible and intangible).
- Develop a hard dollar-based enterprise-wide reporting structure (i.e., "The Intellectual Capital Report") to better measure and manage all knowledge assets.
- Effectively utilize ICM to achieve the value growth goals of the business (with documented impact).

The structural capital component of ICM involves essentially what Dow has been doing in its IAM program over the past 10 years, so very few changes are being made to that portion of the Polyurethanes ICM pilot. The only modifications so far include upgrades to the current Dow technology mapping tools, ICM strategy development, and enhancing the level of integration into the project management process.

The external capital component at Dow is focused on how to both enhance and better utilize our external relationships to maximize future value contribution. "The primary relationship we are targeting is our relationship with our customers," says Near. "We are working to more effectively integrate our customer satisfaction/loyalty drivers with future value contribution to further enhance both elements."

Of the three primary components of ICM, the human capital component is likely to bring the most long-term value, says Near. As we move into the new millennium, not only are human resources going to be in increasingly short supply, but the length of time a person stays with a given job or company is going to decrease dramatically. So the days of the standard 30-year career at one company are most likely over. This means, says Near, "Attracting and retaining human capital is not going to be the only determinant of future business success. How well you utilize the tacit knowledge they bring for the short time you have them will be absolutely critical."

The guiding principle for the human capital element of the Polyurethane ICM pilot is to better manage application of individual and collective knowledge toward the strategic direction of the business. Near elaborates:

> We are essentially focusing on measuring, in hard dollar terms, how well we're utilizing the knowledge embodied in our people. Rather than try to value all the tacit knowledge in a person's head, we're valuing how well we're applying it to our projects and then to strategic needs of the business. In more practical terms we're measuring how efficiently our decision teams align the skills and capabilities of their people with the needs of each project in the business. So we are truly trying to measure a return on investment (ROI) on our human capital. This is not designed to be another metric to measure individual performance, but rather a direct measure of how well our decision teams are utilizing and deploying the human capital in their organizations. This is truly a promising new approach to valuing human capital, and we've partnered with our corporate Human Resources group and outside consultants to codevelop, pilot, and eventually implement the program.

Key Learnings from the Dow ICM Pilot in Polyurethanes

After one year Dow has learned a lot from the Polyurethane pilot, and several other businesses are starting the ICM journey. Near shares some of the key learnings thus far:

- Recognize yourself as a knowledge company.
- Secure upper management understanding, support and commitment.
- Having the right organizational structure is key.
- Put your IPM portfolio and practices in place first.
- ICM must be viewed and managed on a project-by-project basis.
- Timely and effective competitive assessment is critical.
- Apply valuation techniques consistently.
- Stay focused on future value contribution.
- Identify and manage your key IC drivers first and IC reporting second.
- Recognize that ICM is a business issue, not a technical or legal issue.

THE FUTURE AT DOW IS INTELLECTUAL CAPITAL MANAGEMENT

As this book goes to press, the ICM Pilot by the Polyurethanes business is tracking its planned timeline. They are developing a number of first and better practices and are sharing these key learnings throughout the company. "We are definitely breaking new ground," says Near, "but we still have a way to go before we can say that we've fully defined all the invisible equity in our business and, most importantly, how to effectively tap into it. There is no doubt, however, that more proactively managing our knowledge capital via a comprehensive ICM program will have a profound economic impact on the future of our company."

Bruce Story is Director, Intellectual Asset Management, for Dow's Polyolefins and Elastomers business group, one of the largest business groups within Dow. When asked what he viewed as the main benefit of Dow's intangibles management journey, he cited strong connections between strategy, R&D, and legal that helped build the morale at Dow. Story waxes enthusiastic on this point:

> It's a lot of fun. I've never had so much fun in my Dow career as this. There's a lot of impact on the business and across all the functions. One of the joys is watching your inventors get excited as they see their impact on the business. The patent attorneys also get excited because the patents that they spend time obtaining have value and get used. The human capital effect is great. We can always find people that want to work in our business, so attracting and retaining innovative people is not a problem with us. All in all, this whole IAM/ICM effort has been very good for morale.

Senior management at Dow is committed to creating and managing intellectual capital across the entire corporation. Richard M. Gross, Corporate Vice President for Research and Development states, "The chemical industry is a knowledge industry and The Dow Chemical Company is a knowledge company." Because managing intangibles has had measurable impact on the corporation's income and growth, Dow has seen a difference in corporate culture. As Oriel points out, "We have made a long-term commitment to leveraging our knowledge capital. Throughout Dow, we are beginning to see ourselves now not so much as a chemical company, but as a 'knowledge company.'"

"Dow will continue to pioneer the development of intellectual capital management, accounting and reporting so corporations can make visible their full value and potential for growth," says Oriel. These internal efforts are accelerated through external conversations and collaborations with recognized experts Karl Erik Sveiby, Baruch Lev, Leif Edvinsson, and Patrick Sullivan.

The Dow story resounds with success and hard work. How can other companies follow its example? Sharon Oriel offers these points to ponder:

1. *Senior management support is essential.* H.H. Dow put his chief engineer in charge of managing inventions. Today, IAM/ICM has the support of Mike Parker, CEO and his entire leadership team.

2. *Find a way to show real monetary results from managing intellectual capital.* Dow started with saving money on patent costs. We then moved to using patents to create revenues and value for the company. Dollars are a lot easier to understand than patent claims. We show the $$$.

3. *Recognize that Intellectual Capital Management requires dedicated resources.*

APPENDIX A

MINING A PORTFOLIO FOR VALUE

By Patrick Sullivan Jr.

PORTFOLIO MINING IS an activity that has gained prominence on the IP scene in the past five or six years, but it has actually been around for quite some time. In 1991 at ICMG we embarked on our first portfolio mining exercise for a chemical company to identify technology that they were no longer using so that they could abandon patents that were costing the client several million dollars in worldwide patent maintenance fees. We didn't call it mining then, nor were we the first to perform this sort of project in an IP portfolio. However, this practice took some time to catch on in corporations across the world, particularly as managers have searched for low-hanging fruit and potential cost savings. The present day competitive business environment and the reliance on patent protection for protecting a company's product value streams have set the stage for patent portfolio mining.

This appendix will provide a brief introduction to mining and its close kin, portfolio categorization. What follows from there is an explanation of the strategies for mining and various value extraction targets (i.e., types of jewels) for which you can mine, a discussion of the intellectual capital mining process, and a "Then What?" discussion for embarking on the next stage of the IP hierarchy.

The term "mining" is used in the context of IP portfolios because of the assumption that there are valuable "jewels" hidden amidst the legal department's filing cabinets that contain paper patent files. These jewels are presumed to be patents that currently lay dormant (value in waiting) but that have potential to protect products and services that revolutionize a market, or that represent an innovation that has been stolen (i.e., an infringement) and is in use by someone else (for example, by a competitor!). Put simply, just one of these patents may represent an unclaimed lottery ticket.

Patrick Sullivan Jr. is a partner at ICMG, located in Palo Alto.

Let's take a step back. When we think about an industrial mine, three things hold true. First, miners and prospectors must have a good understanding of the lay of their land to know what to do and how to do it. For example, they consider, "Are we in a stream or underground? Are there any unturned rocks, or has this already been picked over?" No Forty-Niner would pan for gold if a water source wasn't there at one time to wash the gold downstream and deposit it in a slow-moving location. Second, the miners are generally looking for something specific, like gold, coal, copper, or some other commodity. Some mining operations are capable of mining for several of these at once because they have a diverse claim, a mix of tools and equipment, and solid expertise. Third, the miners have some limitations they must recognize and figure in to their mining tactics, like the limited size of their claim, their cash position, and the methods and tools at their disposal. Many miners underestimate the time to find that first nugget, or mine for something that isn't consistent with their claim or the region (i.e., mining for coal in an area where emeralds abound). Who hasn't heard a tale of the old prospector who had been working a claim for thirty years by himself and finally struck it rich? The point is that mining involves a good understanding of your own context, as well as a solid grounding in what you have to work with in your claim.

Portfolio Mining is comparable to traditional commodity mining because these truths also apply. The old Forty-Niner terms and problems also apply to present day IP mining. Each of these are addressed later in the context of patent portfolio mining.

Claim.   Your patent portfolio is your claim, and the IP attorneys, business developers, marketing managers, R&D teams, general managers, and even consultants all play parts as prospectors. Knowing your claim is vital to your ability to get value from it. This understanding of your claim is what we call portfolio categorization.

What to Look For.   Knowing what you are mining for is also imperative. However, unlike commodity mining, patents are intangible and the information you learn about a patent portfolio can easily be reused again for a different purpose. Thus that dirt that was thrown out still has value in patent mining because we can track where it came from, and what other "items" it may still contain. Knowing what you are mining for is equivalent to setting your portfolio mining strategy.

How to Mine.   Strip-mining, panning, blasting, using slurries, and plain old digging are examples of mining techniques. All have one thing in common— they are systematically uncovering and sorting through the claim to identify the jewels. Portfolio mining also has a common method, and as many different ways to achieve this as you can imagine.

What Do I Do After I Start?   Finally, when you have completed any stage of mining and you look across your claim, the thought "Then What?" comes up as you see the various piles of dirt lying around your claim. Portfolio Mining has a few "Then What?" stages.

UNDERSTANDING YOUR CLAIM: PORTFOLIO CATEGORIZATION

At some point, you need to roll up your sleeves and look at your claim. Is it a young portfolio? Are there clumps that expire in the near future? Does it contain a broad array of technology with varied applications, or is it narrowly defined in a few specific niches? Are the patents written with broad claims or limited to a few (or one) fields of use? Does the portfolio build on the technologies of others, or are these seminal patents in the industry?

The answers to these questions may be obtained by categorizing your portfolio. Improved software makes many of these analyses quite simple to obtain, such as a histogram of the portfolio showing the number of patents and their years until expiration. Other factors, such as narrow vs. broad claims, require a brief read of the patent—a factor that software as yet cannot determine. The purpose of this categorization is to understand what you are dealing with, and whether or not you can expect many great triumphs from untold jewels, or a handful of good ones. But there are also many auxiliary purposes for this categorization, like an understanding of your overall technology position, your capability to defend yourself in an infringement lawsuit, and the overall management of your aging portfolio (after all, patents are an expiring asset—a fact that the Forty-Niners never had in their path to riches). These auxiliary benefits are not covered here, but certainly knowing what is in your portfolio is the first step towards managing it.

Categorization is also called "clustering." The idea is to look at the portfolio and create various "buckets" that you could use to segment the portfolio. Age of the patents is one, IPC code another, technology family is still another, and so on. Make no mistake—this is an iterative process. Categorization is like peeling an onion: the first pass reveals information relevant to the first management question. The second pass reveals more, and the third, fourth, and fifth sharpen your awareness of the capabilities, weaknesses, and opportunities lying in your patents.

What you are mining for determines which buckets you need. If you want to achieve cost savings by dropping patents that you no longer need by no longer paying the maintenance fees, you need buckets like "Critical to Our Business" and "8-Track Technology." If you are looking for noncore revenue streams but encounter senior managers in divisions of your company who are skittish to let their core technology outside your doors, you need buckets like "Don't Even Think About It," "Core but OK to License Outside Our Field Of Use," and "Free and Clear-Knock Yourself Out." In the end, picking buckets for categorization is iterative, and requires knowledge not only of your portfolio, but in consulting-speak the buckets should reflect your "As-Is" condition as well as your "To-Be" condition. In other words, pick your buckets for future management and action, and don't be surprised if you keep inventing new ones—that's normal.

What to Look For: Mining Strategies

If one day your CEO walks into your office and says, "I read a book about patents and I think we should get more value from our patent portfolio. Get to work!" and then walks out of your office, don't be ashamed if you have a stunned look on your face. This is happening more and more, and although your first answer is to say, "Of course!" after you have time to reflect on your task it can seem daunting. "What should I do? What value should I strive for? Who do I need to involve in other groups in my company?" These are the most common questions immediately after an epiphany like this.

Don't panic. The best thing you can do first is to consider your company's overall business strategy and plot your As-Is condition with respect to your use of IP. "Are we litigious, or are we negotiators? Do we have an NIH mentality or do we license things in and out? Are patents core to protecting our business, or do we need to build a stronger program?" What is most helpful is if your company already has determined what your IP strategy is and the role that IP plays in getting value for your company. This is easy to say, but difficult to ascertain, since 95 percent of the companies we see don't start with a coordinated company strategy to their IP strategy. Consider the various ways you can get value from your portfolio, and whether they are consistent with your company business strategy. Then choose a mining outcome and work towards it.

There are two basic strategies for a patent portfolio mining exercise. One is to pursue patents that can generate the most cash for the bottom line, since licensing revenues are usually booked directly as operating income. This is the first strategy considered since in most circles, "cash is king." Most IP departments are cost centers, so an influx of cash can give them more operating budget to buy more sophisticated software, improve processes, or even simply hire more attorneys to prosecute more patents. Divisions love the cash streams because they improve their return on R&D dollars. And at the corporate level, IP licensing income can be used for additional projects and to seed new entrepreneurial activities.

The second strategy is to use patents to generate noncash value. Licensing a patent to another party may gain access to the other party's technology that in return, can reduce your R&D program expenses and improve your development timeline (a benefit that is often much more valuable than cash). Other noncash objectives include access to markets, access to technical staff and know-how, or obtaining equity or notes from the licensee in return. Noncash objectives require good knowledge of your portfolio so that you can assess the trade-offs between the value of your IP and what you will receive in return (i.e., categorization).

Once you have determined which value extraction type (or types) interest you, determine which of the various types of "jewels" you wish to mine. In patent portfolio language, we call this selecting your value extraction objectives.

VALUE EXTRACTION OBJECTIVES

Here are the most popular objectives (types of jewels) that are used in portfolio mining programs, (i.e., companies use patent portfolio mining to find patents or technologies):

- Infringement candidates
- Noncore revenue streams through licensing, joint ventures, and other strategic alliances
- Core-business licensing
- Merger & acquisition (M&A) positioning strength
- Tax donation candidates
- Abandonment candidates

For each of these objectives, tune your portfolio mining program to find those items that you are looking for. Here is a quick description of some fine tuning for each objective.

Infringement Candidates. Here you are searching for patented ideas that are being willfully (or often unintentionally) used without your permission. You are looking for patents that are broad in claim, and that claim inventions which are being used in another party's products and services. Once you find a patented idea that is potentially being used without your permission, you should find some evidence that it is being used in that product or service. This often requires reverse-engineering, or canvassing stores to find similar products that may contain your idea. The Internet is a very useful tool for researching the product claims posted on company web sites for their products and services. Mining for these opportunities requires a solid legal perspective and team to guide you.

Noncore Revenue Streams.   Here you are searching for patented ideas that have applications outside your current business, and that have sufficient markets to warrant an out-licensing or development program. Defense contractors have terrific technology that was developed for their governments that can be used in the commercial or consumer sectors. For example, GPS technology is making its way from the defense industry to the commercial and consumer sectors rapidly. Ideally your company has patented an innovation that not only solves a problem in your application and market, but also in another application and market. Most significant though, is whether the patent claims are broad enough to protect this alternative application. If the innovation is applicable but is protected by the patent claims in only one field of use, chances are it may be difficult to bring that innovation to market and expect it to be legally protected from competition.

Core-Business Licensing.   Normally this is a hot potato in companies. After all, if you license the rights to the patents that protect your products and services, aren't you cutting off your nose to spite your face? This would be true if your strategy was to remain a product company and to focus your energies on gaining IP just for protecting your products. When IBM licensed technology to Dell computers in the late 1990s, many people outside the IP world were shocked (including many IBM'ers). But IBM's position as a technology company rather than a products and services company is what made that licensing deal possible. These IBM executives realized that they could potentially make more money by leveraging their IP to Dell combined with their product sales, than they could by simply using the IP to protect their products. This is a difficult possibility for many managers based on the intense rivalries that exist between business units.

M&A Positioning Strength.   When mergers or acquisitions occur, they usually are made without a solid understanding of the intellectual property that will change hands. Many corporations assume that their products are adequately protected and that those patents are calculated into the overall purchase price or merger value. However, in most cases the intellectual property due diligence is limited and companies acquire or merge portfolios and don't have any idea what they have shortly afterward. With a solid understanding of your portfolio, you can identify those patents that should be reassigned to the new entity and which ones should stay behind. Also, more sophisticated companies grant licenses for IP, rather than title to it, reserving the right to use those patents in other fields of use. And by knowing the noncore value of your portfolio, you can determine just what income or noncash value you are giving up by including those noncore value-producing patents in the transaction. IP due diligence is extremely difficult if the portfolio is not adequately categorized. Once it is, the possibilities are astounding, since you can pick your M&A targets and suitors based on synergies with your portfolio.

Tax Donation Candidates.   Many people mistakenly think that they can donate IP that isn't worth anything. However, the U.S. Internal Revenue service doesn't give you something for nothing. For an IP donation to occur, you need to have a candidate that has application and value such that the receiving party will gain value from it that is measurable. That measurable value is what the donating company receives as a tax write-off. This means that in patent mining, you are looking for donation candidates that have some value, but that may be better suited for exploitation in a nonprofit entity that can expand it or set standards with it. For example, this can mean donating a technology package for a program that was underfunded, but that still produced good technology and that has no chance of resurrection within your company again.

Abandonment Candidates.   These are patents with only a few years of life remaining, or are not protecting any of your products and services, or are not included in any licenses, or are not current technology that can generate value. As the leftovers in the portfolio, these should be recommended to the IP department for abandonment.

Now that you've considered the jewels you are looking for in the claim, let's discuss the overall process used for all types of mining.

How to Mine

Imagine you are a Forty-Niner. You are sitting on your claim, you see the lay of the land, and you consider what to do next. "How much money is at my disposal? How many people? Do I have to find a certain amount of money in six months, or is this a five-year program?" The answers to these questions address some of the setup and "How-To" parameters for setting up a patent mining program. Before we address these parameters, you need to consider the three basic approaches to mining.

To obtain results with reliable certainty, you can mine every piece of dirt in the claim and run it through your discovery process. At the end of the program, you would have mined everything that there was to mine, could close up shop and return home. Let's not confuse portfolio categorization with mining, since the categorization is used to identify the clusters for later mining. The actual mining is how you are going to reach into those clusters and extract the gems. The actual mining is the separation of the ore from the earth.

In patent mining, two characteristics of patent portfolios differentiate them from commodity mines. First, patents expire, so during your mining process some of your claim will be removed, and as new patents are granted, you obtain new additions to your claim. This means that the mining process is not a static one, but a rolling one, and unless you halt patenting developments, you will never complete the census of the portfolio. Second, in a commodity mine, gold is gold, and diamonds are diamonds. Allowing for differences in grade, these commodities are well-known, their uses well-understood and their properties well-defined. Patents, however, can be used in countless ways, and unlike commodities where an emerald appears in only one setting, patents may be used by more than one person at a time and in multiple settings at a time. This makes their exploitation much more complicated but the possible opportunities far greater. It also forces you to make choices about which opportunities you will consider (Value Extraction Objectives) and whether you have the resources to mine for those objectives in the time allotted. It also raises the question of whether you have mined for every possible objective at the end of your census, and whether a review of certain categories for a different objective will yield different results.

A second approach to mining is to shoot for the low-hanging fruit. Simply put, this is "cherry-picking" and attempts to discover the easiest patents that can be commercialized in the shortest amount of time. The low-hanging fruit approach does not examine every patent, but uses computers and subjective judgment to find the first items that should be commercialized based on your objectives. It is similar to pouring the entire claim into a funnel, sifting it, and seeing what comes out first. At the end of the project, you have a partially completed itemized list of candidates, but a high probability that these will be successful.

The third approach is a statistical sampling method. After the portfolio is categorized, you may sample the patent clusters and mine only those selected to determine the value of each cluster. Using statistics, you may extrapolate some values for the entire portfolio. This is useful if you cannot perform a census and are not confident that a low-hanging fruit approach will accomplish your objective. The end result is the same as the low-hanging fruit approach because you have mined those sample clusters, but you may not have all the intelligence of the portfolio gained through the sifting method.

These approaches have various costs associated with them. Clearly the census approach requires the most resources and the most time, but the benefits are tremendous. And you can be much more proactive with the portfolio as it is being mined. The low-hanging fruit looks for a quick win, and the statistical sampling method is a good middle approach for many value extraction objectives. Once you consider these, it's time to mine.

The Portfolio Mining Process

Any mining operation attempts to stake a claim, select the process for mining that claim, and analyze the area in the claim for the desired objects. This analysis occurs in the following manner.

Cluster to Prioritize Groups

If you have not already categorized the portfolio, basic clustering by technology, age, and so on is useful to understand what is in the claim. Later in the process you can return to the categorization and fill in the next level of categorization based on your findings, but for now your goal in this phase is to understand the portfolio enough to prioritize which clusters you want to start with, which ones to eliminate from the program, and so on.

Review the Technical Merits of the Patents

Once the clusters are selected, engage internal and external technical experts to examine your technology embedded in the patents. Based on your objective, you are looking for technological traits like broad technical application, hot technology, old eight-track, and also examine/document the state of the technology, that is, is it on the drawing board, is it reduced to practice, is it protecting a working product or service.

Review/Verify the Legal Strength of the Patents

Most companies assume that the patents are valid (not a bad assumption). However, some may be quite susceptible for challenge, and if you are mining for infringement candidates your legal team should assess this risk. Legal departments do this usually as a matter of course.

Review the Commercial Applications of the Technology

Knowing what the technology may be used for helps you determine what problems it can solve. This is the creative phase where your team must evaluate the myriad possibilities to apply the technology and whether any of those are viable. Despite the daunting challenge, it isn't as hard as it sounds because many ideas are not viable, although I've often heard myself saying "Wow! If we could modify this thing to do this . . ."

Assess the Potential Revenues/Value of the Patent

These applications should be prioritized and then evaluated based on the patent claims, technical strength, and technology development. Your revenue estimates should address the various scenarios that are consistent with your mining objectives. At the end of this phase you will have an idea of what the cash/noncash value is for each patent that is run through this last phase, and possibly, of your entire portfolio.

Then What?

Once you've mined the portfolio for any value-extraction objective, you will find that you hold an immense amount of knowledge that accumulated from your assessment of the portfolio. The final "Then What" isn't really final, because this claim is a living, growing thing, and requires careful nurturing, growth, pruning, and management. These activities are usually continued in the Integrated and Visionary levels of the IP Value Hierarchy.

APPENDIX B

COMPETITIVE ASSESSMENT

By James R. Ewing and Jill M. Rusk

INTRODUCTION

If asked, most executives would agree that intellectual property has value, and that, in fact, their own organization is the holder of valuable pieces of intellectual property. It is likely, though, that many of these same executives would not be aware of the pieces of intellectual property or the intellectual property strategy of its closest competitors, let alone organizations that may rise to become new competitors in the near future. We have learned that performing competitive assessments using intellectual property as a primary basis for the assessment provides organizations with valuable insight that can be used to help companies better position themselves in the future vis-à-vis their competitors.

Today's knowledge-driven economy has presented companies with never-before-seen opportunities and threats. Given the pace of technology innovation, it is imperative that a company today develops and exploits any possible advantage it may have over its competitors. Knowledge capital, intellectual assets and intellectual property have become the name of the game. A company benefits by being a leader in innovation and technology. A company must set the direction and trends for the future and be able to adapt to the ever-changing marketplace.

A company must also be willing to investigate never-before-used channels and links to its customers. The easier and more direct methods of procurement have required companies to expand beyond traditional supply bases. The global economy has also created the need and opportunity for businesses to market and sell to companies around the world. Web-based purchasing, sole-source supply chains, vertical integration and a host of mergers, acquisitions and divestitures have created the need for companies not only to investigate and pursue other avenues of communication and functional lines of business, but to expand their operating networks and supply networks, as well.

James R. Ewing and Jill M. Rusk are both directors in Andersen's Chicago office.

This speed of innovation, technological development and business integration requires strong management direction and alignment of a company's strategic objectives with its intellectual property objectives. A company cannot be a leader in technology or innovation, if it is not a leader in the development of intellectual property. Making a decision about the direction of innovation, the depth and breadth to which a company will go to be an innovation leader, makes the competitive and technology assessment methodology an irreplaceable tool in today's marketplace.

Competitive and Technology Assessment

A competitive assessment provides a broad overview of the client's competitive marketplace, emphasizing the technology landscape, current innovation(s), trends in the market and potential competitive threats. It provides strategic insight to senior management of a company on its strengths, risks and opportunities, as well as those of its competitors, that can be used to make effective business decisions. It will answer questions such as:

- What are my competitors doing?
- What patenting trends are happening in my industry/market?
- What is the current pace of innovation? Of my company? Of my competitors?
- What white space might be available to the company?
- What companies might be possible licensing candidates?

The competitive assessment requires sifting through the myriad of publicly available information and focusing on that information that is helpful and specific enough to provide insight into a competitor's operations. Most companies house some type of competitive assessment business unit. The personnel within this unit scour the marketplace for new products, attend trade shows, study industry guides and magazines for information on the developments of its competitors. Unfortunately, this type of competitive intelligence is reactive rather than proactive. The competitor has created a product, a service or an opportunity for itself and it is now willing to share that information with its industry. The competitor may also have perfected its monopoly rights, through patenting, for its new innovation. The rest of the industry must now react to these developments, when, through some competitive research and strategic analysis, the company might have been made aware of the competitor's activities, months if not years ahead of its release to the public.

A technology assessment, while narrower in view than a competitive assessment, answers specific questions regarding a technology or technology platform, while looking at the players, markets and trends in innovation. It may uncover recommendations for opportunities to expand existing markets or create new markets by identifying candidates for acquisition, joint venture, partnership, licensing or recruitment. While much of the same information is studied in a competitive assessment, a technology assessment provides a comprehensive analysis of the given technology or technology platform, rather than looking at an industry, marketplace or specific companies. It will answer questions such as:

- What companies/competitors are playing in the same technology space?
- What technologies or companies might I acquire given the technology areas in which we are currently active?
- What about technologies in which we want to be active in the future?
- What inventors are prolific in a given technology?
- Is my technology the seminal technology? Are other companies learning from my company? Or is my company learning from others?
- What appear to be the future technology trends?

While a technology assessment may not provide quite as much information as a competitive assessment, it will provide insight into a competitor's innovation, research and development, usually months, if not years, before the results of that innovation are released to the public. It can highlight the direction all competitors are moving, including those companies not considered competitors in the most general sense.

This appendix will provide a brief introduction to competitive and technology assessment, including the definition and applicable uses of each, the importance of the derived information within the current economy, possible indications of need, the information that is most commonly found, and the use and application incorporated in the analysis of that information.

WHY PERFORM A COMPETITIVE ASSESSMENT

Why should a company use intellectual property competitive assessment techniques? Although there are any number of reasons, here are three important ones. First, intellectual property has value. IP allows a company to differentiate itself from its competitors. This IP, which is a legally granted monopoly over some form of creative expression, translates into market power for the holder of IP which can allow a company to earn a greater than equilibrium market rate of return. Any organization should be interested in how its competitors gain competitive advantage. Second, IP can be very disruptive. A patent on technology that predates your technology in the marketplace, providing a monopoly right for a competitor, may cause a rapid decline in market share and profits. Drug companies are aware of these dangers and fight this battle every day. The majority of companies, though, don't find out about disruptive technologies until it is too late. Third, performing a competitive assessment is easy. The rise of the internet and the bevy of databases full of IP related information, especially patent information, has made performing competitive assessment techniques more cost and time effective. The remainder of this article discusses a number of different areas where one can focus its competitive assessment efforts. In addition, the discussion will be focused on patents, which for most companies is the most significant type of intellectual property in the portfolio.

Various departments within the company will benefit in different ways, of course, from access to new information about competitors. The research, development and innovation departments will be able to look at topics related to innovation, technology direction, advances by competitors, key inventors in the fields and other similar topics. The legal department may be able to identify possible infringers, determine filing patterns of competitors, and make strategic filing decisions (publish, patent, trade secret, copyright). The marketing department may be able to identify other players in the marketplace or it might be used to identify trends in the market. The business development organization will be able to identify possible licensing targets as well as possible new market innovations. The mergers and acquisitions departments may be able to analyze competitive technology portfolios for complimentary assets while identifying possible targets. Most importantly, it will provide the entire company with information about its own company or its competitors that it might not have available (or might not gather) on a continuing basis.

A competitive assessment might be considered by a company because it has been caught by surprise in the past and wants to protect itself in the future. A competitor might have launched a particular product or developed a particular technology of which the company was not aware. A new competitor might arise from a non-traditional source. For example, a supplier of component parts suddenly manufactures and sells a completed product. A competitive assessment will identify areas in which a competitor has patented various technologies, but where its products might not yet be in the marketplace. A company may need to add inventors given its future personnel needs. This could be due to either a change in innovation direction or attrition.

More confidence may be placed on strategic decisions if a company has access to certain competitive or technology information. Acquisition targets may be identified. Divestiture decisions may be made without fear of "selling" core technologies or intellectual property. Partners for strategic alliances or joint ventures may be identified or eliminated. A company may be able to identify potential licensing targets. Given the direction of a technology, strategic decisions may be made about the future research, development and innovation within a company, as well as its reliance on a given technology.

Company Position

We have described the general need for competitive information and defined competitive assessment. Now, we will explore various scenarios where a company would benefit from using competitive assessment techniques.

There are a number of areas to focus competitive assessment efforts that can be termed as offensive applications of competitive assessment techniques. Offensive is an appropriate term as these scenarios all relate to adding to the organization, either through bolstering the existing IP portfolio or directly impacting the bottom line. A later section deals with defensive techniques that focus on protecting the existing IP portfolio.

Offensive

One very common application of competitive assessment techniques is in identifying acquisition targets. Acquisition targets is being used here in its broadest sense as it relates not only to companies but also to individuals and individual technologies. As an example, a certain company that has been successful in the overseas markets is looking to enter the US market, but is lacking in certain key components of technology to make a successful entry. A logical first step for this organization should be to analyze US patents. Through this analysis, the company can identify whether there have been patents issued in the US relating to the desired technology. Once identified, the organization can proceed down a number of paths. It could try to acquire the technology directly from the patent holders, through such vehicles as license, sale or joint venture. It could also try to acquire the company that holds the technology. Finally, there may be a desire to acquire the talent (the inventors) that developed the technology. This may be an especially attractive strategy in instances where a direct match to the desired technology has not yet been patented but inventors who have worked on developing patented technology in a similar field can be identified. The company benefits by being able to weigh various "buy versus build" options, and can decrease the amount of time it would take to develop the technology.

Competitive assessment techniques are also used to identify entities that are in markets where access to your technology may be attractive. Distilling your intellectual property down into a handful of key descriptive words and searching the patent databases for matches is a good starting point. That way, you will be able to identify companies who have invested development time and money in areas related to your own technology. Performing similar searches on other documents, such as technical journals and publicly available corporate documents of competitors or other companies, could also surface potential buyers of your patented technology. Another technique that has become much easier with the software technology advancement in the area of patent information is forward citations (subsequent patents where your patents have been cited) to see who may be building on your technology, at least tangentially. This technique can prove especially valuable in identifying entities that are not currently on your radar screen. In many circumstances, licensing protected technologies provides companies the opportunity to generate additional, sometimes significant, revenues without jeopardizing current market position.

Finally, competitive assessment techniques can be used to focus development and patent activity in the future. As we will discuss in more detail in the next section, competitive assessment techniques can be used to identify the technology development trends within competing companies. One can project future development efforts using these trends, and make decisions reacting to these projected trends through such varied actions as expending funds to create competing technologies to acquiring entire companies to help compete more effectively against the projected technology advancements. In addition, certain available software packages, such as Cartia's Themescape, can help create technology maps. In the case of Themescape, one can create a map of all key competitors, built upon the key concepts described in patents. Often, this type of map points out areas of technology underdevelopment. These areas of underdevelopment may become important areas of technology development in the future. Having a more clearly focused development and patent strategy increases the likelihood of developing protectible technologies that will protect or even enhance market share.

Defensive

As discussed in the previous paragraph, profiling your competitor's patent portfolios can be a powerful tool for your organization. In the defensive mode, understanding the make-up of these portfolios provides a window into the future strategy of your competitors and allows your organization the time to react to these strategies. The technology maps explained above play an important part in this profile. Besides pointing out white space, these maps can clearly describe your competitor's areas of technology competence. Creating these maps in a time sequence allows one to obtain the added perspective of which technologies have been the focus of the more recent development efforts. Armed with this information, your organization is in a position to decide whether it needs to react, for example, by redirecting its own technology development into areas that a competitor is building a competency, or by working to create a patent shield to prevent the competitor's development efforts from further encroachment upon your space.

We just described how profiling a competitor's portfolio to identify technology competencies might trigger responses from your organization. Another technique starts with looking at your company's own technology competencies and determining whether these may be under attack by other organizations. The type of analysis could start by identifying the technologies that your organization believes will be key to its future success. After boiling these technologies down into key words and concepts, one can search patent databases (in addition to other information databases), looking for matching concepts, and ultimately, entities whose technology developments appear to suggest that they might be players in this technology in the future. Again, armed with this type of information, an organization can develop a strategy to react, possibly by acquiring access to the patented technology through such avenues as cross-licenses for design freedom to acquiring companies outright.

KEY INDICATORS OF NEED

We have described fully a number of scenarios where a company could benefit from employing competitive assessment techniques. At a more basic level, though, there are a number of key indicators that may help an organization determine whether building competitive assessment competencies and engaging in competitive assessment techniques is worthwhile. These include the following:

Size of Patent Portfolio

A company's patent portfolio represents a significant investment. Considerable time and money was spent taking the underlying patented technology from concept to working model. Obviously, additional time and money was spent as attorneys and other executives considering the patent worthiness of the invention, crafting the patent application and maintaining the good-standing of the patent, possibly even protecting the patent against infringement. Having a competitive assessment capability helps a company protect and improve this important asset.

Size and Changes in Competitors' Portfolios

Just as it is for your company, the patent portfolio of your competitors acts as a competitive weapon, protecting valuable market space and providing the opportunity to charge premium pricing. If a competitor has a significant patent portfolio and/or if the size of the portfolio has been changing, your organization should want to know what is in that portfolio. As described earlier, the information contained in these patents can provide a window into a company's future strategy.

Pace of Innovation

If you are in an industry where the pace of innovation is very rapid, especially where market changing innovations have become commonplace, you will want to employ some competitive assessment techniques. In these types of markets, although holding patents may be valuable, it will likely be most valuable to hold patents that represent the major market-changing innovations as opposed to the incremental inventions that will likely make up the vast majority of the patent portfolios of the companies in the industry. You will want to be combing through the portfolios of your competitors for hints of their next major innovations, as well as searching through the general population of patents to identify entities that may be developing technology that could impact your own major innovations.

Size/Structure in Relation to Competitors

Companies that have competitors with large patent portfolios or companies that are privately held competing against publicly held companies often draw much of their competitive advantage through distinct, protected technology innovations. These types of companies will engage in competitive assessment to help protect against encroachment into their technology space, while also looking for white-space opportunities.

Heavy M & A Activity

Those companies whose growth is fueled at least in part through M&A activity can use competitive assessment techniques to identify and screen potential acquisition candidates, especially those where one of the main drivers of the acquisition is access to technology.

Innovations Existing in Other Parts of the Supply Chain

Oftentimes, your company exists in the middle of a supply chain where patented innovations can have either a positive or negative impact on your business. For example, you may have an exclusive arrangement with a supplier that has a superior product, in part protected as intellectual property. This gives your product a competitive advantage in the marketplace. Or, there may be a supplier whose intellectual property allows it to extract a price premium from your company and others. Competitive assessment techniques allow companies to better understand and take advantage of the dynamics at play in the supply chain.

GENERAL APPROACH

So, now that we have described various drivers of need, we want to at least provide you with a high-level approach for performing a competitive assessment. Although these are just the basics, we hope that the general framework described will help your company begin to implement competitive assessment techniques.

Define the Scope

Not surprisingly, the most valuable insights and solutions will come where one has taken the time to clearly define the scope. Many times, the scope can be created in the form of a question. For example, one could pose a question such as, "What are some potential acquisition targets?" A more valuable answer will surface if one spends time crafting a question that more directly meets the needs of your company. As an alternative, how about, "What potential acquisition candidates exist that could help bring technology x to our North American market?" What you have now is a scope that is more actionable.

The scenario described here was precisely the scenario facing a European-based technology client. We were initially approached by this company with a need expressed very generally as a desire to gain a foothold in the US market. Past attempts to take a product line to the US that had been very successful in Europe had met with failure. Through our initial discussions with the company, it became clear that what had been missing was some very specific technology necessary to convert the European product to a product that would be saleable in the US. The company had tried repeatedly to develop the technology competency internally, as the culture of the company typically demands, but had no success. When we as a group were able to change the scope of the need from entering the US market to acquiring the technology competency in order to successfully compete in the US market, our work became highly focused and we were able to quickly arrive at a solution. Some very basic patent searches focused on the missing technology that identified a number of acquisition candidate companies.

Brainstorm

Organizations have significantly more useful knowledge than they typically realize. That said, after the appropriate scope has been defined, it is very important that the organization gather together individuals who can provide input and start filling in the answers to the questions posed. As an example, the organization may have scoped out the question, "Which organizations have products that could compete with our product and what are the patent positions built around these products?" A team built from across multiple functions would be perfect for a brainstorming session about this question. Marketing can describe the product and the attributes that make the product appealing for customers. Technologists will explain the underlying technology that comprises the product. Legal can describe aspects of the underlying technology that are legally protected through patent or trade secret. Business developers will be able to start a listing of known competing companies. The results of the brainstorming session will be used to gather additional information about competing products and patents for the final analysis.

Prior to a brainstorming session we had related to a consumer products client, we purchased bags full of our client's and competitors' products. We captured the similarities and differences between the products in such characteristics as size, shape, smell, color, design, consistency, and efficacy. Furthermore, we also grouped products by company to determine where the gaps in the product lines existed. We documented which of the products were on their face covered by patent or trademark protection. These points all became key inputs to our data gathering and analysis during the later project phases.

Gather Data

With the project scope and the results of the brainstorming session, we are prepared to perform our formal data gathering. The place to start is a database of US patents. (Any patent database will work, but using a sophisticated search, retrieval and analysis package, such as Aurigin's Aureka, makes the data gathering and final analysis easier.) A good starting point is key word searches using the product descriptions surfaced during the brainstorming session. Another important search is one that uses the patent class code(s) of any relevant patents that your company holds. Of course, the patent portfolios of any companies identified during the brainstorming session should be examined. Ultimately, you should have built a data set of patents that relate to the product of interest.

You can also gather together non-patent data during this phase. Gathering organizational, financial and product information about each company is a simple exercise. Company web sites, as well as research sites such as Hoovers, Compustat, and ABI-Inform are all terrific starting points for gathering this type of information. Also valuable are basic searches of the World Wide Web or of proprietary information bases using the product descriptions created during the brainstorming session.

Just compiling a listing of companies who appear to be patenting in your technology space can be very enlightening. It was for one of our recent clients. A handful of simple key word and patent code searches helped produce a listing of companies including a number of suppliers and one distributor of our client company. The existence of the distributor on the list was particularly disturbing as our client believed, as most would have believed, that the distributor had no technology development or manufacturing capabilities. It turned out that the distributor was using outsourcing to obtain these capabilities to produce a product that directly competed with our client's product.

Analysis

Once the data has been gathered it is time to turn it into valuable information. Graph each of the companies' patent portfolios over time to see each company's development trends. (See Exhibit 1.) Segment the companies into three groups: significant patent protection, limited patent protection and no protection. See if there seems to be any relationship between the level of protection each company has and the prices / margins / market shares that are enjoyed. Determine who the

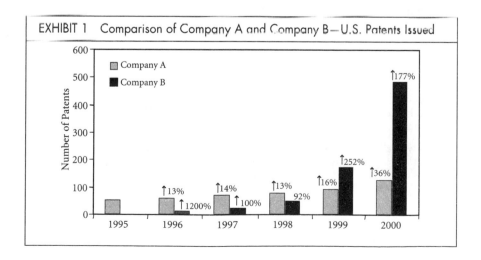

EXHIBIT 1   Comparison of Company A and Company B—U.S. Patents Issued

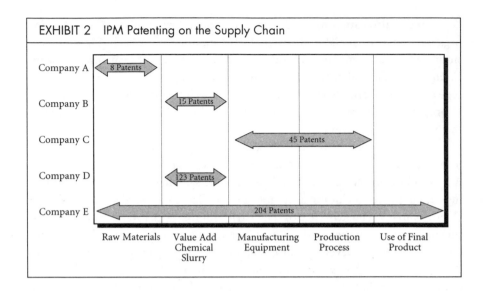

EXHIBIT 2   IPM Patenting on the Supply Chain

Company A — 8 Patents

Company B — 15 Patents

Company C — 45 Patents

Company D — 123 Patents

Company E — 204 Patents

Raw Materials | Value Add Chemical Slurry | Manufacturing Equipment | Production Process | Use of Final Product

key inventors are so that their efforts and movements can be tracked more closely over time. Place each company on a supply chain to clearly portray where each patent holder exists in relationship to your company. (See Exhibit 2.)

The key to performing the analysis is to be as creative as possible. Think about the ultimate audience of your analysis and how to simply yet effectively communicate your findings to this audience. Ultimately, having this type of analysis available to your organization will help improve its strategic decision-making ability.

CONCLUSION

The fast-paced, ever-changing marketplace forces a company to use all tools available to protect and enhance its competitive position. Gaining knowledge about a competitor's position within the marketplace, its technological advances and future direction provides a yardstick to which a company may measure itself. Knowing what to look for, how to interpret the available data, what the analyses indicate, and how to recognize recurring and forward thinking themes will allow a company to gain critical knowledge of its competitors and, hopefully, use this information to set its own strategy and tactics.

APPENDIX C

INTEGRATED PERFORMANCE REPORTING

A GUIDE FOR ASSESSING PERFORMANCE REPORTING TO
SENIOR MANAGEMENT AND THE BOARD OF DIRECTORS

CO-SPONSORED BY THE
CANADIAN PERFORMANCE REPORTING INITIATIVE
OF THE
CANADIAN INSTITUTE OF CHARTERED ACCOUNTANTS
AND THE
CREDIT UNION INSTITUTE OF CANADA

1999

PREPARED BY

ROB MCLEAN
MatrixLinks International Inc.

TABLE OF CONTENTS

1. BACKGROUND AND OVERVIEW

Background

This Issue Paper provides senior management and members of Boards of Directors with an overview of key trends affecting performance reporting, and a means of assessing their organization's current practices and capabilities with respect to "integrated performance reporting."

The focus of this paper is on "internal" performance reporting: that is, reporting to senior management and the board of directors. All other aspects of performance measurement and reporting, while important, are beyond the scope of this paper. Specifically, this paper does not address:

- External performance reporting or disclosure to investors or creditors
- Performance measurement of individuals or of organizational units
- In-depth performance measurement with respect to particular aspects of performance, except insofar as these are relevant to performance of the organization as a whole
- Performance reporting for entities other than business organizations

At the outset, it is useful to clarify what we mean by *performance measurement, performance reporting,* and *integrated performance reporting.*

Performance measurement refers to techniques for distinguishing various levels of a business organization's performance. Typically, these techniques focus on a particular aspect of performance, such as quality or customer satisfaction. The measures may be: qualitative or quantitative; absolute or relative; related to particular time periods; and so on.

Performance reporting refers to methods for summarizing and communicating information about performance to a particular audience—in this case, executive or senior management and the board of directors. We choose this audience because it is this group that is accountable for performance of the organization as a whole, and has the authority to make decisions concerning the quantity and scope of information it receives. For convenience, this group will henceforth be referred to in this paper as SMBD.

Integrated performance reporting refers to methods for synthesizing information so as to convey, in as efficient a manner as possible, the overall performance of the organization.

The point of departure for this paper is the observation that over the past 10 to 15 years, the quantity and range of information that is regularly provided to SMBD has increased dramatically.

At one time, financial statements were considered the main vehicle for providing SMBD with an overall picture of the organization's performance. In the late 1970s and 1980s, an increased emphasis on quality led many organizations to add quality issues to the board agenda. In the 1980s, many jurisdictions passed legislation which made SMBD members personally liable for the organization's compliance with environmental and health and safety regulations. Consequently, compliance reporting became an additional board responsibility.

In many companies today, SMBD receives reports on topics as diverse as:

- Financial performance
- Market share
- Quality
- Health and safety
- Environmental compliance
- Customer satisfaction
- Employee satisfaction

Many leading companies have added other performance "domains" to this list, such as:

- Intellectual capital management
- Risk management
- Shareholder value
- Environmental performance

This proliferation of reporting has led to a new challenge—that of synthesizing this wide range of information into a comprehensive or integrated view of the organization's overall performance.

Many SMBD members feel overwhelmed by the quantity and diversity of the information reported to them. They are looking for a way of grasping the organization's overall performance without having to read dozens of detailed reports. They want to know how various aspects of performance interrelate: for example, how does employee satisfaction affect customer satisfaction and vice-versa? They want to understand what weighting should be placed on different aspects of performance: that is, what are the most important determinants of overall performance. They also want to understand the organization's performance as perceived by shareholders and other key stakeholders.

Given this context, the cosponsors of this initiative believed that it would be useful to provide SMBD members with a basic framework for assessing their own organization's progress with respect to performance reporting. It should be recognized at the outset that performance measurement and reporting is a dynamic field, with many organizations working to expand the boundaries of current practice. Another objective of this paper is to identify areas for continuing research and development.

About the Cosponsors

The cosponsors' objectives in supporting this paper are complementary but distinct.

Until recently, the main focus of the Canadian Institute of Chartered Accountants was financial measurement and reporting. However, in its 1996 Vision project, the CICA recognized that its members would be held increasingly accountable for measuring and reporting not just on financial performance, but on other aspects of performance as well. This led to the launch of the Canadian Performance Reporting Initiative, which provides an opportunity for collaborative research and experimentation into various aspects of performance measurement and reporting, and has subsequently led to the formation of TVC International Inc., an entity created to enhance value creation measurement and reporting.

The Credit Union Institute of Canada is the national education association for Canada's $48 billion credit union system. One of CUIC's areas of responsibility is to provide support for training members of credit union boards of directors. This provides an opportunity to influence the expectations and capabilities of board members with respect to performance measurement and reporting. As a result of this interest, CUIC undertook to test the approaches described in this paper with leading credit unions across Canada.

Overview

This paper is organized as follows.

Section 1 provides a background and overview.
Section 2 describes an overall framework for exploring various approaches to Integrated Performance Reporting (IPR).

Sections 3 through 7 describe the various components of this IPR framework in greater detail.

Section 8 provides an assessment guide that shows how the IPR framework
can be used to evaluate an organization's practices and capabilities.

Section 9 provides concluding comments and proposals for continuing research and development relating to integrated performance reporting.

2. A FRAMEWORK FOR EVALUATING INTEGRATED PERFORMANCE REPORTING PRACTICES AND CAPABILITIES

Performance reporting practices and capabilities can best be described by lo-
cating them within a continuum. Given the developments of the past two
decades, we can differentiate among five major locations along this continuum:

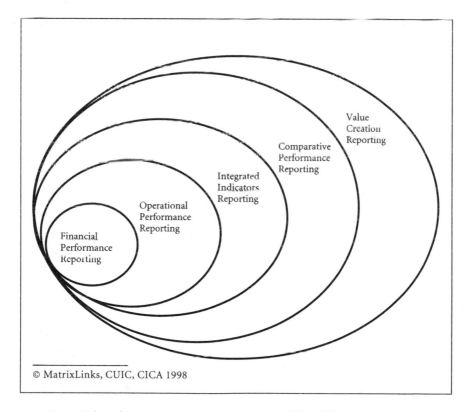

© MatrixLinks, CUIC, CICA 1998

Financial performance reporting is a basic building block for any attempt at
integrated performance reporting. As discussed in Section 4, we have seen in
recent decades the development of increasingly sophisticated techniques for
analyzing financial performance, return on investment, and risk.

Operational performance reporting consists of the organization's practices and capabilities relating to nonfinancial information. Over the past two decades, techniques for measuring and reporting operational performance have become much more sophisticated. Most organizations have systems that track such things as quality and productivity. Section 5 points out that leading organizations today employ comprehensive performance management systems that track performance against targets covering all aspects of operations.

Integrated indicators reporting refers to the techniques for linking financial and nonfinancial performance measures. The best known approach is the "balanced scorecard" initially made famous by Kaplan and Norton. Developing a balanced scorecard is a logical step, based on today's practices, for an organization that wishes to integrate financial and nonfinancial information to get a comprehensive picture of its overall performance. This and other approaches for integrated indicators reporting are discussed further in Section 5.

The term *comparative performance reporting* is used to refer to various approaches for benchmarking the organization's performance against competitors and/or comparable organizations. These approaches are described in Section 6.

Value creation reporting refers to techniques that link performance to the creation of value. There has been considerable interest in recent years in measuring and reporting on the creation of shareholder value. As described in Section 7, the CICA is currently engaged in an exploration of a broader concept of value creation, referred to as Total Value Creation™ or TVC™.

3. Financial Performance Reporting

Financial reporting has many shortcomings, but its virtues become evident when one looks seriously at alternatives which don't share these same virtues.

The great strengths of financial reporting are as follows:

- Reliability: most of the numbers in a set of financial statements originate in a transaction with a third party. By contrast, many other performance measures are indicators-based rather than transaction-based.
- Comparability: the basic unit of measure for financial reporting is derived from currency—in Canada, the Canadian dollar. This facilitates comparisons among different companies.
- Defined standards: in Canada, the standards for financial reporting are defined by Generally Accepted Accounting Principles, which are codified in the Handbook of the Canadian Institute of Chartered Accountants, and in the United States, the equivalent standards are defined by the Financial Accounting Standards Board.

Financial reporting has been referred to as a "universal language," since virtually anyone trained in business has the ability to read and understand a set of financial statements, at least at a basic level.

The main weaknesses of financial reporting are all related to the fact that it is designed to look backward at the past rather than forward to the future. There is an active ongoing debate about whether in the final analysis, every-thing that is relevant to assessing the performance of a business enterprise eventually affects cash flow. Even if one concedes this point, one must agree that by the time something has affected actual cash flows, it is too late to do anything about it.

One of the main complaints about the current accounting model is that it does not incorporate leading indicators of performance such as management of intellectual capital, which is increasingly important in a knowledge-based economy. Another concern is that financial reporting focuses on the firm as a discrete entity, and does not therefore reflect the complex interdependencies among business organizations that in many cases are critical determinants of business success.

Virtually all of the alternative approaches to integrated performance re-porting are responses to these perceived deficiencies. Nevertheless, its strengths are such that financial reporting will continue to provide the "bedrock" on which all other approaches build.

Financial Reporting Practices

Within financial reporting, there is a broad spectrum of practice. In general, it is possible to distinguish among:

- Companies that provide SMBD with a fairly basic comparison of finan-cial performance against budgets or forecasts
- Companies that provide SMBD with a more detailed analysis of finan-cial return on investment generated in various business units
- Companies that incorporate comprehensive risk/return analysis into their reporting to SMBD

4. Operational Performance Reporting

Modern companies have always used some form of measurement system to track operational performance, whether those operations involve resource ex-traction, manufacturing, retailing, or providing services. Over the past 20 years, the sophistication of these operational measurement systems has in-creased dramatically. This is due to several factors:

- As computing power became increasingly accessible and inexpensive with the development of PCs, it became possible to track performance at a more detailed level than would have been possible without this technology.
- Experience gained in the "quality movement" in the 1980s led to a greater understanding of how measurement can be used systematically to improve performance.
- The performance measurement and management techniques perfected in the quality movement have gradually been adapted and applied in a wide range of other performance domains, including:
  —productivity
  —customer satisfaction
  —health and safety
  —environmental performance
  —employee satisfaction
  —intellectual capital management

Within operational performance reporting, the spectrum of practices now includes:

- Organizations whose operational performance reporting practices are driven mainly by the requirements of suppliers. For example, many companies require their suppliers to acquire ISO 9000 or equivalent certification, which includes a requirement to report on various aspects of quality assurance.
- Organizations where SMBD has chosen to receive regular reports on a set of strategically significant operational performance indicators. This enables SMBD to monitor performance, and also signal to the organization the importance that is placed on the chosen areas of performance.
- Organizations that have implemented a comprehensive performance management system.

5. Integrated Indicators Reporting

Integrated indicators reporting refers to approaches for linking together financial and nonfinancial or operational indicators.

The Balanced Scorecard

The balanced scorecard is traditionally associated with Robert Kaplan and David Norton, who are recognized as its most active promoters. Over the past five years or so, it has emerged as the most widely practiced method for integrated performance reporting to SMBD.

The balanced scorecard was designed to overcome some of the limitations of traditional financial reporting, in that it focuses on:

- A limited number of performance measures which should be linked to an organization's strategy
- The present and the future, rather than the past

In its original incarnation, the balanced scorecard was intended to focus on performance from four key perspectives:

- The financial perspective
- The customer perspective
- Internal processes
- Innovation and improvement activities

In recent years, there has been a great deal of experimentation and development building on the initial concept. Some of the approaches that have emerged include:

- Using the balanced scorecard approach for performance management at various levels in the organization, in some cases all the way to individual performance.
- Using the balanced scorecard as part of a feedback loop in a system to promote strategic learning.

The Skandia Navigator

The Skandia Navigator is another approach that links financial and nonfinancial indicators. While initially introduced as a method of managing intellectual capital, the Skandia Navigator is in reality a potential approach for integrated indicators reporting.

Skandia and its first manager of intellectual capital, Lief Edvinsson, have become well known in recent years among those who are tracking developments in the field of intellectual capital. The Skandia Navigator was originally conceived as a tool for "navigating" through information relevant to assessing Skandia's performance in managing its intellectual capital. The Skandia Navigator is fully described in Chapter 4 of Leif Edvinsson's book, *Intellectual Capital*.

In simplified form, the Skandia Navigator focuses on five areas:

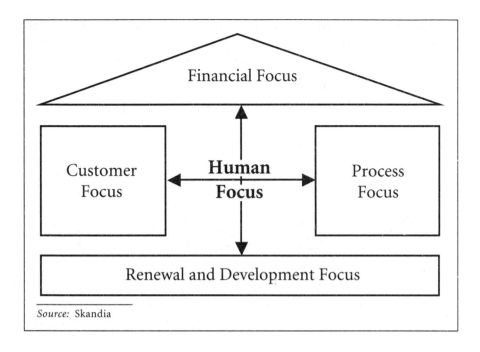

Source: Skandia

As Edvinsson explains, "These are the areas upon which an enterprise focuses its attention, and from that focus comes the value of the company's Intellectual Capital within its competitive environment."

Skandia has developed a set of indicators to measure performance with respect to each of these areas of focus. Its 1994 supplementary report on Visualizing Intellectual Capital included 111 indicators as follows:

Financial focus:	20 measures
Customer focus:	22 measures
Process focus:	16 measures
Renewal and Development Focus:	19 measures
Human Focus:	13 measures

Skandia continues to experiment with these measures, evaluating others, and adding them to its reporting structure as they prove useful.

Further information on Skandia's approach, and on measuring intellectual capital in general, is available in a separate CPRI publication entitled *Intellectual Capital Management: Challenge and Response.*

Identifying Causal Relationships

Among the more important developments in the last few years are initiatives by a number of companies to identify the causal relationships among various indicators of performance. Some of these initiatives were documented in a recent Conference Board of Canada report entitled *Loyal Customers, Enthusiastic Employees and Corporate Performance*. The report refers to work undertaken by the Royal Bank of Canada and Nortel, both of which have created statistical models to enable the company to predict the changes in customer satisfaction and financial performance that will occur as employee satisfaction increases or decreases.

The report notes that at Nortel, every percentage point change in employee satisfaction increases will yield a predictable change in customer satisfaction, which will in turn lead to predictable revenue and margin increases or decreases.

Spectrum of Practice

Within integrated indicators reporting, we can summarize the spectrum of practice as follows:

- Organizations that use a technique such as the balanced scorecard or Skandia Navigator to report integrated financial and non-financial performance information to SMBD.
- Organizations that use techniques such as the balanced scorecard or Skandia Navigator to manage performance at various levels within the organization.
- Organizations that are undertaking the research necessary to understand the causal linkages among specific financial and non-financial indicators of performance.

6. Comparative Performance Reporting

Many organizations recognize that measuring performance using only their internal information runs the risk of missing important quantum shifts in relative performance. Benchmarking emerged in the mid-1980s when it became evident that some companies were getting 100 percent and 200 percent performance improvements as a result of process redesign—far beyond the incremental changes that used to be the norm. Their competitors were able to respond to these nonincremental performance improvements only if they realized where they stood in relation to their rivals.

Benchmarking is now a commonly used term, but there are differences in the depth of analysis undertaken and/or reported to SMBD by various companies:

- Some companies focus their benchmarking analysis on market or customer data.
- Others use a benchmarking approach to get detailed intelligence on comparative performance of various functions or business units at an operational level.
- A third category extend their benchmarking focus to include comparative information about value creation. (See Section 7 below for more about value creation reporting.)

7. VALUE CREATION REPORTING

Value creation reporting is a very dynamic area, in which there have been important recent developments.

Reporting on Shareholder Value Creation

The topic of shareholder value has been thoroughly explored in two recent publications prepared for the CPRI by Julie Desjardins:

1. *Shareholder Value Measurement in Canada 1997 Survey,* a report cosponsored by the CICA and the Financial Executives Institute Canada.
2. *The Measurement of Shareholder Value Creation,* a commentary on various approaches.

Consequently, this section will be limited to a brief consideration of shareholder value reporting in the context of integrated performance reporting.

In general, current approaches to shareholder value reporting are derivatives of financial reporting, but are focused on the implications of financial results for the owners of the business. Various techniques are used to show whether the business is generating returns that exceed the cost of capital employed. To the extent that shareholder value approaches are based on the current financial accounting model, they share its shortcomings and strengths as previously described in Section 3.

Some approaches to shareholder value are promoted as performance management tools. So far, these approaches focus on influencing behavior to increase returns to shareholders.

In considering shareholder value reporting as a means for evaluating overall business performance, it is important to recognize the distinction between:

- Optimizing the returns available to shareholders given a specific funda-mental underlying performance of the enterprise; and
- Improving the fundamental underlying performance of the enterprise, which increases the returns available to be optimized.

At present, many shareholder value management techniques address the former, not the latter. Nevertheless, reporting on shareholder value creation is, we believe, an essential task for most companies. In the context of integrated performance reporting, the key question is whether to focus solely on share-holders or to focus on value creation for other stakeholders as well.

Value Creation for Key Stakeholders

The CICA sponsored a study by John Waterhouse of the use of nonfinancial measures by Boards of Directors of Canadian corporations, entitled *Strategic Performance Monitoring and Management: Using Non-Financial Measures to Improve Corporate Governance.* The study included a survey of over 100 board members and CEOs, and case studies of the performance measurement ap-proaches of five leading Canadian companies.

One of the important insights in the study is the importance of perfor-mance measurement with respect to all key stakeholders. Waterhouse argues that there is a crucial link between an organization's strategy and the stake-holders whose support is essential for successful implementation. Each of the major companies studied in depth—Nortel, the Bank of Montreal, Nova, Syncrude, and Noranda—identified a variety of stakeholders that were re-garded as key to future success. The stakeholder groups most often identified by these companies include: shareholders, customers, employees, the commu nity, and suppliers and business partners.

We conclude that in many companies, SMBD will be interested in under-standing value creation from the perspective of all key stakeholders.

Total Value Creation™

Reflecting these insights, the CICA is currently experimenting with a model for internal reporting called Total Value Creation™ or TVC™.

TVC™ is based on the notion that just as market value normally exceeds book value in most companies, so does the total value created by an organiza-tion likely exceed the market value that is applicable to shareholders. The total value created by an organization includes value created for all key stakeholder groups, which normally include:

- Customers
- Employees
- Business partners and suppliers
- Community/society
- Shareholders

TVC™ integrates financial and nonfinancial measures that, in combination, provide insights into long-term value creation. Intellectual capital-related measures are integral to value creation and incorporated as appropriate into the measurement framework.

The TVC™ approach is flexible to allow companies to make their own decisions on the relative importance of key stakeholders and the measures which best reflect long-term value creation.

TVC™ addresses many of the limitations of other approaches to integrated performance reporting. For example, one of the features of the balanced scorecard approach is that this scorecard is intended to be customized to the needs of each individual organization. As a result, it is not possible to directly compare the balanced scorecards of different organizations. TVC™ includes both company-specific measures, and generic measures that facilitate making comparisons across organizations.

Similarly, the model for TVC™ combines information about strategic direction, operational performance, and value creation to provide an overall perspective of performance.

Further development of the TVC™ approach is taking place under the auspices of TVC International Inc. Further information is available from its web site at http://www.totalvaluecreation.com.

Spectrum of Practice

Within value creation reporting, we can summarize the spectrum of practice among organizations as follows:

- A large number are currently practicing some form of shareholder value reporting to SMBD.
- A somewhat smaller number are beginning to measure value creation from the perspective of other key stakeholders as well;
- The CICA, with the participation of other accounting institutes, is experimenting with an approach to measuring Total Value Creation™— which enables organizations to assess overall organizational performance from the perspective of all key stakeholders.

8. Integrated Performance Reporting Evaluation Matrix: A CPRI Self-Assessment Guide

The following is an outline of an evolving self-assessment guide which is intended to help organizations assess (1) their current positioning with respect to Integrated Performance Reporting, and (2) priorities for future development. This should be considered a "beta" version: feedback and reactions are encouraged.

This latest version of this guide can be accessed through the CPRI web site at www.cica.ca. Using the web-based guide, you can compare your organization's position with that of other organizations that have tested the self-assessment guide.

The Integrated Performance Reporting Self-Assessment Guide asks a series of questions related to each location along the IPR Continuum described in Sections 2 through 7 above. On the basis of these questions, you are invited to identify your current position within the continuum (positions 1 through 4 for each location along the continuum), and also identify your desired future position within the next 12 to 18 months.

Financial Performance Reporting

Positions:

1. The organization provides financial statements to senior management and the Board of Directors on a regular basis.
2. The organization regularly provides senior management and the Board of Directors with analysis of financial performance against forecasts/ budgets.
3. The organization regularly provides senior management and the board of directors with analysis of financial return on investment generated in all business units.
4. The organization provides senior management and the board of directors with detailed comparative analysis of risks and returns for all business units.

What is your organization's current position with respect to Financial Performance Reporting? _____

If this position is not optimal for your organization, what position would you set as a target to move toward in the next 12–18 months? _____

Operational Performance Reporting

Positions:

1. Senior management and the board of directors rely mainly on financial reporting and do not receive regular reports on operational performance.
2. The organization provides senior management and the board of directors with quality and/or customer satisfaction performance reporting in accordance with standards set by customers or standard-setting organizations such as ISO.
3. The organization tracks a set of strategically significant operational performance indicators and reports these regularly to senior management and the board of directors.
4. The organization has a comprehensive performance management system that sets targets and tracks performance for a full set of operational performance indicators, with appropriate monitoring by senior management and the board of directors

What is your organization's current position with respect to Operational Performance Reporting? _____

If this position is not optimal for your organization, what position would you set as a target to move toward in the next 12–18 months? _____

Integrated Indicators Reporting

Positions:

1. The organization reports financial and/or operational performance to senior management and the board of directors, but does not have a mechanism for integrating financial and nonfinancial performance indicators.
2. The organization prepares a regular report for senior management and the board of directors that integrates financial and nonfinancial indicators using approaches such as the balanced scorecard or the Skandia Navigator.

3. The organization uses approaches such as the balanced scorecard or Skandia Navigator to set performance targets and monitor performance at all levels in the organization, in addition to reporting a high-level synthesis to senior management and the board of directors.
4. The organization is actively engaged in research concerning the causal linkages among various financial and nonfinancial indicators of performance (e.g., linkages between employee satisfaction, customer satisfaction and revenue growth).

What is your organization's current position with respect to Integrated Indicators Reporting? ___ _____ _____ ___

If this position is not optimal for your organization, what position would you set as a target to move toward in the next 12–18 months? __ _____

Comparative Performance Reporting

Positions:

1. The organization tracks performance using primarily internally generated data.
2. The organization reports comparative performance with respect to market share and customer satisfaction to senior management and the board of directors.
3. The organization reports comparative performance with respect to productivity, efficiency, employee satisfaction, and other operational factors to senior management and the board of directors.
4. The organization reports comparative performance with respect to value creation to senior management and the board of directors.

What is your organization's current position with respect to Comparative Performance Reporting? _____ _____

If this position is not optimal for your organization, what position would you set as a target to move toward in the next 12–18 months? _____

Value Creation Reporting

Positions:

1. The organization does not report on value creation to senior management and the board of directors.
2. The organization reports to senior management and the board of directors on value creation performance from the perspective of shareholders.
3. The organization reports to senior management and the board of directors on value creation performance from the perspective of all key stakeholders.
4. The organization is experimenting with leading-edge approaches to value creation performance reporting, such as the CICA's TVC™ approach.

What is your organization's current position with respect to Value Creation Reporting? _____

If this position is not optimal for your organization, what position would you set as a target to move toward in the next 12–18 months? _____

Feedback about the Self-Assessment Guide

We are interested in any comments you have about this Self-Assessment Guide, including whether you found it useful, and what changes you would suggest to improve it. You may contact us through the CPRI web site at http://www.cica.ca, or the TVCI web site at http://www.totalvaluecreation.com.

NOTES

Introduction   The Edison Prophecy

1. *The Papers of Thomas Edison: The Wizard of Menlo Park,* Ed. Paul B. Israel, Keith A. Nier, Louis Carlat (Baltimore/London: Johns Hopkins University Press, 1998), pp. 844–850. This entry appears in the journals of Francis Upton, recording (presumably faithfully) the words of Thomas Edison. The editors note that Edison "signed and dated these notes." (See p. 850, note 1.) They also state that in this and surrounding passages, "Upton appears to be recording Edison's thoughts." (See p. 852, note 20.)
2. The number of worldwide patents exceeds this number greatly. Non-U.S. patents passed the 6 million mark nearly 20 years ago: "The Scientific Library of the Patent Office contains . . . over 6,000,000 volumes of foreign patents in bound volumes," quoted in "Patents, Law of," *Encyclopedia Americana* (Grolier, 1982), p. 386.
3. Uniform Trade Secrets Act, Section 1ff., 14 U.S.C.A. 541.
4. Margaret M. Blair and Thomas A. Kochan; editors *The New Relationship: Human Capital in the American Corporation* (Washington, D.C.: Brookings, 2001), p. 1.
5. As stated in note 1, this passage comes from *The Papers of Thomas Edison.*
6. From encyclopedia.com, under Edison, Thomas Alva.
7. This history is based on a variety of sources, including the Edison books cited in other notes to this chapter. The portion on Langmuir comes from Robert Buderi, *Engines of Tomorrow: How the World's Greatest Companies Are Using Their Research Labs to Win the Future* (New York: Simon & Schuster, 2000), p. 76.

Chapter 1   Level One—Defense

1. This court is one of 13 federal circuit courts of appeal. (The other dozen serve the 12 main legal regions in the United States.)
2. Federal Courts Improvement Act of 1982 (Pub. L. No. 97–164, 96 Stat. 25 (1982)).
3. Patrick Sullivan, *Value-Driven Intellectual Capital: How to Convert Intangible Assets into Market Value* (New York: John Wiley, 2000), p. 129.

4. Hisamitsu Arai, "The Facts Behind Japan's Technology Explosion," *Managing Intellectual Property*, May 2000, pp. 19ff.

5. This quotation is based on an interview conducted by the authors. From now on in this book, all quotes are from interviews, unless otherwise identified.

6. The following section is adapted with permission from an Andersen source: Solange L. Charas, "Eureka: How to Recognize and Reward Innovation," *HR Director: The Arthur Andersen Guide to Human Capital* (New York: Profile Pursuit, 1998–1999), pp. 140–145. For the complete text of this article and other articles on human capital, see us.andersen.com/human capital/resources.

7. Id. [Charas].

8. Bush is quoted in Kevin G. Rivette and David Kline, *Rembrandts in the Attic: Unlocking the Hidden Value of Patents* (Boston: Harvard Business School Press, 2000).

9. Karen Hall, "Genome Ground Zero," *Corporate Counsel*, July 2000, p. 62.

10. Stephen Fox, "Intellectual Property Management: From Theory to Practice," quoted in Patrick Sullivan, *Profiting from Intellectual Capital: Extracting Value from Innovation* (New York: John Wiley, 1998), p. 147. In his more recent interview with the authors, Fox confirmed the continuing vigor of this program.

11. Hall, op. cit., p. 62.

12. Hisamitsu Arai, "The Facts Behind Japan's Technology Explosion," op. cit.

13. Paul Israel, op. cit. (note 1), p. 318, reports that by 1888, Edison had become discouraged about patents, and had vowed to avoid them entirely. "Thus, his plan to develop many of his inventions as trade secrets."

14. This list is reprinted from Alexandra R. Lajoux and Charles M. Elson, *The Art of M&A Due Diligence: Navigating Critical Steps and Uncovering Crucial Data* (New York: McGraw-Hill, 2000), p. 297.

15. Krysten Crawford, "Robot, Esq.," *Forbes*, October 2, 2000, pp. 60ff.

16. Rivette and Kline, op. cit., p. 104.

17. Summary of all reported patent damage awards from 1982 through 2000, compiled from a proprietary database maintained by Kathleen M. Kedrowski and Jennifer L. Knabb of Andersen.

Chapter 2 Level Two—Cost Control

1. Press release dated June 16, 1998, from BTG in Gulph Mills, Pennsylvania. See also *Technology Licensing: Corporate Strategies for Maximizing Value,* Ed. Russell L. Parr and Patrick H. Sullivan (New York: John Wiley & Sons, 1996), pp. 79 and 107.

2. For more on these practices at Xerox, see Joe Daniele, "The Intellectual Asset Manager," in Patrick Sullivan, *Profiting from Intellectual Capital: Extracting Value from Innovation* (New York: John Wiley & Sons, 1998), pp. 186–204.

3. D.K. Smith and R.C. Alexander, *Fumbling the Future: How Xerox Invented, Then Ignored, the First Personal Computer* (New York: William Morrow & Company, Inc., 1988).

Chapter 3   Level Three—Profit Center

1. The estimate of ignored technology assets is based on the following findings: The National Science Foundation found that U.S. companies spent $550 billion on research and development from 1993 to 1998, that 60 percent of companies' R&D was spent in-house, and that of this research, 35 percent went unused. This is a conservative estimate, since $1 spent on R&D usually yields more than $1 in sales.
2. Del Jones, "Business Battle Over Intellectual Property Courts Choked with Lawsuits to Protect Ideas—and Profits." *USA Today*, August 2, 2000.
3. Russell L. Parr and Patrick H. Sullivan, *Technology Licensing: Corporate Strategies for Maximizing Value* (New York: John Wiley, 1996), p. 87.

Chapter 4   Level Four—Integration

1. See detailed story in Kevin G. Rivette and David Kline, "Discovering New Value in Intellectual Property," *Harvard Business Review*, January–February 2000, p. 63.
2. Id., p. 62.
3. Id., p. 59.
4. For example, the Economic Espionage Act of 1996 makes the theft of trade secrets a criminal offense punishable by fines to the corporation, as well as fines and imprisonment of corporate officers. This Act could place employees and corporate officers at risk of criminal indictment for theft of such trade secrets.
5. Lisa Naylor, "Procter & Gamble's Next Product: Advice," *The Industry Standard*, April 3, 2001.

Chapter 5   Level Five—Vision

1. This chart is adapted from two boxes appearing in a presentation by Robert McLean, President, MatrixLinks International, Inc., on "Turning Knowledge Into Profit . . . Turning Intangible Assets Into Cash" McLean, a consultant to the Canadian Institute of Chartered Accountants, spoke at the June 29–30, 2000, seminar on intellectual capital management hosted by The Conference Board.

Chapter 6   The Dow Chemical Company—A Case Study

1. William S. Stravropoulos, Chairman, Dow Board of Directors, current; President and CEO, 1995–2000; interview, 1999.
2. The ICM Model used by Dow was developed by the ICM Pioneers: G. Petrash, H. St. Onge, L. Edvinsson, C. Armstrong.
3. Disruptive Technology terminology applied by Dow was developed by Clayton Christianson at The Harvard Business School.

INDEX